PRAISE

WHAT HAPPENED

"Heather's story is a must read for parents, teachers, and clinicians. As both an educator and a parent of a child affected with PANDAS, Heather has a uniquely personal and insightful perspective that can guide others through their own experiences with this illness. She shares, not only coping strategies and tips on navigating this debilitating illness, but also the transformation that she and her entire family underwent on this journey of healing and recovery."

~ Dr. Hatha Gbedawo, Clinical Director, Founder Vital Kids Medicine PLLC

"Heather Korbmacher shares her family's raw story about saving their son from the debilitating symptoms associated with PANDAS. Full of tips and resources, this is a must-read for anyone focused on healing their child from this challenging illness."

~ Dr. Sandy Gluckman, PhD, Author of Parents Take Charge, *Founder of* Parenting That Heals

WHAT HAPPENED TO MY CHILD?

Believe!

♡ Heather

Contributed by Heather Korbmacher

A Parents' Guide to PANDAS, PANS and Related
Neuroimmune Disorders: Information, Support and Advice

WHAT HAPPENED TO MY CHILD?

A MOTHER'S COURAGEOUS JOURNEY TO SAVE HER SON

HEATHER KORBMACHER

Published by Author Academy Elite
P.O. Box 43, Powell, OH 43035
www.AuthorAcademyElite.com

Editing by Carla Atherton
Cover design by Rob Allen, @n23art
Book design by Chris O'Byrne, jetlaunch.net

Library of Congress Control Number: 2018954585

ISBN 978-1-64085-413-0 (hardcover)
ISBN 978-1-64085-412-3 (softcover)
ISBN 978-1-64085-414-7 (ebook)

Available in hardcover, softcover, e-book, and audio book.

DEDICATION

The obvious dedication of this book is to my children and husband who have been on this odyssey with me, but it's the warrior mommas who have gone before me that I must acknowledge here. Their commitment to raising awareness and making information available allowed me and countless others to find our way to diagnosis and healing. I thank you for your courage, your persistence, and your unwavering belief that we *can* make a difference. And to the parents who are just beginning this journey...

Believe. Inhale. Exhale. One breath at a time. One step at a time. You are not alone.

"To avoid criticism, say nothing, do nothing, be nothing."

Elbert Hubbard,
*Little Journeys to the Home of the Great,
Vol. 3: American Statesmen*

CONTENTS

PART 1 – ONSET: THE ROAD TO HELL

PART 2 – DIAGNOSIS: THE SOLITARY PATH

PART 3 – TREATMENT: THE LONG JOURNEY

PART 4 – RESOURCES: THE ROAD MAP

FOREWORD
BY DIANA POHLMAN

"Never doubt that a small group of thoughtful, committed citizens can change the world. Indeed, it is the only thing that ever has."

Margaret Mead

"In the final analysis, the question of why bad things happen to good people translates itself into some very different questions, no longer asking why something happened, but asking how we will respond...Will you be able to recognize the ability to forgive and [love]...and live fully, bravely, and meaningfully in this less-than-perfect world?"

Harold Kushner,
When Bad Things Happen to Good People

Currently, PANDAS/PANS/AE is a newly acknowledged, under-recognized group of illnesses that asks us to understand a relatively uncharted area in research: the brain. How does the brain and how we behave as humans intersect with the immune system? Doctors, neurologists, immunologists, *until just a few years ago*, believed that the brain and the immune system *do not interact*. Only a few years ago, neuroscientists began to realize: the Brain, Central Nervous System, and Immune System are closely connected.

When I started the PANDAS Network ten years ago, it was an incontrovertible fact that both of my children, each at age 7 years old, had acute personality changes together with neurologic anomalies after a strep infection, and that they healed after eradicating the infection and calming the immune response. I could not fathom, at that time, that the medical system would be suspicious of the clinical diagnoses of PANDAS/PANS/AE in children, and that it may occur in adolescence into adulthood; and if left untreated, the effects could be catastrophic. Here I am, a decade later, stunned at the great lengths it seems to require to create consensus around, what appears to me, to be common sense clinical medicine.

Our PANDAS/PANS/AE community has worked hard to gather thousands of cases, and we have evidence that healing can occur with immune modulation treatment. Our community has a gift of hope to offer the world of neuroscience. The numbers of papers on PANDAS/PANS/AE number in the thousands, and parents have drawn a lot of attention to the illness through the media.

We know this: science for our families is the crucible of need. Medical equipment and blood/biomarker tests must be made available to "boots-on the ground" doctors. Currently, there is not one specific biomarker test to explain the neuro-immuno attack that impacts a person's brain and causes neuropsychiatric changes. But open-minded and inquisitive researchers are asking questions and attempting to answer these very questions.

Briefly, here are some of the ways our decade-of-community has helped to affect the science of PANDAS/PANS/AE. New research in neuroscience has proven that the immune system and, in separate research, illness (i.e., streptococcus bacteria) can create concomitant alterations in the immune system and impact the blood brain barrier.[1] Dr. Susan Swedo's groundbreaking identification of PANDAS focused on the psychiatric manifestations of an illness etiologically similar to Sydenham Chorea (SC) that, prior to her work, was not recognized by doctors.[2] Dr. Madeleine Cunningham, microbiologist and strep expert, used her interest in SC and its impact on children in the developing world to isolate potential antibodies rising in PANDAS/PANS/AE children's brains.[3] Her work on autoantibodies in Rheumatic Fever (RF), SC, and PANDAS lead to an understanding of how strep impacts the brain and the heart. In PANDAS Network's observations, a 200 -year- old illness called Sydenham Chorea, triggered by strep, is often poorly diagnosed in the U.S. for a variety of reasons. Primarily, it has not been often seen in the U.S. due to the wonders of penicillin and its wider use as an intervention for RF in the 1940's.

The PANS Consortium has created pathways to clinical treatment and diagnosis in newly published guidelines [4], and new immune markers, together with experimental PET and MRI testing, are bearing fruit as excellent diagnostic tools. However, until these are readily adopted, we parents must trust ourselves, as Heather Korbmacher shares in her story, to toggle together treatment for our children as many doctors are overburdened and treatment is evolving. It is a terrible reality we face as a community and, at PANDAS Network, we face it daily.

I believe we will open important new doors in psychoneuroimmunology, far beyond PANDAS. A handful of PANDAS children in 2007 has grown to an over 13,000 family network, globally, and has expanded to include PANS and AE as we see the spectrum of this illness broaden. Although we have a long way to go, diagnosis and treatment are being applied worldwide, not only in the U.S., but also in Turkey, the U.K.,

Netherlands, Australia, Greece, Brazil, Italy, Canada, South Africa, Russia, Mexico, and elsewhere.

Below, I outline a small brushstroke of a few avenues of broader research that our community is opening. We are not alone in untangling this "Gordian Knot" of neuro-immuno science. However, we don't have enough awareness or diagnostic criteria in the medical community...yet. In neurology, often *no biomarker is found* in autoimmune encephalitis, even in very severe cases where death and permanent disability occur.[5] We call upon science to do its diligence in identifying a biomarker, and we must find funding for this research.

In 2018, the Mayo Clinic published an analysis of cases in Minnesota dating from 1995-2015. They observed an increase in autoantibodies in the past decade with autoimmune encephalitis increasingly being recognized as a common treatable cause.[6] The detection of AE is likely to increase over time as more providers learn to recognize it. And it is anticipated that further neural antibodies will be discovered in the future. This brings me hope. Hope that science will be the avenue of early detection, treatment, and deep healing.

The intersection of immunology and potential genetics of autoimmune diseases and psychiatric presentations was investigated by a group of researchers in London. They conducted a meta-analysis of medical papers to determine if there was a relationship between non-neurological autoimmune (NNAI) disorders (like arthritis, Grave's Disease, and more) and psychosis. "We observed a positive overall association between NNAI disorders and psychosis. And the finding that...autoimmune disorders that would not be expected to directly target the brain, but nonetheless generate substantial immune system activation in the peripheral systems that might ultimately affect the brain is particularly important."[7] Clinicians and researchers around the world are looking into better understanding the connection between immune response and the brain. This continued exploration will open doors even further to early diagnosis, treatment, and ultimately, healing.

And, lastly, the bacteria we understand the most, streptococcus, was reviewed in depth in 2015 for the first time in a meta-analysis. A group of researchers in Scotland reviewed papers around Sydenham Chorea and its lasting effects on mental health. They report: "there is good evidence of neuropsychiatric comorbidities in Sydenham's Chorea. In countries with a high prevalence of rheumatic fever, the early recognition of salient cognitive and psychiatric symptoms may aid in the management of Sydenham's Chorea."[8] In my humble estimation, the developing world is much better at recognizing the sometimes more subtle nuances of Sydenham Chorea. U.S. doctors have missed many opportunities for arresting Sydenham Chorea and PANDAS that have more subtle presentations. But that is another essay for another day.

So why aren't more researchers exploring these connections in the United States? A study looking at encephalitis hospitalization rates and mortality suggest that more research dollars are needed to substantiate real change and alter the suffering of these patients. The Mayo Clinic study in 2018 observed that "the cost of hospitalization in the United States in 2010 for encephalitis (2 billion U.S. dollars) illustrates its severe disease burden." We know there is a connection; there is ample research to show that. And the evidence supports the obvious need for additional research, if not on a humane level, then certainly on a cost burden level. But quality research costs money. It is time for that research to be fully funded so that the confusion and controversy can be ended at last.

Despite the undeniable evidence, to date, that PANDAS/PANS/AE exists, there are some doctors who refuse to help our children; I imagine a paradigm shift is threatening. A recent report by three neurologists, who admit only seeing "mild PANDAS cases," criticizes the PANS Consortium Guidelines, created by experts in Pediatrics, Neurology, Immunology,

Rheumatology, and Psychiatry, and suggest they not be followed.[9] Yet no solutions are offered other than treating the symptoms as solely psychiatric in origin.

Paradigm shifts *are* difficult. Therefore, we must persist and continue to assemble our stories, both anecdotally through advocacy and awareness efforts, and also statistically via patient registries. We need to report *every single precious life and each child's outcome.* Our community, each parent, has made their efforts meaningful because we are helping each other and the next generations. I put the "critics" of these efforts in my rear view mirror most days; because when all is said and done, we have these children in front of us to heal, and we know we *can* heal them.

Our job, now, is to clarify the overlap of PANDAS/PANS/ AE and help *more* doctors feel confident enough to reach out when children are suffering. I would like PANDAS Network to stop receiving emails filled with a frantic fear and hopelessness. Moms and Dads who are searching for answers to why their child is suddenly changed. Children who have seen many doctors and still aren't getting any relief. Typical encephalitic symptoms being missed by providers who aren't more inquisitive. Families begging for help.

Because of our network of parents and their persistence in raising awareness, we are beginning to hear a different tale. Some families, whose children have sudden onset of symptoms, are finding providers who recognize PANDAS/PANS/AE and will treat it. Often, with early diagnosis and treatment, comes rapid healing. It's really – wonderful! Our goal is to have more of these stories and fewer stories of children being misdiagnosed and mistreated.

After a decade of listening to the families and clinicians, of sharing information and forging relationships, of doing all that I can to raise awareness – I search for meaning in all of this. I ask myself, just as Harold Kushner does, *how will I respond?* Will I live fully, bravely, and meaningfully? Learning to walk with my "unwanted companion" is both deeply painful *and* meaningful. It has connected me to others who have walked a similar path with the same "unwanted companion;" it has connected me to others who have had a similar experience. These experiences also touch the lives of many people we love and care about (friends, colleagues, neighbors, and even strangers); they make living each day with sincerity and purpose more important than ever before *for all of us.*

We still struggle to raise funds for research and need broader treatment for our children, but we have uncovered research that is so much bigger than I ever wanted to imagine. So, we need to p – a – c – e ourselves. This is a hero's journey, and it is a marathon. This illness can be particularly painful, so for what it's worth to the person reading, I have three ideas to sustain us on this journey:

1. Our happiness doesn't mean the absence of grief or struggle or loss in our lives.
2. Empathy and caring for others is what makes us truly human and alive.
3. Community is a treasure where we find healing for our children, and we are that community.

Heather Korbmacher's story is important because she gives a voice to the unrepresented families. For nearly every day of the past decade, I have heard stories of family tragedy, children's lives under attack from debilitating mental and physical torment, financial ruin, confusion, anger, terror, nightmares – and it has changed me. On the other side, I see the heroism of families like Heather's and the medical professionals who treat and have a hand in healing these children, and I am grateful. I have learned that money and science are only truly useful if they are used with loving kindness to improve the lives of humanity and the world at large.

Lastly, sometimes it feels bad. It feels lonely. And sometimes we feel unloved and misunderstood by everyone, including our friends, family, and even the very children we are trying to save. It does feel this way, but don't ever give up. We love our children, and they love us. We have this community, and we are liberating ourselves and our children from this tormenting illness. We are opening the doors for our children to walk through, and we can do this, parents, together!

~ Diana Pohlman, Executive Director PANDAS Network

SECOND FOREWORD
BY CARLA ATHERTON

When I sat down to read Heather Korbmacher's book *What Happened to My Child?*, a riveting account of the author's son's intense struggle with PANDAS/PANS/AE and her heroic journey to heal him, I didn't stop until I was finished. I was educated by her medical explanations; I was moved by the pain her experiences caused her; I was inspired by the fact that, although she never knew what to expect, she got up every day to face whatever was to come. I call Heather a hero, but she would tell you that she just did what she had to do, what she *chose* to do, that the word that would best describe her would be *mom*.

What Happened to My Child? is a book about hope, strength, and determination; and it is also about the pain, fear, worry, and exhaustion that is inevitable when our children get sick, struggles that are all part of the healing process. It is about those pivotal moments that show us parents in no uncertain terms that nothing you have imagined for your life or for the lives of your children will ever go perfectly as planned; we just find it within ourselves to handle whatever life throws our way. It is how one mother simultaneously hung on with formidable grip and focused with unwavering vision, while at the same time, had to let go of what she had foreseen as the perfect life, to let go of what her family's future, their focus, their everyday existence was going to be. Not stopping there, however, we readers get to witness how their family then *transcends the new expectations* that could have come out of their devastating difficulties.

Heather Korbmacher is no victim: she is a revolutionary mama who would not give up, who knew there were answers even when no one solution was the panacea or cure, even when doctors and practitioners could not or would not help, even when she was told that PANDAS/PANS/AE did not exist, even when various therapies did nothing or made things worse. This book is not only about strength, it goes beyond that: it is about love, hope, and recovery. It is an essential message every mother or father with a child who has serious health challenges needs to read and take, not only to heart, but also to spirit.

Heather's story is about making it through the storm, adjusting to an ever-changing new normal, and then recreating yet another normal as they continue to reclaim their son's health, to reclaim their family life, and take the power into their own hands to create a brighter future for their own family and for other families like theirs. A phoenix rising from the ashes.

~ Carla Atherton, MA, FDN, TNC, Director of The Healthy Family Formula, Certified Yoga Instructor, Epidemic Answers Certified Health Coach, Host of the bi-annual Children's and Teen Health Summit, Children's Health Advocate, and Revolutionary Mama

AUTHOR'S NOTE

As an educator, I have often joked with my colleagues about doing my best thinking and planning when I wake up in the middle of the night and can't get back to sleep. Those of you who share this mixed curse and blessing understand the humor in this. My mind starts on a topic and then wanders, often finding inspiration for the classroom or whatever project I may be working on; sometimes lulling me back to sleep. And so it was one early morning as I was imagining what I would say in front of a crowd of people, sharing with them the story of this chaotic, complicated medical and psychiatric condition called PANDAS, PANS, or AE. As I pictured this scene in my mind, I had the realization that I needed to write this story down so that other parents and families could read what we had experienced and know that they were not alone in a time that feels incredibly isolating and terrifying. I wanted them to know that they were not crazy in a medical and psychiatric world that suggested they were. I needed to share with families like ours that there was hope!

I was first excited about this idea, and then I wondered where it would lead, because this journey hasn't been just a medical journey for our family. And it hasn't been just the healing of our son. It is my healing, also. Although I felt that telling the personal part of the story was important, I wondered if it would somehow make the medical part less credible. But I knew that it was the whole story that made this experience so incredible: that it was, in fact, a journey of the body, mind, and soul. We are multi-faceted beings existing on levels some of which I am likely not even aware of, and if our story could help even one other person attain physical, emotional, or spiritual healing, or at the very least, could help a family find the medical supports they need to get proper treatment for their child, then it will have been worth it.

During the first three years of living with PANDAS/ PANS/AE, I took copious daily notes and kept a spreadsheet of symptoms and impact of treatments on these symptoms. Most of the dialogue and events are taken directly from my notes. I changed the names of some people to protect their privacy. I omitted the names of anyone I spoke derogatorily of so as not to damage their reputations. Most importantly, all the names could be replaced with the names of any other person, and the story would be the same. But this is *my* version of *our* story. It is intended to give hope, to provide a starting place for families facing a similar experience, to raise awareness and challenge currently held beliefs about mental health, and to inspire intrigue. It is not intended to provide medical advice. Anyone who suspects they or their child are dealing with this illness, or any other mental health challenges, should seek the advice of a professional. I share how I, like so many parents, stumbled across this illness through countless hours of searching for understanding. I share resources that helped us with diagnosis and treatment. If you are searching for answers for your child, then I hope these resources will give you a place to start. I share how we moved beyond our own journey to touch the lives of others. You may be moved to join us in raising awareness and breaking down the stigma of mental health so our children and our loved ones can have deep healing. I tell our story. If you are reading this because it is fascinating, *and it is*, then I hope you will see how wrong it is that parents must work so hard to get help for their children in a country that should be blazing a trail for healing.

I recognize that this story is written at a time when this illness is still considered controversial in the wider medical and psychiatric fields. I hope that the day is near when this will not be so. I understand that providers don't always have time to read the latest research, and so they haven't heard of this illness, or they haven't read past the controversial debate over the name and treatment recommendations. I am enraged that influential doctors contend that this illness isn't real, or if it is real, that it is rare, and that the symptoms should be treated by psychotropic drugs.[1] It is my observation that many of these same doctors serve as consultants for, and are funded by, big pharmaceutical companies, yet they report no conflict of interest. They cite a lack of rigorous human studies by clinical researchers as their primary reason for not substantiating this diagnosis, yet they have never contributed to research themselves to prove or disprove it. I believe this will change as those clinical researchers they discredit continue to do the heroic work of investigating while treating and healing our children. But currently, the controversy continues.

The name, alone, has several acronyms, which can be confusing. PANDAS (Pediatric Autoimmune Neuropsychiatric Disorder Associated with Streptococcus), PANS (Pediatric Acute-onset Neuropsychiatric Syndrome), and AE (Autoimmune Encephalitis). The progression of the name changes indicates, to me, a shift in understanding as research emerges and clinicians grapple with the urgent reality that these children need early diagnosis, and with appropriate treatment, can heal. Symptoms and triggering factors have been expanded on. Treatment options have been identified and continue to be explored. The search for a biomarker is underway. The name debate has raised barriers for families seeking answers, it has handicapped providers trying to accurately diagnose and treat our children affected by this illness, and it has slowed awareness. To us, the parents, this is criminal.

Throughout this book, I use the different labels interchangeably. Our son met the diagnostic criteria of PANS, but it was Streptococcus that was identified as the triggering pathogen, indicating PANDAS. In my opinion, AE of the basal ganglia best describes this illness. A pathogen has triggered an autoimmune response resulting in encephalitis or inflammation in the brain. Specifically, the basal ganglia, a group of subcortical nuclei responsible primarily for motor control, as well as other roles such as motor learning, executive functions and behaviors, and emotions.[2] This inflammation is causing symptoms that are far beyond a child's ability to control, yet these symptoms are often misdiagnosed and, therefore, mistreated.

Scientists have been exploring the connection between pathogens and mental wellness for more than a century.[3] In the late 1800's, syphilis-induced madness, now referred to as neurosyphilis, was plaguing the asylums of the time. Medicine and psychiatry worked together to try to understand the bacteria-induced delusions of grandeur, erratic behavior, and eventually paralysis and death. Even then, there was skepticism between the two fields, but the exploration of pathogen-induced mental illness was underway as it was evident to science that this was more than just a "scourge from God." With the development of penicillin in the 1940's, the accounts of syphilis dropped dramatically, and again, medicine and psychiatry unzipped. As researchers continue to explore the biological factors of psychiatric disorders, today, the body of evidence grows, supporting the revelation that neuroinflammatory and immunological abnormalities are present in psychiatric disorders. Fortunately, once again, the distinction between medicine and psychiatry is fading.

Recent discoveries in 2015, by multiple scientists, showed that the lymphatic system in mice extends into the brain.[4] This discovery was considered so significant that they would have to "rewrite the textbooks." These findings were confirmed in humans in 2017. The lymphatic vessels serve as a highway throughout the body to circulate key immune cells and return metabolic waste products to the bloodstream and back into the brain. This discovery is significant because it asserts that the lymphatic system plays a vital role in immune response *within* the brain. With this new knowledge come implications for treating and preventing brain disorders and mental health problems involving immune-related inflammation.

In this exciting time of learning, there is still so much that we don't know about the intricacies of the brain, the immune system, and the impact of pathogens and inflammation on mental health. As clinical researchers are doing their best to diagnose and treat our children, they have voiced a need for a biomarker that can definitively identify if a child does or does not have PANDAS, PANS, or AE. To answer this call, some scientists are doing the meticulous work of trying to understand the mechanisms of this illness in order to identify the best diagnostic tools. Providers are courageously treating our children, and clinical researchers are collecting data that can be used to further the advancement of diagnostic and treatment options. In a medical community of specialists that often work in isolation from each other, findings are not always shared, and connections are not always made. This slows the process. Research takes time and resources, and it is critical that every study meet scientific criteria in order to be credible. We understand all of that; yet, we, the parents, want and need answers and help *now.* We are afraid, and we are frantic. But we are also courageous and determined. We will not stop until the science has done right by our children. We will continue to raise our voices...for awareness, for diagnosis, for treatment, and for insurance to cover the costs. We will raise the money needed for the research to continue. We will lead the way with legislation. We will connect providers and researchers. We will create the data bank of information. We will be the change.

I ask that, as you read our story, you have an open mind. And if you are moved by our story, add your voice to the cause. Tell others. Thank you for going on this journey with us. Thank you for being a part of our healing and inviting us to be a part of yours.

ACKNOWLEDGEMENTS

I would like to acknowledge the generous contributions of friends and family who supported the writing and publishing of this book through our Kickstarter campaign. Specifically, I would like to thank Joseph and Adrienne Doucette, Oriana & John Burns along with their children John and Aria, and my husband, Arnold Korbmacher. If I hadn't met my Kickstarter goals, I don't think I would have completed this book. Thank you *all* for supporting this endeavor!

I mention our team of providers throughout the story, but I must pay tribute here to the incredible people who helped us get diagnosis and treatment in order to save our son from a lifetime of mental illness. I would like to thank Jordana Hawkins for truly listening to us and running the original diagnostics to help us uncover what was going on in our son's body. Thank you also for being willing to collaborate and order tests and treatment in our area to make it easier for us to access. I would like to thank Hatha Gbedawo for being strong and unwavering in the belief that we would heal our son. Thank you for guiding us through the many treatment options to find what was needed to help our son's body heal and for your continued investigation into learning what others are doing to treat their patients. I would like to thank Carla Atherton for providing invaluable information through the Lotus Health Program and Healthy Family Formula Programs. Your training helped me clean out our home, clean up our diet, and to know what questions to ask. I would like to thank Sandy Gluckman for teaching us how to be parents who heal by reducing the stress response while gently rewiring the brain. I would like to thank Ted Putvin for helping us fine tune all the supplements, antibiotics, essential oils, homeopathies, and energy treatment to best meet the needs of our son's body. And I would like to thank Diana Pohlman. Your leadership in the world of PANDAS was crucial to helping us get information and guidance during each stage of this journey. Don't ever doubt that you are saving children's lives! Thank you, also, for your friendship and commitment to making a difference.

The support of family and friends was so helpful during a time in my life that was isolating and terrifying. I am so grateful to all those who showed up for us in the many ways that you did. I am especially grateful to Peg Mazen (Nana). I couldn't have wished for a more generous and strong stepmom. Thank you for your gift of living near us for six months when things were their hardest. Thank you for spending time with our boys and with us on a daily basis. Thank you for all the research you did to help me get resources and for brainstorming with me. Thank you for the last minute runs into town to get something that Hans would eat. Thank you for the lattes, hot cocoas, and steamed milks. Thank you for your unconditional love and support. You are a gift to my family and to this world!

Finally, I would like to thank my husband, Arnold, for supporting me in writing this book. Not once did you doubt my ability to pull this off. You trusted me with our most precious task of healing our son, and I thank you for standing with me through the most difficult thing we have ever done together.

LIST OF ABBREVIATIONS

AE – Autoimmune Encephalitis

CBD – Cannabidiol

DIBELS – Dynamic Indicators of Basic Early Literacy Skills

EEG – Electroencephalogram

IVIG – Intravenous Immunoglobulin

LDN – Low Dose Naltrexone

MRI – Magnetic Resonance Imaging

NIMH – National Institute of Mental Health

PANDAS – Pediatric Autoimmune Neuropsychiatric Disorder Associated with Streptococcus

PANS – Pediatric Acute-onset Neuropsychiatric Syndrome

PET – Positron Emission Tomography

RF – Rheumatic Fever

SC – Sydenham Chorea

PART 1

Onset:
The Road to Hell

"The Edge... There is no honest way to explain it because the only people who really know where it is are the ones who have gone over."

Hunter S. Thompson,
Hell's Angels: A Strange and Terrible Saga

CHAPTER ONE

FLIGHT 471

Flight 471 had a perfect landing at SeaTac airport that Sunday evening in April, 2014. We were returning from a weekend wedding celebration in southern California, honoring my Uncle Anthony's union with his beautiful bride, Christina. Our plan was to have dinner in the airport, pick up our car, then drive the hour and a half home to Bellingham. My husband, Arnold, our two boys, and I would get to bed a little later than usual that night, but we would be off to school and work the next day, a little tired, but totally doable. We joined the single-filed crowd in the aisle of the Boeing 737 to work our way off the plane. Emerging from the jet bridge, we began looking for a restaurant where we could sit down and get some food. I asked our 10-year old son, Hans, what sounded good to him.

"I don't know."

This inability to make a decision had become a common response recently, and I was tired of guessing.

"Okay, we'll go have a burger."

"No, I don't want a burger."

"Alright, how about pizza?"

"No. I don't know what I want! Oh, never mind!"

We continued walking, my frustration mounting as every restaurant we came upon was adamantly declined. We were approaching the food court, and I thought with some relief, *everyone can have exactly what they want.* But Hans couldn't decide what he wanted. I was impatient, offering suggestions. Then Hans walked over to a post, began banging his forehead against it and crying.

"I don't know! It's too much!"

He looked up at me with a tear-streaked face, turned, and walked briskly away. Just like that, he walked away from us in a crowded airport.

"Leave me alone!" were his parting words.

And there I was, standing in the food court of the SeaTac Airport, and time slowed for a brief moment. My oldest son had just bolted in a crowded public place. *This is really happening*, I thought to myself. *Put on your work hat.*

I am a Special Education teacher by degree, specifically trained to work with students who present with challenging behaviors. I've had students run from me, hit and kick me, call me names, and fall apart. I know misbehavior, and I know how important it is to stay calm.

I looked at my husband, Arnold, who had a questioning look on his face.

"Take Andre to get pizza and noodles, find a table, and I'll bring Hans back here."

I knew I needed to keep my eyes on Hans. In my mind, it was no different than a man overboard, and I didn't want to lose my child in the sea of people. I also wanted assistance. As I kept my eyes on Hans, I began to scan the crowd looking for security. I thought that maybe Hans would respond to me with a security officer. He had always been enamored with police and soldiers. It occurred to me that I had never paid attention to whether there were security officers present in an airport, and now that I was looking for one, they seemed to be everywhere. For some reason, this slow motion string of thought struck me as funny. I saw a lady with grey hair and a bit overweight. No, not her. There was an older man, not very friendly looking. Not him, either. Then I saw a young man with a kind face, physically fit. I approached him.

"Are you a security officer?"

"Yes."

"My son has a disability," I lied, "and has just bolted. I need you to walk with me while I follow him." I knew the disability word would get sympathy and support.

I pointed out Hans, the 10-year old boy in the skinny jeans with the tie dye pink t-shirt and baseball cap. The young security officer told me that he was about to go on his break, but he would walk with me. He also told me that he couldn't touch my son. I assured him that I didn't need him to. I was confident that if Hans needed to be restrained, I could do that. In addition to being a Special Education teacher, I was also a Right Response trainer for the school district that I worked in. I'd had to restrain and escort children who were unsafe. Hans wasn't being unsafe, other than bolting from his family, and I didn't want to lay hands on him unless it was absolutely necessary. I have experienced that laying hands on a child in crisis only escalates the behavior.

"Do you want me to call the police?"

"No, I don't want to involve the police."

I was pretty sure that Hans would respond to just having a security officer with me, and I did not want this to become a bigger situation than it already was. As I called to Hans to wait for us, he turned around; his face clenched in anger.

"Leave me alone!" he yelled, then kept walking.

I told the security officer, "we've never had this happen before."

"This is a safe place for this to happen, there isn't really anywhere he can go."

What had just felt overwhelmingly scary to me suddenly became completely manageable. We were approaching Hans.

"Hey, do you like baseball?"

Hans stopped and replied, "no."

"He likes the Seahawks!" I interrupted as I told myself to be quiet and let this guy engage Hans.

The security officer laughed, "yeah, who doesn't love the Seahawks right now?" Seattle fans were still enjoying the high of winning the Super Bowl.

They exchanged small talk about sports, and he was able to get Hans to walk back with us to the food court. Hans didn't want me within 100 feet of him. I assured him that I would follow 100 feet behind him, knowing that he really just needed space. I needed him in front of me so I could keep my eyes on him.

When we got back to the food court, Arnold and Andre were waiting, pizza and noodles in "to go" boxes and worried looks on their faces. The security officer told Hans he needed to stay with his parents. Later, I wished I had asked him for his name so I could have thanked him. I quickly explained to Arnold and Andre that Hans didn't want us near him. He would follow Arnold and Andre, and I would follow Hans. Arnold and I exchanged looks.

"What's wrong with Hans?" asked Andre, our 8 year old.

"I don't know, sweetheart. He's upset, and we're going to give him space while we go back to the car."

We proceeded to lead Hans through the airport to baggage claim to pick up our luggage; Arnold and Andre, followed by Hans, followed by me. After retrieving our bags, we continued to the bay where we waited for the shuttle to pick us up and take us to the parking garage. Hans immediately hid behind a large pillar. I placed a box of pizza on the bench next to the pillar.

"Here is your favorite pizza, Hans, pepperoni. You can eat it if you want to. I will leave you alone."

Once I had moved away, he peered around the pillar and then stepped from behind and sat on the bench. He ate a few bites. The shuttle arrived, and he boarded first, walking directly to the back of the bus. Arnold, Andre, and I sat in the front. The shuttle filled. Every seat was occupied, and my son was surrounded by strangers. I watched with my peripheral vision, pretending to look out the window. I was terrified. What was going on?

We arrived at the parking garage. The passengers filed off the bus to gather their luggage. Hans left with them, and I was worried he was going to bolt again, and this time there were lots of places to go and none of them were safe. I kept my distance pretending to be calm until our car was brought to us. I let Hans climb in first, followed by the rest of us.

"We will give you as much space as we can."

He was not in control, kicking on the driver's seat, pulling on Arnold's seat belt, and swearing. Arnold asked him to stop. I told him to keep the driver safe, and that if he didn't, we would have to call the police. He didn't care, and my statement just became an empty threat as I was unwilling to involve the police. I tried to engage him with the iPad. He refused. I pulled up a game and handed it to him. He finally settled playing Dragonvale, eating pizza, and talking to himself, interspersed with the angry outbursts of kicking the seat and yanking on the seat belt. Had I known then how bad it was going to get, we would have gone directly to Seattle Children's Hospital Emergency Room and checked in. Instead, we endured an hour and a half of what seemed like crazy behavior. But thank goodness we didn't go that night, as I would later learn that SCH wasn't open to the diagnosis of PANDAS or PANS at that time, and he would have likely been misdiagnosed and put in a psych bed.

We arrived home, even later than planned. Arnold unloaded the bags. I ushered Andre into the house and up to the bathroom to get ready for bed. Hans went into his room, slammed his door, and went to bed in his clothes and with his teeth unbrushed. I snuggled with Andre for a few minutes, kissing him on his nose as I did every night.

"Why is Hans acting this way?"

"I don't know, honey. But I'm going to find out. Let's get some sleep. It's been a long day."

I checked on Hans. He was disheveled, but sleeping. I climbed into my own bed, exhausted and afraid. The sleep that had already overtaken Arnold finally gave me a reprieve.

CHAPTER TWO
PERFECT PARENTS

I have never been what I would consider an intuitive parent. This is not to say that I can't tell when my child is hurt or sad, but I have always read books and looked to the science and research to tell me what is best for my children's development. I was committed, from the beginning, to establishing a sleep routine, and I kept sleep logs on both of my boys as infants. Our first son, Hans, was a "textbook" baby. He met all the developmental milestones and "learned" to sleep just as the books taught. Our second son, Andre, taught me that not all children follow the books. He, too, met all the developmental milestones, but his sleep habits were not as easily trained as Hans's had been. With Hans I would think, *didn't you read the book?* when I heard moms share their stories about walking their child or putting them in the car to get them to sleep. With Andre, I realized that though I had read the book, he hadn't, and I found myself walking up and down our stairs every night, quietly singing lullabies trying to get him to sleep. I began to learn not to judge other parents who were doing it differently; there may be a very good reason why. This lesson would present to me over and over again with what was to come, until I could no longer ignore the significance of it. Releasing judgment and embracing compassion would become two of the most significant life lessons I would finally learn through this isolating experience with Hans, an experience that changed everything I had once believed to be true.

I continued this pattern of textbook parenting throughout all of the decisions we made. Our children didn't have any sugar before the age of one. There were no sodas in our home and rarely juice. The television was never on if the boys were in the room, and we were extremely careful about what they were exposed to as they got older. We ate all of our meals at the table together and expected good manners. We interacted with our children, reading books, singing songs, playing games, and we spent time outside. When the boys were old enough for pre-school, we chose Waldorf education, initially because of the costumes and beautiful set up in the classroom. Both boys loved dress up and imaginative play and spent countless hours with neighborhood kids donning costumes that I had sewn for them and creating worlds filled with adventure as they played on the hill behind our home. With the Waldorf preschool, we found teachers and a group of parents who shared our beliefs about preserving the innocence of the child. We filled our home with natural fiber products and became those difficult parents to shop for. We created our gift lists, and I even unwrapped gifts to see what they were before our children did and would return things we didn't want to have in our home. To my family who may read this, I'm sorry.

Although we were controlling and somewhat rigid in our systems and routines, we loved our children very much. We played with them, building elaborate forts, creating "work sites" outside for their trucks, providing many opportunities for artistic expression, searching through the Legos for that one needed piece, riding bikes together, playing catch, and so on. I spent the first four years of Hans's life and the first two and half years of Andre's life at home. It was never easy for me, but there were many joyful moments. Arnold and I would joke that we were the perfect parents before we had children! Early on, a friend shared with me that just when you get it all figured out, they move on to the next developmental stage, and it all changes. I was told that these years go by so fast. I thought they were the slowest fast years I had ever experienced. For me, it was hard work. I read a lot, wanting to make the right choices for my children.

The year that Hans would turn five and Andre would turn three, I returned to the classroom, and Arnold quit his job to stay home. I needed to renew my teaching certificate and had decided that I would go through the process of getting my National Board Teacher Certification to do that. I wanted a year back in the classroom before starting. During those first years back teaching in a high school program for our district's most challenging youth, I was very protective of my schedule. I made sure I was home as soon as I could be every day to maximize my time with my children and husband. My family was my primary focus, and my friends and extended family could share many stories of what an interesting set of parents Arnold and I were. We were rather controlled by having children and trying to always do it right, yet feeling that we were falling short so many times. I struggled to learn how to balance work and being a mom. Arnold learned to manage the home.

We moved into the years of schooling. We chose to continue with Waldorf education, greatly appreciating their approach to early childhood. Both Hans and Andre had fabulous teachers, and in the Waldorf education system, the teachers typically stay with them through the 8th grade. They complained from time to time about school, as children are apt to do, but they were doing well in their classes and had close friends.

The kids were healthy and thriving. They played soccer, learned how to ice skate, went to horse camp, and swam at the neighbor's pool. We enjoyed impromptu neighborhood BBQ's and dinner parties, Easter egg hunts at the park, and lots of play time between all eight kids in the neighborhood and classmates.

Hans and Andre were typical siblings, sometimes cooperating, other times fighting. Arnold and I continued to implement systems at home to encourage positive interactions. These systems were really to encourage us, as parents, to acknowledge them when they were playing nicely and supporting each other rather than always correcting their sibling rivalries. The boys "earned" their screen time, which was limited to one hour per week. Gradually, we gave them responsibilities, clearing their dishes, unloading the dishwasher, helping fold laundry, making their beds. We kept to a daily schedule and seasonal rhythm.

The boys were moving up in the grades. Field trips to the farm turned to overnight camping trips. Finger knitting advanced to knitting small animals and crocheting hats. The stringed instruments were introduced. The math became more complex. Reading for learning emerged as they researched their projects and homework was assigned. I became more immersed in my work, taking a new position as the district's behavior specialist working with a team of six. Instead of being in my own classroom, I was supporting teachers and their students who presented with challenging behaviors across the district. I began extending my days beyond the contracted hours as I was apt to do, but still found time to be with my children, working after they went to bed and sometimes late into the night.

We spent our holidays camping in our RV, our home away from home. In the winter, you would find us up at Mt. Baker or Snoqualmie Pass, skiing, building snow patios, and sharing early night campfires under the stars. In the spring and summer, you would find us along a river or lake, visiting family, and exploring the national parks. Our friends knew *The Flair* and we enjoyed many camping experiences together, the kids playing and the parents playing, too. When we had opportunities to celebrate with family afar, we hopped on a plane and joined in the fun. Arnold and I learned to loosen up a bit about our daily schedule as we travelled to other time zones and had to adjust. The boys were exposed to more technology with their cousins, and again, Arnold and I learned to loosen up a bit more. We were accustomed to traveling together and were familiar with the joys and frustrations that brings.

When the boys were 8 and 10, we enjoyed a momentous trip to Europe for a week-long family reunion in a castle in Ireland followed by a week in Paris to visit my sister and her family, a week in Chatel hiking in the French/Swiss Alps, and finishing up in Germany visiting with Arnold's extended family. The boys managed the many checkpoints, bag searches, flights, hotels, rented cars, new foods, and re-packing their backpacks. We enjoyed the intrigue of different cultures and languages while gaining a new appreciation for the comforts of home. We had our joy-filled and frustrating moments and were an exceptionally blessed family.

CHAPTER THREE
THE FLU

We returned from our fun-filled summer in Europe to the securities of our routines and schedules as we began to look forward to the new school year starting. In late August, Arnold's mom was diagnosed with cancer for the second time. Both of our fathers had passed away from cancer before the boys were born, and my mom had passed from cancer the previous spring. We were blessed to have been with each of them as they transitioned from their earthly bodies. Each passing had been unique to the individual and was as mysterious to me as birth; reminders that what we have is precious, and life is to be cherished, in all of its complexities. Arnold and I fully understood that spending time with our parents, while we could, was something to take advantage of rather than take for granted. We decided that Arnold would fly down to California to be with his mom through her treatment, spending two weeks of each month with her in her home.

September was filled with mixed emotions. There was the excitement of starting a new school year. Hans would be in the 4th grade and Andre in the 3rd grade. But there was also the anxious worry about Oma. Arnold flew down to California for what we thought would be his first of many visits supporting his mother during her chemotherapy. Unfortunately, it turned out to be his last visit with his mom. While he cared for her in her home, the boys and I developed a routine that would accommodate my work schedule. I would drop the boys off at school, then go to work. After their school day ended, they would go to after care, and I would pick them up as early as I could. Not too different than most working parents, just slightly different for us as we had always had a parent at home to manage the routines. At the breakfast table, we would skype with Arnold and again at the dinner table, having him with us as much as possible. Arnold stayed with his mom, caring for her in her home until she was moved to the hospital. He was with her, along with his two brothers, when she passed the night before the boys' school held their annual Michaelmas celebration. This had been a favorite occasion for our family over the years, dressing in red, gathering with the other families, and enjoying the activities and treats prepared by the loving hands of parents and children. Michaelmas is a festival of inner strength, when we conquer fear, and awaken ourselves to the eternal within.[1] The boys and I attended this favorite celebration, honoring and mourning Oma, a fitting tribute to a graceful lady.

Oma's passing was hard on all of us. As Arnold had just lost his mom, I was reminded of the fresh pain of recently losing my mom, and our boys were sharing in our grief as Oma had been very much a part of their lives. One night, shortly after Arnold had returned home, Hans was crying in his room.

I went in to see what was wrong, "Hans what's got you sad?"

"I just realized that you and Poppa aren't going to live forever, and I can't take it," he sobbed. I ached as he had his first realization of our mortality.

"Yes, sweetie, some day that will be true. But I want you to know that we are both healthy and strong, and we have a long life ahead of us."

"I know, but I will miss you when you're gone." How true I knew that to be. I held him tight until he settled, and I stayed with him until he was asleep. I let my own feelings of loss consume my thoughts as I missed my parents deeply, especially my dad. He was bigger than life, and he had been my rock. He taught me to see the world with wonder and curiosity and to find the magic in all things. He had a huge heart, and those who knew him felt seen and loved by him. His death left a hole in my life.

Other than the stress of this emotional loss, everything was pretty much as it had always been. We settled into the rhythms of the year. Halloween was followed quickly by Thanksgiving, and then it was early winter. Ski passes were purchased, and our weekly pilgrimage to Mt. Baker for a weekend of skiing began. We would roll into Heather Meadows Friday evening, and I would make dinner while Arnold started a campfire and the boys dug caves in the hillside snow bank. Often we were joined by friends or would make new ones, and I was especially excited to use my new glow-in-the-dark bocce ball set, a beautiful and magical site on the snow under a star filled sky! This winter, the snow was slow to come, and the boys would seek out their favorite runs, checking to see if "Death Star" or the "Canyon" were open, elated when they finally were! We marked off the days of skiing on our calendar, excited for that first run that was "free." I treasured my mornings, waking up to the majesty of the mountains surrounding us, watching as the sun first kissed the American Border Peak a blushing pink. After breakfast, I would sit on our snow patio sipping a cup of coffee, listening to Diana Krall, and snuggle into my down coat, a soft smile reflecting the beauty of nature and the peacefulness of the moment.

Flu season was upon us. We didn't get flu shots, understanding that it was a "guess" which flu viruses might be circulating each year. Mid-December, Hans was sick and had a high fever of 103.7. I knew that a fever was an indication that the body was fighting something and that it was working hard. I knew it wasn't usually necessary to give something to bring the fever down unless it was interfering with sleep, but I was concerned about how high his fever was, so I called the triage nurse and was told to monitor him and that it was likely the flu.

"Give him plenty of liquids," was the advice she offered.

That night, Hans awoke shortly after going to sleep and was making distressed sounds in his room. He was wild-eyed in bed, yelling at Arnold who was the first one to respond to his wake up.

"Get away from me!"

He was rigid. Looking at both of us, he got out of bed, pushed past us both, and walked to the hallway biting on his tongue and grunting. Arnold ran downstairs to get a glass of water while Hans stood there biting and scraping at his tongue with his teeth.

"Hans, Poppa is getting you water. Momma is here. You are safe," I tried to assure him as he was looking distressed.

Arnold gave him a drink of water as he and I exchanged worried looks. Hans drank the water, walked downstairs, stood up on the couch, and raised his arms straight up in the air.

"Sweetie, come on down."

I coaxed him off the couch, and he began fiddling with Arnold's laptop that had been left on the ottoman when we went up to see what the matter was. We gently removed the laptop from his hands.

"Come back upstairs, honey, it's sleep time."

He allowed us to guide him upstairs. Arnold and I decided to put him in our bed so we could keep an eye on him through the night. He settled in our bed and was asleep quickly after that.

We were both a little freaked out about the whole thing. Hans had had fevers before, but we'd never seen a response to being sick like this. I got onto my computer to see what

I could learn about fevers and the unusual behaviors we had seen. I searched credible sites that I felt contained trustworthy information about common health symptoms. Between WebMed, Parent Magazine, and the Mayoclinic, I concluded that Hans had experienced a fever-induced hallucination, and that if he continued to have a fever, we should take him in to see his doctor. The next morning, Hans woke up and looked at me somewhat perplexed.

"What am I doing in here?"

"You woke up feverish last night, and you were acting a little strange. We wanted to keep an eye on you through the night. You're going to stay home today, and we'll see how you're doing." He was fever-free that day and returned to school the following day as if nothing had happened. I was relieved. Two weeks later, right after winter break had started, he presented again with a high fever and had a similar episode.

This time, when he started making distressed sounds in his room shortly after going to sleep with another fever, I tried waking him up.

"Hans, wake up. It's momma. You're in your room. Tell me your name."

He didn't respond to my prompts but settled back into a feverish sleep. That night, I slept on the floor in his room so I could keep an eye on him throughout the night. The next day, he was again fever-free and fine. Both experiences were noteworthy and out of the normal for us, but with his returned health, we assumed that all was okay. We didn't think anything more of it. We brushed it off, not anticipating any further problems, and moved on.

By late December, Arnold and I began to notice some subtle changes, which we thought must be the "12-year change" happening a little early or the onset of pre-pubescent hormones. He seemed almost depressed. The things that previously brought him joy were not so interesting. As we set out on our annual Christmas tree-cutting excursion, Hans expressed that he didn't really want to participate this year. Andre bounded between trees pointing out all the ones he liked. In contrast to Hans's lack of enthusiasm, Andre's joy for this tradition was evident.

"What do you think of this one?"

"I don't really care what tree we get," Hans mumbled. "There aren't any good ones."

Andre's enthusiasm was not to be dampened, and we made a choice with Andre's input, cut our tree, dragged it back to our car, and brought it home. But the joy wasn't there for me as it had been in years past as I was beginning to worry more and more about Hans.

Christmas and the New Year came, and we spent the holidays with family. Christmas morning was bright and early in our home as we all experienced the excitement of what Santa might have left under our tree. Hans was questioning Santa, but Andre was still an adamant believer.

"How could Momma and Poppa hide all these presents in the house?" he would say.

I have always believed in the magic of Christmas. The boys grew up believing in Santa. I knew that one day Santa would no longer be real, but the magic of giving and creating wonder and excitement would always be. One of my favorite books is *The Polar Express*. I love the idea that if you believe, there is always magic. I had certainly experienced enough magical moments to know that to be true. And I fostered that in the boys, just as my dad has fostered that in me.

After the morning excitement, breakfast, and presents, we packed ourselves and our gifts for extended family into our minivan and travelled down to Seattle to join my sisters and brothers and their families for "Second Christmas" at Nana's house, complete with filled stockings and more presents from our Kris Kringles and from Nana. Nana is my step-mom and has been a formative person in my life since she and my dad joined families when I was seven. They each brought two children and then had a fifth together when the four of us were in our early teens. We are an interesting mix of full siblings, half siblings, and step siblings, exemplifying the notion that blood is not a prerequisite for a family. Nana's love for the holiday season greatly influenced the traditions I was continuing in my home. We loved heading to her home to continue our Christmas day.

The boys enjoyed the time with their cousins, and we all celebrated with good food and drink and being together. Two days later, we were back home to welcome Arnold's brother, Uncle Bruno, and his girlfriend, up from California, to spend the New Year with us. We celebrated a "Third Christmas" with an Xbox One accompanied by driving and dance games. Both were games that Uncle Bruno felt certain Arnold and I would approve of. He was right. We enjoyed more good food and drink together, laughing at the videos of our sometimes awesome and sometimes awkward dancing!

New Year's Eve we donned the customary hats, blew on our horns, and set off poppers for the midnight hour. It was nice to have had so much time with extended family. Through all of the revelry though, I noticed that Hans didn't seem completely himself. I couldn't exactly pinpoint it, just that he seemed a little down. I brushed it off and let the festivities carry me. Winter break ended, and we returned to the routines of school.

CHAPTER FOUR

DIS-EASE

As January faded into February, Arnold and I continued to notice changes in Hans's behavior. He became particularly sensitive to criticism or corrections. I especially noticed it at family dinner time. Asking him to sit up in his chair or use his silverware would result in swearing and leaving the table. These seemed to be extreme responses to simple and normal requests.

My reaction to this was to delve into the resources I had access to. I read Ross Greene's *The Explosive Child* [1] and asked Arnold to read it, as well. I began to think about all of our expectations as falling into one of three categories or "baskets." Basket A was the non-negotiables, and safety was the only thing that fell into that category. Basket B was those things we could teach problem solving skills around. When Hans became angry at being called to the table for dinner while playing a video game, I would respond, "I see you're frustrated that it's dinner time, and I'm wondering if you are wanting to finish this round, maybe you could ask if you could come to the table as soon as you're done?" to which he would usually reply with the prompted request. And Basket C contained those things that really weren't worth the escalation, such as eating with your fingers or slouching at the table. This was particularly hard for Arnold who wanted to continue with our expectations as they had always been. When Hans would lean back in his chair at the table, Arnold would tell him to sit up, even though every time it would end with Hans swearing and leaving the table. I began to dread mealtimes, and Arnold and I began to have our own disconnect as I would get frustrated, feeling that he was creating problems rather than just letting problems go. As we began to disagree over our approach to parenting, the frustration in everyone increased.

"I can't discuss parenting with you until you read Ross Greene's book because it is more than I can try to explain to you."

"I just want my kids to have manners and show respect."

"Isn't that what we all want, but at what cost?"

It felt like we were spiraling out of control in disagreement. When I think of the term *dis-ease*, we were already there. Our home was definitely a place of dis-ease.

In addition to the marital strains that Arnold and I were having over parenting, the relationship between Hans and Andre was also becoming more strained. Andre is a year and a half younger than Hans. He is full of energy and loves to experience life in a hands-on way. He is a classic extrovert.[2] He has also always craved his brother's attention and approval. Hans has always been more of an introvert,[3] preferring quiet time alone while he reads a novel or figures something out, and especially not being "bugged" by his younger brother. This is not to say they don't ever interact positively. They have enjoyed many years of typical sibling experiences, playing together, arguing, working it out, and moving on. But Hans was becoming more physical with his reactions towards Andre, pushing him or going after him with a raised fist, saying "I'm gonna' murder the little jerk." I had needed, on several occasions, to physically come between them. I would send Hans to his room. He would go yelling and swearing. Removing privileges and assigning consequences weren't making a difference. I would resort to yelling in anger at these outbursts. This wasn't making a difference, either. But the aggression towards his brother was in Basket A, the non-negotiable category of safety.

"You do not get to hurt your brother!" I would yell in frustration, all my mirror neurons[4] firing.

As a behavior specialist, I knew that I was responding as my brain was wired to do, mirroring the behavior I was seeing. I also knew that I had a fully developed prefrontal cortex that I should be able to access with intent and that I needed to be in control of my own emotional responses. As a parent, I was experiencing how hard it is to do. As big emotional responses were becoming more frequent and the stress that comes from living in that environment was high, I was struggling to practice my own words of instruction I had provided countless times to others. I was getting caught up in the emotional crisis and making the situation worse time and time again.

It was at this time that I started to think, maybe I should have Hans evaluated. He was displaying aggressive behaviors that were far more extreme than we had seen before, and Arnold and I thought maybe with an early onset of pre-pubescent hormones and a family predisposition for mental illness, we may be seeing something emerging. I looked into where I could get a pediatric neurological-psychiatric evaluation and learned that there was only one person in the Bellingham area who offered this service, and she didn't take Molina, the state insurance coverage we had for our boys. I would find this problem again and again! I contacted Seattle Children's Hospital and was sent a list of providers in my area. I was familiar with this list; these were the organizations I referred families to who didn't have private insurance: Catholic Community Services, Interfaith, Whatcom Counseling and Psychiatric Clinic. You call a central number and are referred on. My own biases emerged. I didn't want to be in this group, waiting in the office with the same clients that I served through the school system. We weren't in crisis. So I stalled.

CHAPTER FIVE

DIFFICULT STAGES

As winter fades into spring in Whatcom County, those who don't spend their weekends driving East on the 542 to head up to the mountain and play in the snow are usually pretty tired of the long months of rain that deluges the lowlands. The months spent indoors result in jubilation when the first rain-free days occur and the crocuses emerge. At the first opportunity, folks head outside.

March arrived, and the *dis*-ease in our home was being managed by our letting go of previously held expectations, particularly manners at the table and swear words. Arnold had finished reading *The Explosive Child*, and we had agreed to ignore certain behaviors. At the same time, I was trying to provide emotional coaching to Hans when issues would come up that could be turned into learning opportunities. I would verbalize that I saw him feeling a certain way and was wondering if maybe he needed something. Then I would offer a way for him to problem-solve with me. Problem-solving consisted of giving a little to get a little and required that we both give. I was the one who had to come up with several solutions until we could agree upon an outcome because he simply couldn't problem-solve, himself. Most of the time, his response would be an angry, "I don't know!"

One afternoon, one of the neighbor boys was over playing outside. Hans came in the house in a crying rage.

"He needs to go home now! Make him go home. He's an imbecile. If he doesn't go home in 5 seconds, I'm gonna kill the little jerk!"

"I hear that you are very upset. Tell me what happened."

"He just needs to go home now. He's an idiot. I don't know, just never mind! Make him go now!"

I tried to understand what had happened, but he wasn't making any sense.

"Okay, I hear that something happened to upset you, and it's time for our friend to go home. I'm taking care of it. You take a break here, while I explain that it's time to go home."

I found Andre and Trevor outside.

"Hans is very upset. Can you tell me what happened to make him so angry?"

They both seemed baffled by Hans's response.

"I have no idea. We were playing, and he just ran into the house."

"Ok, well let's call it a day for now, and we'll get together again soon."

I went back into the house and found Hans at the top of the stairs with his Nerf gun, seething and ready for battle.

"Hans, Trevor is going home. You and Andre will have some space from each other. You can put the Nerf gun down."

"Good," he said and returned to his room.

I was questioning my response. We had been experiencing these extreme behaviors in the home, and now I was seeing this same overreaction occur with a friend. I was worried about what he would do. I wanted to help him get calm so he didn't get aggressive with Andre or their friend. My training was conflicting with my mother intuition. Was I encouraging this behavior by giving in to his demand, or was I preventing a crisis? Or both? I told myself that preventing his aggression was the right thing to do. I trusted my intuition and sent Trevor home.

Two weeks later, Arnold and I celebrated our 18th wedding anniversary. Arnold spent the day bike riding with our good friend, John. The boys and I spent the day with his wife, Abigail, and their two kids. Not the most romantic anniversary, but we've always felt that celebrations can be flexible as to when we honor them. This was a family that our boys had grown up with. We'd spent time together camping, dinner parties at both homes, 4th of July celebrations, birthdays, and impromptu get-togethers. When our boys were toddlers, our friends celebrated the birth of their first child, Jay, followed two years later by their daughter, Arial. Hans and Andre were idolized by their son, and in turn, they were both good role models. So I was surprised when Hans came into the house as he had done two weeks previously with our neighbor. Again, he was in a crying rage saying the same things, but this time it was about Jay.

"They need to go home right now! Jay and Andre are being mean! I don't want them here anymore!" each sentence delivered between the sucking air of sobbing.

"Hans, I see you are upset. Tell me what you are feeling." I was troubled by what was beginning to feel like a pattern.

"They are being mean!"

"What did they do that was mean?"

"They only want to do what *they* want to do."

"Ok, and that's got you upset. How about you do something you would like to do in your room, and then we'll see how you're feeling in a bit."

This time I was able to talk him through his feelings and give him quiet time to calm down. After about twenty minutes, he was able to return to playing with Andre and Jay. Abigail and the kids stayed until Arnold and John came home, and we enjoyed a BBQ together, though I was ever so watchful.

No one else had noticed Hans's outburst, and he had gotten over his extreme reaction fairly quickly. I was relieved and thought this was progress, but I was still concerned. I was hoping that we were in an awkward stage and that, with continued emotional coaching, Hans would develop skills to deal with his big emotions, and we would get through this rough time. I was looking forward to having fewer of these responses as he continued to develop skills. Was I in denial or hanging on to hope?

Impromptu BBQ's with the neighbors were events the family was used to. A week later, it was no surprise when Hans, Andre, and the neighbor boys came in from playing on the back hill asking if we could invite their parents up for dinner. It was a resounding *yes* from all the parents as we were all ready to shake off the winter greys and enjoy the beginning of spring. The boys continued their play outside, while the adults enjoyed a glass of wine, the grill working its magic. Dinner was ready to be served, and I had gone in to open another bottle of wine when Hans came in the house crying and yelling.

"Trevor needs to go home now! They all do! Make them go home!"

I was feeling more than annoyed by this repeated behavior. We had gone from big emotional responses in the home to social situations outside the home, and they were becoming more frequent.

"Dinner is ready, and we invited our friends up, so we will feed everyone and then they will go home."

Hans began swearing and insisting that they go home.

"You're not my mother! You don't care about me."

I was at my worst, having had two glasses of wine, feeling impatient with this recurring scene, and needing to get dinner served. As I walked away, I muttered to myself, "you're right, I'm not your mother, you're from Mars." I don't think

I could have done worse emotional damage than that. Hans became hysterical.

"I told you! You said it yourself! You're not my mother! I hate you! This isn't my family!" He was hyperventilating, and I was horrified at what I had just said and what was happening. Arnold came in the house to see what was going on as he could hear the commotion from outside. I briefly explained how I had botched what was already becoming a bad situation. We put food in to-go containers, and I went outside, crying, to hug my neighbor.

"I'm sorry, but we're going to have to call it a night." She knew that things had been tough recently and was very understanding as she gathered her family to walk the two blocks home.

It took some time to help Hans get calm, and I apologized for the hurtful words I had said. I reassured him that I was his mother and that I loved him dearly. His hurt reply was a dagger in my heart.

"How do I know you're really my mother?! How can you prove it?!" I got his birth certificate, thinking it would be physical proof for him, though I was worried he might tear it up. Then I told him the story of his birth, a story he had heard many times over the years.

Arnold and I had tried to conceive for six years unsuccessfully. With the intervention of In Vitro Fertilization, we got pregnant with Hans. We were beyond thrilled to have this precious soul in our lives. The morning that Hans was born was the biggest explosion of love that I had ever experienced. I will never forget that first moment of holding him in my arms. I never knew I could feel love that deeply. We've called Hans our miracle of science. Eight months later, when we got pregnant with Andre naturally, we referred to him as our miracle of nature, and that deep love became twofold.

I slid his birth certificate under the door and began: "the night that you began to come into this world I awoke feeling the tightness of contractions. Poppa breathed with me and supported me at home until it was time to head to St. Joe's. They had a beautiful room ready for us. Our wonderful doctor joined us, and we labored through the night until the early hours. When you were born and they put you on my chest, I felt the most amazing sensation of love. One of my favorite pictures is you all snuggled up with me sleeping peacefully. We were so happy after so many years of wanting you. You will always be our miracle. And we will always have that deep love for you."

Hans had stopped crying. He accepted my apology by opening his door and handing me back his birth certificate. It was a somber dinner and bedtime routine that night. Hans didn't want to read with Andre and me. Instead, he chose to stay in his room alone and read his own book. That night, I lay awake reflecting on the evening and how poorly I had handled it. I decided that since we were seeing a pattern in Hans's behavior, I needed to be clear-headed so I could be there for him in a more supportive way. I felt that if I had not had several glasses of wine, I wouldn't have responded the way that I had. I was accustomed to having a glass of wine with dinner, but I was aware that it affected my judgment. I made the decision to stop drinking. I shared this decision with Arnold the next day, and he supported it. It would be a surprise to my friends as I was the one who was always trying out new cocktails and serving up drinks at our social gatherings, but I needed to do this for Hans and for myself.

That was Friday, and Sunday was the annual Easter egg hunt and party at the neighborhood park. Between the neighbors on our street and friends, there are more than fifty children who converge in the park to search for eggs filled with goodies. This tradition was started by two families on our block when our children were all toddlers together. The parents would gather the day before to fill the plastic eggs and donate gently used treasures for the "golden egg table" where kids would trade in their golden eggs for a new-to-them delight. After all the excitement of hunting for eggs, the kids would enjoy fun activities hosted by the parents. Tug of war was always a favorite as kids pulled hard to topple the parents in heaps of laughter. The games were followed by a potluck and social time for parents, while the children played. This year I was on duty for mixing Bloody Mary's to be served from our neighbor's backyard that opens onto the park. As Arnold and I prepared for the event, we discussed how we would keep an eye on Hans. We were concerned that he might have another angry outburst. I told Arnold I wasn't going to drink.

"But you're making Bloody Marys!"

"I'm making them. That doesn't mean I have to drink them!"

Along with other parents in the neighborhood, we both had assigned tasks for ensuring that the event would run smoothly. Our plan was that we would carry our cell phones and make sure that one of us was always nearby to keep an eye and ear on Hans.

One of my neighbor friends, who likes to tease my drinking habits, asked me, "what's in the glass?" a favorite question.

"Iced tea. I'm not drinking today. Hans has been having some big emotional responses to frustration, and I need to be clear-headed in how I approach it."

He smiled, and that was that. We made it through the event with no mishaps. Hans enjoyed the games with the neighbor friends, and again, I hoped that we were just going through one of those difficult stages.

CHAPTER SIX
IT'S HAPPENING

One week later, Hans joined in the celebration of a classmate's birthday at one of the bowling alleys in town. When I arrived to pick him up, Hans was the last one remaining, and they were playing with some of the new toys his classmate had received at his party. Hans asked if his classmate could come home to play Monsuno at our house. I checked in with the mom who said that would be fine. I explained to her that we were going to the home of another classmate's parents later that evening to celebrate the completion of his national board certification in psychology and would take her son home after that. She agreed. Arnold, far more intuitive than I, wasn't sure we should go. I really wanted to honor this accomplishment and pushed.

"It will be fine, and they're going to have pizza there for the kids."

Arnold agreed reluctantly, and we took the three boys with us to the party. Upon arriving at the front door, the guest of honor welcomed us in with a new hat on his head. Hans promptly knocked it off his head, a mischievous smile on his face.

"Hey that's my new lid, hands off," Ethan laughed as he jabbed Hans in the ribs with a playful gesture.

The three boys went around back to join their friends in play. Arnold and I mingled with the parents we had grown to know so well over the past five years. Looking out the large windows, we could see past the deck to the yard below where the children were playing. Beyond that was the bay, with Mount Constitution standing proudly on Orcas Island. I have always loved the views of the San Juan Islands, their mystical blue layers deceiving the eye of all the evergreens that cover these Coast Salish islands. Upon entering the main room, I was greeted by my friend who was hosting the party to honor her husband's hard work. She handed me a crafted cocktail, wanting to know what I thought of it. She and I had enjoyed exchanging recipes and trying new seasonal drinks. She knew I wasn't a big fan of shrubs, which is a sweetened vinegar-based syrup, but she thought I might like this one. I sipped it, giving her my nod of approval, making a note to myself to sip slowly. I still wanted to stay clear-headed, but the social pressures of this group of parents had me wanting to cover up what was going on in my family. I reasoned that having one cocktail would be manageable; this would be my one drink for the evening. I was surprised that I liked it and told her so. I joined several of the moms discussing their gardening needs. As I listened to how hard it was to find a good gardener, I was thinking to myself how trivial it all seemed. I was feeling like my life was beginning to unravel, and here I was pretending that everything was fine and that standing around drinking cocktails and discussing gardener issues was normal. It felt superficial and somehow meaningless to me in that moment.

Then I heard Arnold's voice from across the room, "it's happening."

I knew exactly what he meant. Putting my nearly full cocktail glass on the nearby table and looking out the window, I saw Hans standing on the deck yelling down at his schoolmates and seething with anger.

"What's happening?" I heard one of the moms say as I quickly went outside.

"Hans, stop."

Standing behind him, I ushered him to the side of the house by reaching my arms out on both sides of his body and walking so that he had to walk with me. He was swearing and yelling in between his sobs.

"I'm going to kill those fucking imbeciles! Those jerks!"

"I can hear how angry you are. Tell me what happened."

Between his angry sobs, he was able to tell me that two of the girls had taken his hat and were throwing it around. I immediately saw the irony in this after our entrance. He had put one of the girls in a headlock trying to get it back before he realized that she didn't have it. I found out later that Andre, knowing that Hans wasn't having fun, had told them to stop, gotten the hat back, and had given it to Hans. Hans remembered differently, that after he released the girl from the headlock, *he* found the person who had his hat and grabbed it from her. This was a pattern I had seen unfolding, Hans remembering situations differently from others present or others not understanding what he was so upset about. After Hans got his hat back, he made his way up to the deck and was yelling and swearing down at them. He told me that the classmate, whose birthday party he had attended and who had spent the afternoon with us, had said something that made him mad, but when I asked what he had said, he wouldn't tell me.

"You don't need to know!"

As we were sitting there, he had gathered up a handful of small pebbles and clenched them in his fist. One of the other dads came out the front door and looked over towards us sitting on a low wall at the front corner of the house. "Are you mad, Hans?"

I cringed as Hans threw the pebbles at him. I forced a smile on my face.

"Yes he is. Would you please go tell Arnold that it's time to go home?"

He turned around and re-entered the front door he had just come out of. Within a few minutes, Arnold appeared. Hans was crying.

"Take me home now!" he sputtered in between the catching breath of expired sobs.

We walked to the car, and Arnold shared with me that he had already arranged for Andre to stay and he would return to pick him and Hans's friend up later. I appreciated that he had the foresight to do this. At the same time, I felt angry and embarrassed. Arnold had suspected this wasn't going to work, and I had pushed to go. I had hoped that Hans having a good time at the birthday party was a sign that he could handle this event, as well. I had wanted to just go to a party and enjoy myself. Now I was feeling badly that I hadn't listened to Arnold. I was mad that I couldn't enjoy a social gathering. And I was worried about what these parents that we had grown so close to would be thinking. This was not the Hans that they knew.

It was a quiet ride home, other than the leftover sobs from Hans in the back seat. I was grateful that Arnold didn't ask Hans to tell him what had happened as I had already done that and didn't want to re-trigger his emotions. Arnold dropped us off at home and left to gather up Andre. I trusted Arnold to have a good explanation upon his return to the party. I knew there would be some inquiry as we had just disrupted what was supposed to be a celebratory party. I could picture Arnold's half smile as I imagined him explaining that we were working through some big emotions with Hans lately. I wondered what the other parents would think, but I trusted them to be understanding.

At home, I fed Hans dinner and began our routine for getting ready for bed. Arnold and Andre returned home. The boys bathed and brushed their teeth. Andre and I climbed into Arnold's and my bed to read together while Hans read by himself in his room before we all went to our own beds for sleep. It had been a hell of a long day. As I lay there, I recounted the past several months. We had gone from big emotions occurring in the home to them also occurring in social settings, and now they were happening more frequently. We had gone from once a month, to several times in a month, to weekly. I was concerned about the patterns we were seeing. Later, I would be told that this progressive pattern of behaviors was what is called a *subacute onset*. It would be explained to me that the onset of symptoms had occurred when Hans had presented with, what we had called, fever-induced hallucinations. My training as a behavior specialist had made it possible for me to manage these symptoms as they were emerging and increasing until they were so big that I no longer could.

The next day was Arnold's birthday, and that night was a wedding shower for my youngest sister, Nicole. We drove down to Nana's house joined by our sitter who would watch the boys while we all attended the party. Kaylene was our preferred care provider for the boys when Arnold and I had a date or would both be gone. She had been caring for the boys for several years and engaged them in creative activities, knew and supported our family values from her own time as a student at the Waldorf school, and genuinely cared about our kids. We were typically very confident in leaving the boys in her care. This night, however, I felt apprehensive as I told her not to hesitate to call if Hans became at all agitated or unmanageable.

The wedding shower was a lovely event, hosted by the close friends of my soon-to-be brother-in-law's mother. There was fine whiskey, good food, and the company of both families and friends commingling in celebration of these two amazing people! I had witnessed the development of their relationship over the past years as they had travelled the world together. Their love for each other was evident in the way they communicate respectfully and honestly with one another. I adored Nicole and was confident in the man she had chosen to spend the rest of her life with. Their relationship was one that we could all model after, and I was so happy to honor them. Typically, I would have tried each of the fine whiskeys being served in celebration, but tonight I slowly sipped on my one glass, determined to enjoy the warm flavor without clouding my judgment.

During the festivities of the evening, I was sharing with my brother's wife a little bit about what had been going on with Hans and that we were concerned. She talked with me about Spiritual Response Therapy and the healing it had provided for her daughter, my niece. Essentially, SRT is examining our soul history; past, present, and future; and clearing any patterns of negative energy[1] from the Akashic records,[2] releasing pain and restoring harmony. I was intrigued and made a mental note to check in with my acupuncturist and healer to see if she did SRT. I had been seeing her for several years, working on many levels of healing. I sometimes referred to her as my "woo woo" doctor, but really she is an intuitive healer, addressing many layers of health through multiple modalities. I have always believed that we are more than just a physical body and that there can be many factors affecting our health; emotional trauma, relationship patterns, family history, just to name a few, so I was interested in her suggestion. This intuitive side of me co-exists with the scientific side of me, keeping me open to complementary approaches to health, never assuming that there is only one way to solve health issues.

After the party, we returned home to Nana's, and I was surprised that both boys were still awake. Typically, Kaylene would have had them in bed and asleep. They had been reading in their own beds, so it wasn't a terrible thing, and I went upstairs to get them to put their books away. There was no complaining as both Hans and Andre were tired. I gave them both good night kisses, and they were asleep quickly. I went back downstairs to get the report from Kaylene. She said all had gone well. I admired the beautiful eggs the boys had colored, and we laughed that last year she had done the same with them when Arnold and I had celebrated our anniversary. We thanked her, and she left for her drive home to Bellingham.

We awoke the next morning, Easter Sunday, to baskets filled with goodies. The extended family came over for brunch, and as I poured mimosas, the kids went downstairs to play and build forts. I was nervous about Hans not being supervised, and I didn't want an incident that would spoil this time with the extended family. I shared briefly with my brother, Eric, that Hans had been having some difficulties recently and about my concerns that he might get mad and over-react. I asked if he thought it would be okay if I talked with his son, who was several years older than Hans. He heard me out and thought that Ryan would be responsive. My siblings were used to me micro-managing my children, so I don't think he understood the full impact of what I was sharing. *I* didn't even realize the full scope of what was going on yet. Eric wasn't concerned by what I was asking of Ryan, so I pulled Ryan aside and shared with him that Hans had been having some big reactions to his frustration and that if he seemed like he was getting mad, would he please come and get me? He promised that he would, but all the prepping wasn't needed. The kids played without incident, and the adults socialized around the Easter brunch buffet.

I tried to relax a bit. I talked with my sister, Nicole, who is a Licensed Marriage and Family Therapist. I told her what I was observing and asked her what was the difference between a psychological evaluation and a neuropsychological evaluation. [3] She shared that a neuropsychological evaluation would also assess his cognitive abilities. I didn't need that done; he was at the top of his class. I asked if she thought an evaluation would be helpful. She said it wouldn't hurt. I made a mental note to look into getting a psychological evaluation done soon. I felt that it would be useful information and I was needing some insight. Later that day we returned home, and I had a plan to start investigating.

Monday morning, we began our routine of getting dressed, having breakfast, making lunches, and heading out the door. Except that Hans was still angry about the incident that had occurred on Friday. As Arnold made breakfast downstairs, I was trying to coax Hans into getting dressed. In my mind, staying home from school was not an option.

"I'm not going to school or I will pummel those imbeciles. You'll have to fight me to get me dressed."

"I hear that you are still upset. I know you can get yourself dressed. Go ahead and do that and come eat breakfast. We can talk more after that."

He began crying, "I don't know! It's too much!"

Tears now streamed down his face as he looked at me with panic in his eyes. I went downstairs frustrated. Arnold and I talked briefly about letting him stay home so we could talk with him more about the incident. It was getting late and it was time to leave, and he still wasn't dressed or fed. Arnold took Andre to school. I stayed with Hans and asked probing questions, trying to get at what he was still mad about. I got the all too familiar response.

"You don't need to know!"

I explained that I couldn't help him if he wouldn't tell me what he was so upset about. Arnold returned from dropping Andre off, and I had to get to work. We talked briefly, agreeing that something was not right. Later that day, I returned home to get the report that the day was without incident. That night we reminded Hans that he had a field trip the next day and that it was something he had been looking forward to.

Tuesday morning I awoke wondering what the day would bring. Arnold was scheduled to chaperone, and I had a full day scheduled, as well. I hoped that the allure of the field trip and the preparation the night before would be enough. Hans was still angry at "the jerks" in his class, but he was looking forward to going to the Woodland Park Zoo. He got himself dressed, but was quickly frustrated when asked what he wanted for breakfast.

"I don't know. It's too much!"

This was another pattern that had been emerging, his inability to decide what he wanted to eat, and his frustration over being asked. Arnold made his favorite: egg, ham, and cheese on an English muffin. Arnold took Hans and Andre to school and stayed to chaperone the field trip. Hans's day went well. There were no harsh words exchanged or extreme behaviors. We hoped we were back on track. He made it through the rest of the week; the only incident being what appeared to be a misunderstanding which resulted in Hans swinging his sweatshirt at his best friend.

Homework was due on Friday. Hans had been doing his homework independently all year with me checking his work the night before it was due. I went in his room to check on his progress.

"How's homework going?"

"It's stupid," he mumbled. "I'm not doing it," and he began to scribble angrily across the page of long division.

I stood there quietly watching him, alarm bells going off in my head. I had certainly seen this behavior often in my work, but never from him. Hans had always taken pride in his school work, especially enjoying math. When he would complete a page of computation, he would often write himself an even longer problem to compute. What I was seeing was so out of character for him.

"Let's skip the math this week." I gathered the work and removed it from his desk.

"Can I help you practice your spelling?"

"I guess so."

We went through his list then called it enough. I didn't want to create stress. We were leaving the next day for our big camping trip weekend in southern California to celebrate the wedding of my Uncle Anthony.

Friday was an uneventful day, and I was relieved. I had taken half a day off, and we were all packed and ready to head to the airport after their school assembly. I loved the Friday school assemblies. Each grade would take turns highlighting the work they were doing. The parents would join in the end to sing our school songs and support our children. It was a gathering of community, and it always filled me up. Today it felt good to be part of this weekly tradition. I didn't know that this would be the last assembly that would feel this way for me.

CHAPTER SEVEN
LAS FLORES RANCH

Arnold had secured an RV that would be delivered on site at Las Flores Ranch, near Camp Pendleton, California. It was a long awaited event, but instead of feeling excitement, Arnold and I were nervous. Even though the week had ended well, Hans's extreme behaviors made us cautious. We arrived at the Orange County/John Wayne Airport; much larger now than when I was a little girl visiting Grandma with my sister, Oriana, in the summers of my childhood. In those earlier days, we would get off the airplane on a roll-up staircase and be escorted by a stewardess across the tarmac to the open arms of our Grandma. It always made me feel like a movie star. Now, it was no different than any other large airport. After disembarking the plane, we went to pick up our car. It was muggy, and all I cared about was A/C and a comfortable back seat for the boys. While we waited to get our car, the boys were jumping over the railings, parkour-style. I watched to make sure they could safely clear the railing; I did not want a trip to the hospital because of a broken bone!

As we pulled out of the airport, the palm trees and heavy air brought back happy memories of my childhood summers, long drives to Disneyland, and trips to the beach. We drove the 45 minutes to Grandma's house. When we pulled in,

Grandma and the family were still out at the rehearsal dinner. We went to our rooms and unpacked what we needed for the night. The boys would sleep in the bunk beds, Arnold and I on the futon in the same room. My sister, her husband, and their two-year-old would be across the hall in the other guest room. The wedding party returned home, and we exchanged hugs and kisses and excitement over the next few days. I took the boys into their room and ran them through their bedtime routine; putting on their soft music, rubbing their backs, and sitting in the room until they were both asleep. I had learned from years of travelling that they did not bring out the best in each other at bedtime in a shared room. Andre didn't like going to sleep by himself in new places, and Hans didn't like listening to Andre as he tried to settle in. After some arguing and name calling, they were both asleep. I joined the adult festivities on the back deck, the smell of Jasmine wafting through the warm nighttime breeze. We stayed up late telling stories, laughing, and finalizing plans for the next day.

In the morning, we all had breakfast together and packed up our things. The boys helped load the car with the linens we were borrowing from Grandma and other wedding things we would need for the weekend. We headed south on Interstate 5 to Camp Pendleton Army Base. The boys, especially Hans, wondered if we would get to see any drills. We inquired with the soldiers who checked our ID upon entering, and they replied that it was always a possibility. We drove down the winding road to the ranch where we found our RV, level and open, and we unloaded the car.

While Arnold helped begin the setting up process for the wedding, directing the many camping rigs rolling in throughout the day, the boys and I drove back off the base and found a nearby Walmart where we would pick up all the other necessities that didn't come in the RV; plates, plasticware, cups, napkins, paper towels, food, coffee, beer, and activities for the kids. I was used to having all our things ready to go in our personal RV at home, this was really the bare bones. The boys chose water guns, glow-in-the-dark bracelets, bubbles, and I picked up a ladder ball set. Hans really wanted a Nerf gun, but I explained that we wouldn't be able to take it on the plane, it was too big. He was pretty upset about this, but he managed to keep his cool when I assured him that the Walmart in Bellingham likely had it, also.

For the bridal rig, I picked up scented candles, potted flowers, Excedrin, Alka-Seltzer, orange juice, Starbucks instant coffee, and Bloody Mary makings. We are a family who enjoys the festivities and sometimes overindulge, and I wanted to make sure the bride and groom had an easy time moving into their mornings after. I was familiar with the "hair of the dog" and knew it would be a weekend of late nights partying. Even though I wouldn't be participating in excess, I wanted to be helpful for those who would.

We returned, making our RV as comfortable as we could with minimal supplies. Everyone had jobs to do, and as more of the extended family arrived with their rigs, the boys found their cousins and enjoyed running errands in the golf cart. I had talked with my three sisters, Oriana, Megan, and Nicole. I shared, briefly our concerns about Hans and asked them to help us maintain "zone defense." As Arnold and I had many tasks to help with, the boys were mostly being supervised by my middle sister, Oriana, and her husband, John, who had a toddler to chase after. I checked in with them periodically and was continually re-assured that everyone was doing just fine. Again, I felt relief, but was still on guard.

We all worked through the day, enjoying each other's company. After the evening meal, the adults were in the ranch house working into the night on preparations and celebrating as they worked. I was with the boys, getting ready for bed. As I cleaned up the kitchen, I heard complaints from the top bunk.

"These beds suck! I am not sleeping in this bed!"

I went over to see what the matter was and, sure enough, the beds really were awful, not much more than a comforter for a mattress.

"You're right Hans, these really are not comfortable. Let's pad them with the comforters we brought from Grandma's, and you can sleep under a sheet. It's hot out, anyway."

"I am not sleeping in this bed."

As I did what I could to put together something more comfortable, Hans put a movie on the iPad. After making the bunk up with comforters, he climbed up.

"I guess this will do."

He proceeded to watch a movie. I was tired.

"Hans, we're not starting a movie now, it's time to go to sleep. Tomorrow is a big day, and you will be up later than normal. Please turn the movie off."

"No, I won't!"

I was too tired to fight over this and decided it was going in basket "C."

"Okay, I'm taking Andre into my bed so he can go to sleep."

The bed that Arnold and I had at the other end of the rig was huge. Andre was asleep within minutes. I could hear the movie from the other side of the RV. I was frustrated that I was letting my 10-year old stay up when I knew he should be sleeping. Yet, I didn't want the fight that I anticipated would follow, and I was too tired to be my best self. I lay there waiting. I could hear the laughter from the party going on in the distance, and I wished that I could share in that joy. Finally, there was quiet from Hans's bunk, and when I checked on him he was asleep. I returned to the ranch house to help with preparations, wrapping candle holders in moss as part of the table decorations. I appreciated the community effort going into making this celebration such a lovely event, and I wanted to surrender to the carefree delight, but I continued to feel guarded and apprehensive.

The next day we woke up later than usual, ate breakfast, and began the tasks needed for the final preparations. Hans, Andre, and their cousin were putting together 200 luminaries that would line the road from where the ceremony would take place to where the reception would be held at the ranch house. While the kids worked on scooping the sand into the bags and placing the battery operated candles, the reggae tunes of the band, *Extra Classic*,[1] surrounded us as they did their sound check and ran through their line-up. They were friends of my uncle Anthony's band, *The Donkeys*,[2] and Hans enjoyed their music, but Andre found it to be too loud.

"Let's take it outside so it's not so loud. We can finish up there," I offered.

"No, it's too hot, and I like the music," replied Hans.

Andre was happy to go do something different. Hans and I finished up the luminaries and packed them in the boxes. Hans went to get the golf cart. He drove it up to the side of the barn and helped me load the boxes. As he drove the golf cart down the road, I laid out the luminaries along the side. We were nearly half way through when Andre came running over wanting to drive the cart.

"No, you didn't help!"

"Yes I did, it was just too loud. I want a turn driving."

"Let Hans finish up this box," I suggested, "then you can have a turn while I put the luminaries in the other box, and we'll rotate." They both agreed. Hans got out, and Andre got in. After the next box was empty, Andre complained.

"Hans got to do more, I want to do the next box." That was too much for Hans. He lunged towards Andre.

"Get out you jerk-ass! It's my turn." Hans put his arm around Andre's neck and tried to pull him out of the golf cart.

"Hans, step back. Take your hands off your brother!" I ran to the golf cart.

"No, he's a jerk-ass! It's my turn!" Hans tried to throw Andre to the ground. I put my arms around Hans' shoulders, securing my hands in front of his body and pulled him off of Andre. Then he turned on me. "I hate you! Get away from me!"

As he attempted to hit me and kick me, I brought his arms around his front, crossing them and holding his lower arms between his wrists and elbows, escorting him behind the ranch house where no one else would witness what I anticipated was going to be a full melt down. He kicked me and swore at me and fought for me to let go.

"I will let you go when your body is still and you stop yelling at me." We were sitting on the ground now, his arms secured, his feet kicking, his body twisting as he tried to wrench himself free between attempts to head butt me.

"You're hurting me, let me go!"

I was hot, and we were near a large open field. The barn was behind us, and my sister, Nicole, was off in the distance, watching.

"I will let you go, but if you start hitting and kicking me, I will hold you again. Keep your hands and feet safe."

As soon as I let him go, he took off across the field. I followed from a distance, looking around. The field ended with a fence that surrounded the ranch grounds. Beyond the fence was the road and miles of open ground, Camp Pendleton base. When he reached the fence, he tried to climb it, but his flip flops were making it difficult.

"Stop!" I yelled to him. "You are on an army base; do you know what that means?" I didn't even know what that meant, probably nothing, but I was hoping that his admiration for soldiers would keep him from running. He stopped and collapsed to the ground. I walked towards him slowly. He was crying.

"I've got stickers in my feet! Get them out!"

I knelt down, noticing that one of his flip flops had come off his foot. I helped him get the stickers out of his foot, found his flip flop, put it back on his foot, and sat with him as he worked through his big emotions. I didn't talk with him. I didn't know what to say at that moment, and I knew that sometimes saying nothing was best. I helped him up, and we walked back towards the barn.

"I want to go back to the RV."

"Okay, I'll finish up the luminaries. Let's get you something cool and see what the other kids are up to."

He seemed calm. We walked back to the RV, he got some water, and then went out to find the kids and play. Nicole, my sister who is the LMFT, had observed the episode. She offered to help finish up with the luminaries.

"That isn't normal, right?" I asked her.

"No. That's not normal."

"Yeah, I didn't think so. Something's not right, but I don't know what it is. I feel like I need to get an evaluation done."

"I really think that would be a good idea."

The rest of the day was without incident, though I was on high alert. Everyone enjoyed a beautiful wedding ceremony. Hans and Andre blew bubbles as Anthony and Christina walked down the aisle, a newly-wed blissful couple! The magic that had been created over the past day and a half was enjoyed by all, and there were no problems during the reception. I kept up the facade of everything being okay, and it was exhausting. When it was dark, I decided to take the boys back to the RV. I found Arnold sitting with Grandma in the newlyweds' rig. I told Arnold I was going to put the boys to bed. Grandma told me to let the boys stay up and go have a dance with my husband.

"Grandma, you have no idea what we've been going through. Arnold can find someone else to dance with. I have to take care of my children."

I knew that wouldn't make any sense as it was true, no one knew what we had been going through. I wanted so badly to get caught up in the magic of this night, but I was exhausted and I was worried. I stepped outside the rig into the warm night, protected by the darkness around me. For a brief moment,

I allowed these feelings to wash over me as the tears finally found release. With a deep breath, I pulled myself together and put a smile on my face. I joined the party, collected my boys, and took them to our RV. They fell asleep easily, and I returned to the celebration, dancing into the wee hours as though everything was fine.

The next morning, April 27th, we enjoyed a camp breakfast with the wedding party, packed up our things, putting what we borrowed into the back of Grandma's car. We said our goodbyes, shared hugs and kisses, then drove to the airport to catch flight 471 home. During the flight, Hans asked for a snack pack.

"No, we will get dinner at the airport. A snack pack would ruin your appetite."

There was just a little complaining from Hans. We landed, and shortly after getting off the plane, all that had been brewing over the past four months erupted into the storm I had sensed was coming. Everything that I had taken for granted, our happy lives, the values that we held, the beliefs we had about parenting, the carefree connections with friends, all this would change. We would be swept up into a hell that would be isolating and terrifying.

PART 2

Diagnosis:
The Solitary Path

"I learned that courage was not the absence of fear, but the triumph over it. The brave man is not he who does not feel afraid, but he who conquers that fear."

Nelson Mandela

CHAPTER EIGHT

YOU'VE GOT TO BE KIDDING ME!

After our nightmare trip home, Monday morning dawned early for me. I woke up, apprehensive about what this day would bring. Typically, Monday mornings I would meet with the members of the Intervention Team for the school district I worked in. This consisted of me as the Behavior Specialist, the Autism Specialist, and six paraeducators. This Monday, I was going to be late because Hans was refusing to go to school again, crying and anxious. By now, I was sure something was wrong. I texted my co-worker to let her know that I would be in by 9:00.

Upstairs in Hans's room I talked with him, asking him questions.

"Do you feel angry?" I wondered if this was still about the incident with the hat.

"Sometimes," he replied, quieting down.

"Do you feel anxious?"

"What does that mean?"

"It's when you're worrying about things a lot or things are making you feel icky in your tummy."

"Sometimes."

"Do you feel sad?"

"Never."

"Do you feel confused?"

"Yes, all the time. I always feel confused."

"Do you feel happy?"

"Never."

"Okay, you're going to stay home today. It was a long weekend, and last night was tough. We'll talk more about this when I get home."

I went downstairs to help get Andre out the door with Arnold. When Arnold got home from dropping off Andre, I briefly shared with him the conversation I had had with Hans and then left for my meeting.

I walked into the room with my colleagues, and I burst into tears. These are good people who work with our district's hardest children. They had been hearing snippets of what was going on and knew we were struggling with Hans's behavior.

"I think Hans has had a mental breakdown. I don't know what's wrong, but I've got to get help." I shared with them what had happened at the airport. They all offered to help in any way. We finished up our meeting, everyone went off to their assignments, and I got on the phone.

I called my friend, the psychologist who had just achieved his national board certification, and explained that I was afraid that Hans was having a mental breakdown and that Arnold and I were wondering if it might be an early onset of puberty hormones paired with a predisposition resulting in a mental illness. He questioned what I meant by a predisposition, and I went over my family history: mother with anxiety, depression, and borderline personality disorder; two sisters with anxiety; another sister and an uncle who occasionally experience depression; two nieces with anxiety; father who self-medicated with alcohol and marijuana. I also shared with him the emotions that Hans had identified that morning.

"Do you think we need to do a psychological evaluation?"

"You've essentially done that already. I think you need a psychiatrist, and he needs medication."

"Do you recommend anyone?"

My friend sent me a list of recommendations, and I began to make calls. Of the three psychiatrists who work with children in our community, one wasn't taking any new patients, the other was only working with adults now, and the third scheduled me for an appointment in June, 2015, fourteen months away.

"You've got to be kidding me!"

I took the appointment that was over a year away, incredulous as we were in crisis *right now*! I knew, from my work, that the field of mental health wasn't very good, yet I had no idea it was this bad! My colleagues rallied around me, and it was suggested to me to take Hans down to Seattle Children's Hospital Emergency Room. They would have to at least assess him and could provide me with resources.

The next day, Tuesday, we were able to get Hans to school. They had another field trip, and at drop off, his teacher told Arnold she wasn't comfortable with Hans only coming to school for field trips. Of course we understood this, but at the same time, we were happy for him to attend school for any reason! Little did we know that that would be the last day he would attend for the remainder of the year. From work, I contacted one of the therapists who works with the psychiatrist who we had scheduled with for 2015. She and I had shared clients over the last couple of years, and I asked if there was any way she could help us get in sooner. She suggested scheduling with a therapist in that office and accessing the psychiatrist that way, sort of "through the back door." I could get on another waiting list and was told the wait would be two or three months. This still was not what I was hoping for, but it was much sooner than fourteen months away. I thanked her.

The next day was Wednesday, April 30th. It was Andre's 9th birthday. After the boys were in the car, I went out to say goodbye like I had countless mornings. I opened the side door to give Hans and Andre a kiss, and Hans bolted from the car, running around back to the deck. I followed him to find him sitting on the steps clutching at the railing and crying.

"I can't do it. It's too much!"

"Okay, something feels too much for you. We're going to figure this out. For today, let's just try to go to school. You're all dressed and ready to go. If it's not working out, you can always call, and Poppa will come and get you." Hans quieted down and walked back to the car with me. Fifteen minutes later, I got a call from Arnold.

"He's under the back seat swearing at me and refusing to get out. He's saying I'm not his dad and that he hates me. What should I do?"

"Bring him home. He can't go to school like that."

When I got home that afternoon, I talked some more with Hans. He was crying and very upset about not being able to go to school. "I know I should, I'm so sorry! I feel so bad!"

"This feels hard, and we're going to figure this out. Can you tell me what is it about school that makes you feel like you can't go?"

"I don't know, I just can't do it." I sat with him, rubbing his back, wondering what was going on with my child who suddenly was unable to go to school on top of all the other big emotions he had been experiencing.

We had planned on going out that evening for Andre's birthday dinner to one of our family's favorite restaurants, *Jalapeno's*. I asked Hans if he thought he could do that, and he did. We piled into the car and drove down to our local restaurant. As we sat outside on their deck, we enjoyed our meals, with Andre adorned in a birthday sombrero. We shared a fried ice cream, and I tried to be happy and upbeat, though inside I was aching. I was aching because we had decided not to have a birthday party for Andre this year due to Hans's unpredictable behavior. Instead, Andre would spend the night with a buddy and take *their* family out to dinner and the movies over the weekend, not ours. I was aching because I didn't know what was wrong with Hans, and I was supposed to be an expert. I was aching, and I was scared.

That night, as Hans was going to bed, he was again crying.

"What are you upset about, Honey?"

"I'm afraid to go to school tomorrow, but I know that I should go and I feel so bad."

"What are you afraid of?"

"I don't know, I just don't want to go, but I know that I should."

I tried to assure him, but he was upset. His bedtime music was playing softly. He had listened to this music every night since he was a baby, but this night it didn't have the effect of soothing him to sleep. I stroked his hair. I rubbed his back.

"Momma's gonna figure this out with you. For now, let's get some sleep. I love you." I continued to sit with him and gently rub his back. He cried softly until he finally settled into a fitful sleep. What usually took minutes took more than an hour, but he was asleep.

CHAPTER NINE

I WANT RESOURCES

It was the 1st of May, when kids go to school and make May Day baskets to fill with flowers that they share with others as a random act of kindness. When Hans woke up that morning, he called for me. I went in to find him crying in the corner of his room saying he was confused and didn't understand what was going on.

"What's wrong with me? What's happening to me? I feel weird in my body and my head."

I decided then that I was taking him to Seattle Children's Hospital Emergency Room. I didn't need to wait for him to be raging. I talked briefly with Arnold who agreed it was the right thing to do. Back upstairs, I let Hans know we were leaving.

"Sweetie, we're going to drive to Seattle to go see a doctor who might know what's going on and how to help. You can bring your iPad in the car."

"Okay mom," he said bravely.

He got dressed, ate an English muffin and strawberries, and we drove the hour and a half south. While we drove, I called my sister, Megan, and we talked for a short period of time about her eight year old daughter's anxiety, what she was taking and how she responded to it. Megan told me that it made a huge difference for her daughter. She had been on Celexa[1] for several years and would never have been able to attend the wedding the previous weekend without it. I thought maybe we could find a doctor who would know what Hans needed.

I had been to an emergency room once before with Andre when he was five. He and Hans had been playing roughly, and he had hit his cheek on the edge of our wooden coffee table. The corner connected with his molar resulting in what was called a "through and through." That night, the Saint Joe's Emergency Room in Bellingham was full, and there was screaming coming from down the hallway. We were brought to a room where we waited for quite a while, distracting Andre with books we had brought from home. The nurse who stitched up the inside and outside of Andre's cheek told us that he was the easiest patient he had had all night. When I reflect on that evening, Andre was a true champion. He had held so still, breathing slowly and remaining relaxed as he locked his eyes onto mine and squeezed my hands. I was so proud of him amidst the chaos of that emergency room.

With this being my only experience, I was nervous walking through the doors into the Seattle Children's Emergency Room. I was worried that it would be chaos, and my son, who was struggling with anxious feelings and confusion, would be unable to deal with it. But it was complete tranquility. The walls and floors were sparkly clean, reflecting the sunlight flooding in through the large windows. The soft pale green color of the chairs was calming, and there was only one little boy checking in with his mom. We walked up to the small counter where only one individual could check in at a time. They took our information and immediately brought us back to a room with a glass wall and door. We met with several doctors, one after the other, assessing Hans's condition. Hans had questions as he assessed the environment.

"What are the rails on the bed for?"

"Sometimes kids come in here that need the rails to help keep them safe," the nurse replied honestly. A doctor came in, unlocked a door on the wall and pulled a small computer out from behind the door.

"Why is everything locked up?"

"If a child is being unsafe, we want to be able to put everything away."

Hans seemed to appreciate both of these precautions and settled in to answering questions while his vitals were being taken. We were asked many questions, but essentially it all boiled down to whether Hans was in danger of hurting himself or anyone else and if there was any violence in our home. We were safe. Hans had never threatened or tried to hurt himself. And though Hans reported that sometimes Arnold and I would fight, and that he didn't like it, these were only verbal disagreements. Arnold and I were never aggressive with each other.

"So, what were you hoping to get from us?" the mental health specialist asked me very matter-of-factly.

"Resources. I can't get in with a psychiatrist for another year, and I need to know what is going on."

The mental health specialist gave me a list of psychiatrists and therapists in the King County area. She also suggested that I schedule an appointment with our pediatrician. Along with the list of resources, our exit papers included a trigger card with instructions and an escalation scale. This scale was identical to the stress cycle we teach in our Right Response classes. The nurse went over the trigger cards with us explaining that Hans would want to identify new coping strategies for when he was feeling stressed. We left this tranquil place, got into our mini-van, and drove the hour and a half home. I was hopeful with my list of contacts.

That night, Hans was again very agitated about going to school the next day and was crying. He climbed behind the couch, wedged up against the wall.

"What's wrong with me?"

"I don't know yet, honey, but we're going to find out. The doctors at Seattle Children's gave me a list of specialists so we can get in with someone who can help us."

I tried to sound confident and hoped that I was telling the truth! Hans was agitated and fearful through the evening until he finally fell asleep with me sitting next to him running my fingers through his hair as I always did when he was sick.

The next morning he was worse. He awoke very agitated. When I went into his room he was sitting up in his bed, his back up against the wall in the corner, his knees brought up to his chest. He was wild eyed and crying.

"Where am I? Who are you?"

I tried to stay calm as my mind was racing. "Honey, you're in your room, and I'm your mom. You're safe."

Hans was panicked. "You're not my mom. This isn't my room. My room has more Legos."

"This is your room, Sweetheart. I'm your mom, and you're safe."

"No, you're not my mom! Oh, it's all too much! What's happening to me? Where am I?"

He wedged himself between his bed and the wall and began clawing at the mattress. I was trying to think of how I could help soothe him, but nothing that I had ever done before was working. He wouldn't let me touch him, cowering as if my touch hurt him. He couldn't follow any breathing coaching.

"What's going on? Make it stop! It's too much!" he repeated over and over.

I told him I would be right back. I went downstairs and told Arnold that Hans wasn't going to school that day and that I would stay home until he got back. I cancelled my meeting that was scheduled that morning at one of the elementary schools and went back upstairs to try and soothe Hans. I decided to just be quiet and sit next to his bed, my gaze averted, focusing on keeping a kind and neutral look on my face. I waited for him to get through this emotional response

59

and settle. He finally quieted and laid still, his eyes almost glazed over. Then he sat up and looked at me.

"What just happened?"

"You were upset. You're safe, and it's going to be okay. Climb up onto your bed. Okay, I'm here with you, Hans. You're safe." I stroked his hair while he lay on his bed quietly.

"Hans, I'm going to get you some food. I'll be right back. Call for me if you need me." I brought him an English muffin and strawberries. He let me feed him. I went to work, telling Arnold to call me if he escalated again.

Instead of working, I spent the rest of the day on the phone calling every psychiatrist and therapist between King County and Whatcom County. I left messages, some of which were never returned. When I did get a call back, I asked when we could get in. If it wasn't a date earlier than an appointment I had already scheduled, I thanked them for getting back to me. I was desperate to get in with anyone and soon. I also called our pediatrician.

We had been reassigned to Dr. Jordana Hawkins after our previous pediatrician had taken a new position. It had been at least a year since we had gone in as we were caught up on our vaccinations, and the boys were scheduled for well checks every other year now. This would be our first visit with Dr. Hawkins. I called the front desk to schedule an appointment, explaining briefly what was going on. The kind woman scheduling was able to get us in on Monday. We only needed to get through the next three days before we would see someone! I was hopeful that she would have answers.

CHAPTER TEN
THE DARKNESS

The next morning was Friday, and Hans woke up extremely agitated and fearful, again. I went into his room to greet him.

"Where am I, who are you?"

I assured him, as I had the day before, "you're Hans, and you're in your room. I'm your mom."

"I'm not Hans, you're not my mom, this isn't my room."

He began to cry, cowering and wedged between his bed and the wall. I again sat quietly next to him, in anguish over what was happening and my inability to help him. I didn't know what was wrong, and I couldn't soothe him. Monday felt so far away. After some time, he settled and came out of it just as he had the day before. I got him some food, and he ate fruit and two English muffins while listening to a book. I worked from home that day.

In the afternoon, he called me to his room.

"You know what I want?"

"What's that sweetheart?" I replied, thinking I would give him anything I could. I was desperate to offer him some kind of relief from this torture I was witnessing. If he could name something that would bring him peace and joy, I would make it happen.

"Not to have to go through this every day."

I felt that place in the core of my gut tighten as he asked for the one thing I had no control over. I felt that pain so many parents have experienced when they wished they could take on the burden of their child. I sucked in a deep breath and held back my tears.

"Me, too. If I could take this from you so you didn't have to go through this, I would!"

He looked at me, but there was no smile, no indication of being reassured. My response felt inadequate to me. Why couldn't I make this all go away? Why didn't I know what to do? I sat with him quietly as he turned the pages of one of his TinTin books. I wondered what this new pediatrician would have to say. I hoped she would have some suggestions for us, how to help him feel relief. The rest of the day was without incident.

That night, he was lying in his bed as I sat with him.

"I can rate this for you. It's like having your arms and legs cut off and left to bleed."

"That sounds horrible."

"It *is* horrible, but it could be worse. It could be like being shot in every part of your body and left to bleed, but not shot in the parts that would kill you. That would be way worse."

"Yes, that would be way worse."

I let that sink into my very soul. He was telling me that what he was experiencing was like being tortured without the relief of death. I was keenly aware of his suffering. I saw what it did to him...on the outside. That this was how he described what he was experiencing on the inside left me feeling shattered and helpless.

After he fell asleep that night, I sat next to his bed and sobbed as though the heavy storm clouds had finally released their torrent of rain. I wanted to know what was happening to my boy and how I could fix it. I was supposed to be the expert in behavior. I had never witnessed anything like what I was seeing in my own child. I desperately wanted someone to tell me what was wrong. I wanted someone to tell me what to do. I was feeling like a hollow shell of myself when I finally climbed into my own bed and fell into an exhausted sleep.

The weekend continued to be distressful. Hans awoke fearful and anxious, seeming confused about where he was. I reminded him again that he was Hans, he was in his room, and he was safe. I assured him that he had had some good times the previous days.

"Part of the day was good when I was playing video games."

I agreed that he could do that again. As he played his game, Boom Beach, I worried that I was letting him have too much screen time, but I also acknowledged that it kept him out of his head and gave him some peace. Later that night as he was going to bed, I told him we weren't going to have reading time together because it was late and he had chosen to use the time playing games on his iPad instead.

"You didn't tell me that! Get out now and leave me alone!"

"Let's problem solve."

I had been doing this daily now using Ross Greene's problem solving strategies.

"I hear that you didn't understand that it was games or reading and that doesn't feel fair. I can understand feeling that way. I was feeling frustrated that you started a new game when I had said we were done. Since you didn't understand, you can say *Mom, it feels unfair, I didn't hear what you were saying*."

"Okay..."

"Let's read in your room, one chapter."

"Okay."

I read the next chapter of his book to him, and I turned off the light.

"I still don't feel good, all over. And I'm still feeling fearful about school."

"You have a doctor's appointment Monday, so you won't go to school that day."

"When I miss the front of school that also makes me feel fearful."

"Let's talk more about this tomorrow, now just relax for going to sleep."

I stroked his hair while he settled into sleep. The gentle sound of the falling rain on the rooftop soothed my nerves as my thoughts took over. My years of training were talking back to me strongly. Was I giving in too much to his demands? I thought of all the parents I had counseled over the years to be strong, commit to the expectations, and follow through. I wondered if there could be a fine line between enabling and supporting. I didn't *believe* that I was enabling, but I was *worried* that I might be. I knew that others would suggest I was. I was feeling conflicted between my head and my heart.

I watched my boy sleep. I watched the soft rise and fall of his chest. I was so grateful for this bit of relief for him. I wanted relief for him. I wanted understanding of what was going on. I wanted direction in what to do. I wanted someone else to be the expert.

Sunday morning dawned, and instead of the crying that I had expected to hear, Hans came into my room to have some snuggle time like we had done for the past ten years. It felt normal as we all lay in bed reading together. Throughout the day, though, he was on edge. He got mad at Arnold when he thought that he had blamed him for something, then he called Andre a jerk and pushed him because Andre had bumped him accidentally, which interfered with his video game.

In the afternoon, Arnold and I decided we would go to Yeager's to get a new family game. We thought it would be good to have something new to do together that didn't involve a screen, and it would still be a mental diversion for Hans. We discussed it ahead of time, and I reminded the boys we weren't shopping for toys, just a family game. Both Hans and Andre agreed. We all went together to the game aisle, but Hans left and went down the Lego aisle.

He came back asking, "Mom, there's a set here I've been wanting. Can I get it and pay you back when we get home?"

"We made a plan before we left that we weren't buying anything other than a family game. I'm glad to know what you've been wanting is here. We can make a plan for another time."

"That's bullshit."

He ran out of the building and into the parking lot. I followed quickly behind, reminded of our experience in the airport. He ran over to our car. I kept myself a ways away from him and watched as he crouched by the back wheel crying. Arnold came out and unlocked the car from a distance.

"Hans, you can get in the car. It's safe there."

Hans got into the back seat.

"Stay out! I hate you!"

Arnold went back in and bought some beef jerky thinking maybe he was hungry. I showed it to him through the window. Arnold went back to get Andre and buy the game. They returned, and we all got into the car. I was worried that Hans might get physical with Andre, but all he did was throw a crumpled piece of paper and some beads at me and call me names, which I ignored. I knew that engaging over these harmless things while he was stressed would only make things worse. When we got home, he didn't want to play the game and went to his room and got on his iPad. That night he was again agitated.

"I still feel confused about school, I'm afraid to go, but I feel bad that I'm not going."

"Tomorrow is your doctor's appointment, so you aren't going to school. You don't need to worry about school tomorrow."

"I feel weird in my head, and I'm hot."

I felt his forehead, but he didn't feel hot. I took his temperature, anyway. It was normal. I set up a portable fan in the hallway blowing in on him and did my best to soothe him to sleep. Monday morning he again came in to snuggle and read. I reminded him about his doctor's appointment. After feeding Andre his breakfast and helping him get ready for school, I went into the living room to help Hans get ready.

"Leave, you scary person!"

He ran into his room. I followed him and found him hiding and whimpering in his bed. When I went in to see what was wrong, he yelled at me.

"Get out, leave me!"

I gave him some time and space, then brought in some food, and sat on the floor reading his book to him out loud. He came out from under his blanket, quieted, and listened while eating.

"What are you feeling today?"

"I'm still feeling afraid about school."

"You aren't going to school today. We have a doctor's appointment. So you don't need to be afraid about school today."

"Okay, that makes me feel better."

Later that morning, Arnold, Hans, and I went in to meet Dr. Hawkins. I explained what had been going on, telling her about our trip to Seattle Children's ER, wondering if there were sensory issues, autism, anxiety or depression. I shared my family history of mental illness and disabilities. She told us that if this was something that had been going on for a while and we were just deciding to do something about it, she would have no problem diagnosing and prescribing medication, but because this was something that had come on so suddenly, it sounded like something different, and she suggested that we keep trying to get in with a psychiatrist. In the meantime, she gave us anxiety and depression questionnaires, directing us to send a copy to her once we had filled them out with Hans's input. She also referred us for an Occupational Therapy evaluation[1] and an Autism evaluation.[2] We left that day no closer to any understanding of what was going on.

That evening, I attended a Family Constellations circle.[3] My acupuncturist had told me about this systemic approach to family healing, and I thought I would like to see what it was all about, especially considering the patterns of mental illness that seemed to run through my family tree. It was an emotional experience as we explored our relationships with our parents. With the deaths of both my mother and father, there were strong feelings of loss. I experienced again the loss of my father, the week before Hans had been born; the loss of my mother, who had not had much of a relationship with my children because of her dysfunction; and now what was feeling like the loss of my son, who was tormented by something that I didn't have a name for yet. Just as the meeting was coming to an end, I received a text from Arnold telling me I needed to come home. I arrived to Hans crying and kicking the wall in his room. Arnold was with Andre in his room next door as things were being knocked off his shelves. I went in to Andre first.

He was crying, "I'm so tired, but I can't go to sleep because he won't stop."

"I'm sorry, my love. I will go help him quiet down. Poppa will stay with you. You are safe, and it will be quiet soon. You will have a restful sleep soon."

I pushed my way into Han's blockaded room.

"Why were you away so long?"

"I was at a meeting. I'm sorry it took so long. I'm home now. Let's go to sleep."

I approached his bed, not sure what to expect. He was looking at me with his dilated eyes, fear in his face.

"Don't leave again."

"I'm here now. You're safe. You can sleep."

I started to turn off the lamp on his desk, but he told me to leave it on, he didn't want to be in the dark. I left it on and then sat next to his bed. I ran my fingers through his hair.

"I'm hot, and my head hurts."

Again, I set up the fan in the hallway and got him some ibuprofen. He settled into another fitful sleep.

The next two days were much of the same. I was trying to work, but instead of attending scheduled meetings, I was phone conferencing from home. I wanted to attend a mental health meeting that was being held by the local NAMI[4] chapter. It was at 6:00 pm.

As I was getting ready to leave, Hans was crying.

"I want this to go away, I can't take this."

He ran to his room and was lying on the floor crying.

"Don't go!"

I thought to myself that I couldn't just give in to this and reinforce this behavior. I talked briefly to Arnold, and we agreed that I should just leave, just as we had done when the boys were toddlers and we were leaving them with a sitter. I heard him screaming in his room when I walked out the door. I got into the car and hesitated. I was feeling conflicted, pulled between what I knew in my *head* and what I felt in my *heart*. I looked up to his window, tears spilling down my cheeks, and drove away. My mother's heart shattered as I followed my head.

I had time to pull myself together and arrived to find a poorly attended meeting. I greeted a few people I recognized from my work and sat in the front near the door. Just as the first speaker began, I got the text from Arnold telling me to come home *now*. I was 15 minutes away. When I arrived, Andre was waiting outside by the corner of the driveway. I saw him say, "yes!" and run towards the car. He looked at me with a scared face.

"You can hear him out here, mom."

I went inside to find Arnold with Hans in a prone floor hold. I had needed to do this with him twice before because of violence towards Andre or one of us. I know that it looks worse than it is, but there was my child screaming and being pinned to the floor by my husband.

"Stop it, you're hurting me!"

I directed Arnold to release him. I would take over if he was aggressive, but instead he curled up in the fetal position and sobbed. I helped him to his room and promised him that I would never leave him again when he was already upset. This was a promise I knew I would keep. My conflicted feelings were shifting to confidence that this was not about enabling. I helped him get into bed and began rubbing his back.

"My arms and legs hurt, rub them, too."

I rubbed his arms and legs, and he fell asleep very quickly. Then I helped Andre to bed and told him how sorry I was that he had to go through this, as well.

"What's wrong with him Mom? He scares me."

"I don't know yet, baby, but we're going to find out, and we're going to get him help. I'm so sorry it's scary. I promise you I will keep you safe," I assured him and lay with him until he fell asleep.

When I went downstairs, I found a mess in the playroom. Hans had taken a stack of games and thrown all the contents all over the floor. Arnold and I spent the evening sorting through all the pieces and putting them back in their appropriate boxes. Arnold told me that he didn't lay a hand on him until he started to go for the books. I shared with him that I would set up a system with Hans so he wouldn't have to rage if he wanted me home.

The next day was even worse. After Andre got home from school, he was playing Xbox, and Hans wanted a turn. He went over and hit Andre multiple times. I pulled him off, and then he hit and kicked me, scratching, head-butting, and biting, while I escorted him to his room. He raged in his room, swearing and banging a wooden sword on the door that I was holding closed.

"I hate you!"

This went on for thirty minutes until he found the iPad in his room. He got on his iPad, which calmed him, and he chose to stay in his room.

Hans ate dinner in his room that night. After finishing up his own dinner at the table with the family, Andre walked by Hans's open door, and Hans ran into the hallway and hit him, still mad, then ran back into his room crying. Andre was crying and calling for me from his room. As I went to assist Andre, Hans was lying on the floor in the hallway sobbing.

"I can't do this anymore! I want to feel better. I don't know what's going on. Please help me. Make this stop!"

Again, I assured him that I was doing everything I could and that we were going to find someone who could help us. I helped Hans back into his room and went to find Andre in his room, trying to soothe them both. I felt like I was being pulled in two directions and didn't know how I could support both my kids. Andre calmed quickly and got himself ready for bed. Hans took much more time to get to sleep that night. Again, he wanted the lamp to stay on and needed the fan. He wanted his arms and legs rubbed to "get the blood back in his fingers and toes," as he put it.

Over the next few days, Hans and I did some work together. We set up a 5-point system of how he was feeling. We used his words to describe each number with a 1 being "everything is okay" and a 5 being "I can't handle this, I feel like I'm going to explode!" The plan was that if he got to a "3," Arnold would text me, and no matter what, wherever I was, I would come home. He wouldn't need to get to the point of feeling like he was going to explode. We also completed the questionnaires given to us by Dr. Hawkins just days earlier. The results indicated depression and generalized anxiety with social anxiety and school avoidance being significant. These results were interesting to me because they were only true of the last two weeks. I felt perplexed and scared. I was worried that my son had experienced a mental breakdown and that we were heading down the path of mental illness, and I had no idea what it was we were dealing with or what we would do.

I didn't want this for my son. I didn't want this for my family. I had grown up seeing the struggles my mom endured and the effects on the family; moving in and out of poor relationships, the inability to make healthy choices, the repeated mistakes. This was not what I thought was in store for my children. They had had a healthy childhood. They were being raised in a functional home. We were giving them the best opportunities we had access to. How could this be happening?

Arnold and I had been intentional in not fostering a relationship between the boys and my mom. It had been a hard decision, but after driving with the boys, then a toddler and baby, the 45 minutes to pick her up, and waiting for an hour in the car only to be told by her boyfriend that she couldn't make the visit, I was done. I knew it would always fall on me to make it happen, and I decided that my children didn't need to grow up with the same dysfunction that I had with her. Our home would always be open to her, but I wouldn't make visits happen. And now I was afraid that my own child might be starting down the road I had intentionally tried to keep him from.

I felt totally inadequate as a mother and as a professional. How many times had I sat at a table with a team of educators, school psychologists, school counselors, and administrators discussing a child with challenging behaviors, and the answer was 'mental illness. 'We don't deal with that, that's the therapist's, psychiatrist's, counselor's job.' I hadn't had answers then, and I certainly didn't have answers now, but this time it was *my* child. I was watching him slip away into a darkness that terrified him and me.

CHAPTER ELEVEN

MENTAL BREAKDOWN

It was the last two months of the school year. It was clear to me that trying to get Hans to school was not an option at this time. This compounded his stress as he felt that he should be going.

"I feel so bad. I know I should be going to school, but I just can't," he told me the next morning.

"Well, you're homeschooling right now. School isn't anything you need to feel badly about because your schooling is at home."

At work, I was trying to meet with school teams when I could, often requesting to phone conference as Hans's separation anxiety was severe. He knew how to use the 5-point scale, and the first time that Arnold texted me and I came home, he was so happy.

"It worked!" he said joyfully, "you really came home!"

"Yes. I promised you I would. There isn't anything that I could possibly be doing that I can't leave, and I'm only ever 15 minutes away."

This would become an invaluable tool, and we only really needed to use it a handful of times. Just knowing I would come home seemed to be enough. My co-workers, bosses, and colleagues supported me in this, even allowing me to duck out during an interview when I got the text.

We had a week filled mostly with anxiety. Hans had gotten to the point that he could feel it coming on.

"It's happening!" he would say in a panic. "Help me, mommy. Do what you do to get me through this. It's a 1, 2, 3, 4…" and then he would be either rocking or hitting his head against the bed as I scrambled to put pillows around him.

Other times, he would wedge himself between his bed and the wall or crawl behind the sofa. Always, he would be crying.

"I feel weird, help me! Please make this stop, I can't take this anymore! It's too much, it's too much, too much…" until it would subside, and he would lie there, exhausted, his dilated pupils staring out of terrified eyes. The wild animalistic behaviors replaced by frightened exhaustion.

Sometimes he would lay there for five to thirty seconds sort of dazed, as if coming out of a seizure, and then look up at me and ask, "what just happened?" Other times, he would just come out of it and lay there and cry while I sat next to him. When he was in one of these episodes, I couldn't touch him or soothe him. All I could do was sit with him, thinking through everything I knew, questioning myself on what I was missing, and wondering what was going on. What had happened?

I scheduled a meeting with Hans's fourth grade teacher. I explained what we were experiencing: that Hans could not come to school right now, and that we didn't know what was wrong. I told her we were trying to get in with a psychiatrist, but that appointments were scarce. We had a parent night coming up, and I asked to have ten minutes to talk with the parents so they would know what we were dealing with when their children came home telling them Hans wasn't coming to school. It turned out that both the 3rd grade and 4th grade had scheduled parent nights that same Tuesday evening so I could share with both of the boys' classes. I asked my friends, the psychologist and his wife, to please sit next to me when I shared with the 4th grade parents. I knew that I didn't want a lot of time because being away from home in the evening was too stressful for Hans, and the last two times I had tried to be somewhere had ended up in escalations. As soon as I joined the 4th grade parents, I was given the floor to share. I immediately began to cry.

"Hans has had what we are calling a mental break down. We don't know what's wrong, but his anxiety attacks are extreme, and he cannot leave the house. When he is mad, he rages. We are trying to get in with a psychiatrist, but no one is taking new patients. We are being transparent about this, because whatever this is, it's treatable, just like diabetes or any other illness. We just don't know what's wrong yet."

One of the parents shared that she worked in the office of one of the psychiatrists in town. I laughed and told her I had an appointment there in June of the next year, fourteen months out. She said she would see what she could do. I thanked her, not very hopeful. Then I left and joined the 3rd grade parents and shared our story, again. I went home that night emotionally exhausted.

It was now the middle of May. We had been living in this hell for 3 weeks, and we finally had our first appointment with a mental health therapist. A colleague had recommended several contacts, and this was the one we could get in with first. I was hoping to get some insight, but Hans did not want to go.

"I am not going! You can't make me."

"This is important," I replied. "We are trying to figure out what is going on. You've been asking me to help, and I need to talk with the experts. We're just going to talk."

"No!" he shrieked as he threw his stuffed animals at me. Then he climbed onto his bed and began kicking the wall.

"I hate you, I'm not going!"

He continued to rage. He climbed off his bed and began pulling all of his stuffed animals, his blankets, his pillows off and throwing them at me. I ignored this tantrum, grateful that the things being thrown at me were all soft. Next to come off was his mattress, and then he began to pull the wooden slats off the bed. The slats were all connected with strong webbing on either side, but I had a moment of worry that the wood might splinter and that splintered wood would pose a potentially dangerous situation. Thankfully, there was no splintering wood, only a splintered spirit as Hans finally lay on the ground exhausted and crying. His negotiation skills kicked in, and he began the first of many deals that we would strike over the next several months.

"I'll go if we can go back to Yeager's afterwards to get that Lego set. I have my own money."

"Deal."

I reasoned with myself that bribery was just another name for positive reinforcement. I wasn't giving it to him before he did what he was being asked; I would be giving it to him after he had completed what he didn't want to do. Hans got himself dressed, walked downstairs and outside by himself. Arnold looked at me with a questioning expression.

"We're going to Yeager's after our appointment, and Hans is using his own money to buy that Lego set he saw there the other day. It's a reward for doing this hard work."

I felt that I needed to explain how I got Hans out the door and why we would be going to Yeager's afterwards.

The three of us piled into the minivan and headed to the therapist's office. We pulled into the designated parking alongside the two-story Victorian, which was located in the "lettered streets" of Bellingham. This neighborhood was filled with colorful cookie cutter houses built close together, some of which had been converted into office space. The therapist's office was located upstairs. The waiting area appeared to also serve as a break room with a mini kitchen for those who shared this floor. I noticed several water glasses turned upside down on a drying towel. The furniture was worn, but comfortable. On the bookshelf were the business cards of the different practitioners sharing this space.

A kind looking man came out, introduced himself, and brought us back to his office. He asked if we should speak first, but I thought it would be fine to have Hans there. Hans had heard me share what was going on with his new doctor and with all the providers who talked with us at Seattle Children's Hospital. We didn't have anything to hide from Hans.

Hans and I sat on a couch next to an end table that had a basket with some small fidget toys. He picked up a wooden puzzle cube. I got out my yellow folder. Arnold sat in a chair next to us, and the therapist was in a chair across from us. Outside his window, just past the cherry blossoms, I could see children playing in the field of their middle school. I wished that my child was out there playing, but instead, I began recounting the past 3 weeks, explaining that Hans had been experiencing severe swings in his behaviors, sometimes raging and sometimes having what presented as almost seizure-like anxiety attacks. We shared that, as a toddler, we would describe Hans as emotionally sensitive, that he had been particular about his clothing and sometimes had a hard time pulling back when he was playing rough games with friends. Arnold shared that Hans had been very sick in December, and that after that, he had seemed kind of down. We told him about the episode at the airport and that he hadn't been able to go to school since then. After an hour, we scheduled a follow up appointment and left.

On the way out to the car, Hans said, "I am never coming back to see him again."

I ignored this statement, knowing that it was futile to argue with him. He was expressing that he didn't like the visit, that it had been hard for him. Arguing with him now wouldn't change his mind, it would only discount his feelings. We certainly didn't have any answers, just another out-of-pocket visit scheduled.

The next day, Nana came up from Seattle to stay with Hans while Arnold and I went to see the psychiatrist whom we had scheduled an appointment with the following summer in June, 2015. Turns out the parent who worked in the office had been able to get us in sooner. I had experienced some feelings of guilt when she called me to say he would see us. I questioned why *I* should get this appointment? It felt unfair. But my son was in torment, I reasoned, and I would do anything to help him get better. When the opportunity presented, I would pay it forward.

Just like before, with the mental health therapist, Arnold and I recapped everything we were experiencing. The psychiatrist took rapid notes and asked many questions. After an hour, he said he would like to meet Hans. He couldn't provide a diagnosis today, but he suggested that it sounded like it might be Obsessive Compulsive Disorder.

I was flabbergasted.

"OCD? I clearly don't know enough about OCD. I see rage, I see anxiety, I see depression, but I don't see OCD."

He explained, "OCD doesn't always look like repetitive hand washing or ritualizing. It can sometimes take years to diagnose OCD in children because kids don't always share what they are thinking or feeling. It's the confusion that's got me considering OCD. Most kids don't describe their feelings as being confused all the time. I'm wondering if he's so worried about making the wrong decision, that it's overwhelming him with confusion."

I pondered that for a moment and concluded that I definitely needed to learn more about OCD. I recalled my own preferences for having things a certain way; these preferences had been jokingly called "Heather's OCD" my entire life.

We left, a little bit hopeful that we might be on the track to having answers.

That night, after the boys were asleep, we stayed up with Nana sharing the past two visits with the psychiatrists and what had been suggested. Nana shared her own observation that we had shifted a lot in our expectations, and it must be confusing to Hans. I explained that we had shifted so much to have peace in the house. This got me wondering if we were part of the problem, and the cloud of self-doubt darkened.

CHAPTER TWELVE

DOWNTON ABBEY

Saturday evening was the Whatcom Hills Waldorf School second annual themed "Downton Abbey" dress-up cocktail party. I was originally going to be on bartender duty along with my friend, but I had given up my responsibilities because of the chaos at home. Arnold and I had 4 tickets to attend, but our guests had to cancel last minute. Nana had stayed for the weekend to be with the boys that night so Arnold and I could attend the party.

That same morning was the Junior Ski to Sea relay race, and Andre was doing the soccer ball leg for his team, "Mustache to the Finish." The Ski to Sea race is a big event in Bellingham. World class athletes come from around the world to compete solo or as part of a team. The first leg in the adult race starts at Mt. Baker with the cross country skier handing off to the downhill skier who must first cut steps up the mountain before skiing down. Next is the runner who hands off to the road biker, then the canoe team, the mountain biker, and finally, the kayaker, who finishes up in Bellingham Bay. Arnold or I had been part of a team in one role or another for years. This was the first year that neither Arnold nor I were competing, and we were thrilled that Andre was. The Junior Ski to Sea is the week before the adult race and takes place at Lake Padden.

It starts with a runner, who hands off to the pair doing the three-legged race, followed by the bicyclist who hands off to the soccer player handling the cone course, and finally the teammate who runs the final obstacle course. It is like herding cats, and the kids love it, but Hans didn't want to go.

"I feel so bad. I know you want to go to watch Andre. I will try mom," he looked at me with big eyes.

"You are right that I would like to go and support Andre. Nana is here to stay with you at home so I can go, if you would prefer."

"No, she probably wants to go, also."

He got dressed, and we all headed to Lake Padden, which was crowded with people. Hans stayed close to me the whole time, saying hi to people we knew, but not leaving my side. We worked our way through the crowd to the area where Andre's leg would take place. We watched him masterfully move the soccer ball through the obstacle course. He is a natural athlete, and his ball handling skills were impressive! I was so proud of him and wanted to lose myself in the joy of celebrating my child. But the elation of Andre's success was clouded by the weight of caution I carried for Hans. I was keeping a close eye on him, ready to leave at a moment's notice. He didn't stray far from me. He was interested in the swag table and asked me to go with him. We stood in the short lines to play the fun games for freebies. When the race was over, we joined the team and their parents for a big cheer, then we all piled back into our minivan, and I allowed myself to feel a little relief.

Arnold and I had planned on stopping by the school on our way home to see if we could find a shirt in the lost and found that Andre had left behind on Friday. It was really just a ploy to get Hans onto the school grounds in a stress-free situation. He wasn't excited about this, but agreed when we said we would also like to show Nana around the grounds. We parked in the gravel lot by the upper playground, and we all got out. I was immediately struck by how quiet it was. I had never been at the school when it wasn't full of children. Hans walked down the stairs towards the wood chip play area where the lost and found was. We couldn't find Andre's shirt. Hans said he was done, no anger, just flat. The quiet didn't feel peaceful to me, it felt depressing. I had hoped that being on the school grounds would have sparked something in Hans, made it feel less scary, helped him see that he could do this. As we made a quiet drive home, the gloomy gray sky out my window reflected the bleak feeling within.

Once home, Hans wanted to play Nerf guns outside with the family. Arnold and I enthusiastically agreed. Kids against grownups! To be outside and active would be a good thing, for everyone. After a fierce round of shooting, missing, running, and hiding, we called it quits. As soon as we got inside, Hans wanted to continue playing in the house. In the living room, he moved the ottoman around to act as a shield and got down on his belly to aim his Nerf gun.

Nana reminded Hans, "There's no shooting on the main floor, remember? And Nana really doesn't like guns, they make me feel unsafe."

"I don't fucking care," he shouted at Nana.

We were all a little stunned as he ran upstairs to his room. I went up after him.

"Hans, Nana was just reminding you that she doesn't like guns. Maybe we can play outside again."

"I don't fucking care!"

He tried to push me out of his room. He then ran past me and out the front door.

"Arnold, follow Hans, he went outside."

I put my shoes on and ran out to join Arnold who was already down the block. A neighbor drove by and asked if everything was okay?

"No, Hans just bolted. If you see him, text me please."

When I caught up with Arnold, he had not seen Hans. I was panicked. Where did he go? My mind was racing. He could be anywhere, and he was angry and would be scared. Bellingham has a network of trails, and access to those trails is only 2 blocks away from our home. Arnold said he would go down onto the trail and then double back. I went home to check around the house. He wasn't responding to my calls outside, and I didn't see him on the hill behind our house. I ran in through the front door and heard Nana talking upstairs. I looked up the hallway, and she was standing there talking calmly to Hans, who was seething, with one of his wooden swords raised as if he would strike her.

"Nana," I said calmly, though I was not feeling calm, "please come downstairs."

She walked down, and then Hans came down and tried to hit me with his sword. He was crying and yelling.

"Get away from me, all of you! I hate you! You're not my family!"

I quickly secured the sword from his hands, tossing it behind me near Nana who picked it up and put it downstairs. Hans then began hitting me. I secured his arms in front of him, and he struggled to get loose, kicking me, and screaming.

"Let go, you're hurting me!"

For an hour we struggled. I moved us to the leather covered ottoman, where I could straddle the ottoman and hold him in front of me, both of us sitting. I knew from my work that this was going to potentially take a long time before he was exhausted, and I needed to keep us all safe. That would require that I maintain my stamina. He kicked, he tried to bite, and he spit all over the side of my face, the floor, and the furniture. Arnold returned and saw him spitting.

"Hans, quit spitting on your mother," he ordered. Hans began spitting even more.

"Arnold, please don't ask him to stop doing anything right now. He won't, and it will only escalate things."

Again, I only knew this because of the work I did. At this point, it was better to say nothing, check my grip so that I wasn't hurting Hans, and avoid bites, kicks, and spit as much as I could. I've always found it interesting the different things that trigger responses in adults. Spit is one of those things that seems to universally really bother people. For me, it's the most harmless. It doesn't bruise or break skin, and it's easy to clean up. But it was really bothering Arnold, and Hans could sense that. He renewed his fight and head butted me in the side of my face, my error in not being prepared for evading that. The part that was the hardest for me, other than the fact that I was restraining my own child who was trying to hurt me, was the statements that were being made. It was breaking my heart to hear Hans yelling such hurtful things.

"I hate you! You are not my mother! I'm going to kill you, and then I'm going to kill myself. I'll calm down when you tie yourself up to a post and give me a machete. Let me go, you're hurting me!"

This went on for an hour before he finally lay there, panting, limp, and exhausted. He was crying softly now.

"It's too much. I just want to die. I can't do this anymore. If you loved me, you would make this stop."

I sobbed inside, feeling like my heart would shatter into a thousand pieces, and all I wanted was to make it all go away and help my precious son! But I didn't know what was wrong! I sat with him, quietly listening to his torment. When he had calmed completely, he looked up at me with his tear-streaked face.

"What's happening to me? I feel like I'm going crazy."

Looking down into his wide eyes, I wanted to assure him that everything was going to be alright, but I didn't know what was happening. I didn't know what to say.

"I don't know, baby. But I am doing everything I can to find out and we will get the help we need."

"Will you help me upstairs Mommy?" he asked quietly.

"Of course, sweetheart."

I helped him stand up and walk upstairs to his room. He climbed into his bed and lay there quietly with his big eyes staring off.

I went downstairs, bruised and sweaty, my hair filled with spit, and looked at Arnold, "I don't want to go to the Downton Abbey party tonight."

Hans heard that and began crying, again.

"It's all my fault! You've been waiting for this party! You have to go!"

I headed back upstairs.

"Hans," I replied calmly, "this has nothing to do with you. I am making the decision that I don't want to go to a party tonight because I just don't feel up to it."

That really was the truth. I couldn't imagine getting all dressed up and attending a party where everyone knew we were having problems and would be asking us how we were doing. I just didn't have the strength for answering those questions. Our son wasn't doing okay, and I didn't know what was wrong. I wasn't doing okay. I felt like a shell of my previous self; battered, confused, and scared. Instead of going to the party that night, we all went to bed exhausted.

CHAPTER THIRTEEN
COULD THIS BE PANS?

The next day was much better. Hans played at the park with Andre and a neighbor friend. That night, however, he became agitated again as he began to worry about school. I reminded him that he was homeschooling and that it was okay. He didn't need to worry about school. Later that night, I shared with Arnold some of my observations.

"Have you noticed that Hans's pupils are often dilated? I'm definitely seeing it at night, but I've noticed it during the day, also. What do you make of that?"

"Yeah, I had noticed that. I don't know what it would be."

"He's also complaining at night that he's hot and his joints hurt. He asks me to rub them out and to get the blood back into his fingers. If I don't do it a certain way, he asks me to start over."

"Weird, maybe growing pains?"

"Maybe," I doubted.

That week we had a second appointment with the mental health therapist. I had called him several days earlier to cancel because Hans was adamant that he was not going back, but the therapist convinced me that I needed to bring him in. He reminded me that our children do not get to make the decisions around their health. I, of course, understood this logically. After all, how many parents had I counseled over the years about making the decisions for their kids and only giving options the parents could live with; about holding their kids accountable for their choices and using natural consequences whenever possible while positively reinforcing good choices and behavior. Now *I* was the one being counseled to do the same. My training and experience supported what this therapist was telling me to do, but I knew it would be difficult. I was getting a better understanding of why many of the parents I had worked with over the years had not been able to follow through. It is tough work forcing something on your child when they are so distressed. I wanted to understand what was happening to my son. My intuition told me this wasn't going to be the answer we were so desperately looking for, but my training won out.

The day of the scheduled appointment, I prepared for what was to come. After 30 minutes of raging in his room, putting a hole in his wall, and splintering his door, we made it out to the car with the promise of a trip to Target to use his money to get another Lego set. We arrived 20 minutes late.

"Hi, sorry we are late."

"Tough time leaving?" he asked.

"That's one way to put it." We talked for a short time. The counselor then turned to Hans.

"Would you go for a walk with me in the neighborhood and talk about what you are thinking and feeling?"

"No, thank you," Hans politely declined and looked at me with a pleading look.

"Ok. Let's talk about missing school," he pressed, "you're probably not getting to do much at home since you aren't going to school."

"That isn't exactly how it's playing out at home," I interrupted. "Hans has access to his iPad often. He does some math with me daily, waters the plants, and bathes once a week. Those are our current goals."

I knew how ridiculous this sounded. I knew that I would think a parent was being manipulated and was enabling their child if I heard this response. I cringed inside at the judgment I was imagining this counselor was having for me.

"Is that right?" he looked at Hans.

"I guess so."

"Would you mind sitting outside so I can talk with Hans privately?" and just like that, he asked me to leave.

I was a little panicked, thinking about how volatile Hans was. I wasn't worried about him raging; I was worried about him feeling scared and confused. I sat outside the office in a corner by a window. I sat in a black vinyl covered chair with the word 'fuck' carved into the arm, a crack in the vinyl. I knew the kid who would have carved that word; I had worked for years with that kid. I sat there, looking around, wondering who else had sat here: moms, dads, kids; all feeling helpless, hopeless, confused maybe? I was worried that my precious baby was in there feeling this way. I knew the kids this counselor worked with, and Hans wasn't one of them. He wasn't dealing with trauma due to abuse. He hadn't grown up in a dysfunctional home. This wasn't due to *typical* behavioral causes. Something had happened that had changed him from the son I had known for the past ten years. I feared that this was not the right course of action.

The hour was up, and Hans came out. I scheduled another appointment and paid for the session, out of pocket. We walked silently out to the car.

"I am not coming back. Period."

It was a quiet ride home.

Later that afternoon, Hans asked me, "Mom, do you think I'm doing this just to get out of school?"

"No, honey, I don't. Why do you ask?"

"That counselor said that maybe I was just trying to get out of school. I feel badly that I'm not going to school."

"I know that sweetheart. I do not think you are doing this to get out of school. I'm sorry he made you feel that way. We won't go back to see him."

In my mind, I had just fired him. I had no doubt that what Hans was experiencing was not something he had control over. He was not making these things up, and he certainly wasn't trying to get out of school.

One week later, we had our second meeting with the psychiatrist. We brought Hans to this session, as well. He did not want to go and told us so in the usual manner, swearing and throwing things at us as he dismantled his bed. Bribery worked again, as I promised him another Lego set, explaining how important it was for us to meet with the experts. He left the house on his own and got into the minivan.

Arnold looked at me with questioning eyes, "How did you get him to come this time?"

"I bribed him."

Again, I reminded myself that if I gave him the reward after complying, it was positive reinforcement, anything to make me feel better about this.

We arrived at the office and went into the waiting room. I was pretending to look at a book of dog jokes, barely reading the comics as I wondered what was going on with my son and what were we going to do. The psychiatrist came out and met with Hans first. After 30 minutes, he called Arnold and I into his office and let Hans step outside to a play area designated for children.

"Has anything changed since we last met?" he inquired.

"Symptoms are pretty much the same, although now we are seeing more anxiety attacks, that's what I'm calling them, and less raging."

"Do you think we should do an MRI?" Arnold asked.

"After meeting him today, I would say there's no need to do an MRI. I want to get our behavior team into your home and set up some systems. You definitely have to get him back in school," he stated.

"Thank you!" exclaimed Arnold, as though he had been waiting to hear these words from someone with authority.

I sat there, a bit stunned for a moment. After all, I was on the school district's behavior team. I had had "systems" in place since the boys were toddlers. I did not feel that this was a "lack of systems" or that we were enabling Hans to avoid school.

"I appreciate the need to get Hans back in school. There's nothing I want more than that, but let me tell you what that would look like. I would have to physically man-handle him to get him dressed, carry him out to the car, restrain him the whole way there, and then when we get there and he's under the seat screaming and swearing and crying, what do you suggest we do?"

"Wait him out."

Waiting him out could take all day. I knew that. But what I was doing wasn't changing anything, and this man was the expert. I resigned myself to go against my gut feeling.

"Okay, if that's what we need to do, we'll do it. I'll have to take a day off from work."

"You may want to consider having someone else take him. That may remove part of the equation, and there may be a more likely chance of getting him to cooperate." I heard the judgment in this statement. It was being suggested that we were, in fact, enabling Hans's behavior or that we were currently part of the problem. I knew that sometimes a change in person, location, routine, *anything* could make a difference in a person's response. I was open to this idea. We discussed this further, identifying a few people who Arnold and I thought might be able to handle things if Hans became escalated. Then I added something we had forgotten to tell him the previous visit.

"There's one more thing we forgot to mention last time that may also be important. Back in December, Hans was really sick with what we think was the flu. He had a high fever, 103.7, with what we called fever-induced hallucinations. I don't know if that might have affected anything, but we thought you should know."

"Well, there's PANS and PANDAS, but they're very controversial, and the long term treatments can be problematic." I had never heard of either of these, so I didn't really register this comment until later.

"Okay, so we have an appointment scheduled with you for a follow-up in two weeks. In the meantime, we will get him back in school. I guess that's it until next time. We'll let you know how it goes. Thank you, again, for getting us in. We really appreciate it."

"Good, I'm glad you've already got another appointment. We'll see you then."

And then we left, with no diagnosis and a plan that terrified me. I was unconvinced.

Later that night, as I was searching the internet for something that would make sense, I found information that would make the visit we just had with the psychiatrist hard for me to forgive.

I read on the Psych Central website that a psychological assessment is a process of testing that uses a combination of techniques to help arrive at some hypotheses about a person and their behavior, personality, and capabilities. Psychological testing is nearly always performed by a licensed psychologist, or a psychology trainee. A psychological assessment should never be performed in a vacuum. A part of a thorough assessment of an individual is that they also undergo a full medical examination to rule out the possibilities of a medical disease or organic cause for the individual's symptoms. It's often helpful to have this done first, before psychological testing, as it may make psychological testing moot.[1] No one had suggested to us that we have Hans undergo a full medical examination, nor had any kind of psychological testing been offered. The plan we had made wasn't sitting right with me. I felt that we didn't have all the information we needed, and I was angry that the experts we were paying out of pocket hadn't suggested we do any evaluations.

The next day, I called Hans's teacher from our backyard where no one in the house would hear my conversation. This had become my preferred place to talk so I could share freely. I told her what the psychiatrist had said. It was not received well.

"Oh, Heather, I don't know about that. Everything happened so suddenly and he hasn't been attending, and the class has really come together, you know? They've really had a lot of life together. Connor is doing really well connecting with other kids. I'm just not sure about this. Let me think about it over the long weekend, and I'll get back with you on Monday before school starts back up on Tuesday. Maybe we start with a home visit and see how that goes."

I was stunned. This was coming from a woman I had admired immensely. She had supported my son academically, socially, and emotionally since 1st grade. I considered her a master educator, and in this moment, I was feeling that she didn't want the burden of my child. She had just told me that the class and his best friend were moving on without him. Now, when things were the hardest they had ever been, when I was watching my son slip through my fingers into something that I didn't understand and I needed support, I was feeling abandoned by the teacher and community that I had invested years of my time and energy into. Later, we would meet and talk about this conversation and how I had received it. Later, I would logically wrap my head around the fact that it wasn't her intent to communicate that Hans wasn't welcome in her class, but in this moment, I was knocked to my knees in grief and disbelief. I was losing my son and was battling to get answers. I had been told by a psychiatrist that I had to get him back in school, even though no part of me felt that it was a humane thing to try and do, and now I was hearing, from the teacher I adored, that my son wasn't welcome.

"Okay," I said quietly, choking back tears, "we'll start looking for a new school."

"No, Heather, that's not what I mean. Let me just think about this, and we'll talk on Monday."

We said our goodbyes, and I wished her an enjoyable holiday weekend camping. I hung up and fell to my knees in the grass sobbing; emptying all of my fear, grief, and anger before I went back inside to face my son and my husband.

That night, I began to research Obsessive Compulsive Disorder. It was clear to me that I didn't fully understand this disorder. As a high school resource teacher, I had had one student who had OCD, and he hadn't been able to finish out the school year, which as I reflect, meant I had not been able to meet his needs. I wanted to understand this disorder better. As I combed through websites, I came across the International OCD Foundation. I clicked on OCD in Kids, and I began to read. And then I came across the words, *What if there's an acute onset of OCD?* Yeah, I wondered, what about that?! I couldn't read fast enough. What I read described exactly what we had been living.

"Arnold! I think this is it. I think this is what Hans has. Listen to this." I read the following words out loud:

"My child was fine last week, last month – and now I have lost her. This is not my child; what has happened??? What do I do??

For every parent of a child with an illness, especially a mental illness, there is a particular story. But when you meet a parent of a child with PANDAS (typically a child between ages 3-14), you will hear the same panicked story

93

over and over. A child who was happy at home and at school and was social and athletic, is now walking in circles for hours, washing hands until they bleed, asking the same questions over and over – and over. A child that used to be comforted by a hug is now inconsolable. They may be begging parents for help, begging for a way to end the horror that exists only in their minds. Imagine a child screaming in terror in a corner and a parent unable to hold them. These parents will tell you in detail about the day or week that their child changed.

Here is what life looks like now – children may exhibit some or all of these symptoms:

- Acute sudden onset of OCD
- Challenges with eating, and at the extreme end, anorexia
- Sensory issues such as sensitivity to clothes, sound, and light
- Handwriting noticeably deteriorates
- Urinary frequency or bedwetting
- Small motor skills deteriorate - a craft project from yesterday is now impossible to complete
- Tics
- Inattentive, distractible, unable to focus and has difficulties with memory
- Overnight onset of anxiety or panic attacks over things that were no big deal a few days ago, such as thunderstorms or bugs
- Suddenly unable to separate from their caregiver, or to sleep alone
- Screaming for hours on end
- Fear of germs and other more traditional-looking OCD symptoms

You will often find these parents on the computer every night, desperate for an explanation that makes sense. They are seeking specialists who can help – and finding no answers. They are starting to feel crazy themselves, because no one seems to believe what they are going through." (http://kids.iocdf.org/ocdinkids/PANDAS/)

"Wow, I think you're right," Arnold replied with his typical grounded curiosity. "So what do we do?"

"I don't know, but I'm going to find out. And we *don't* try to send him to school on Tuesday."

I stayed up into the wee hours searching and reading everything I could; the controversy, the debate, the case stories, the symptoms, the diagnostic testing, the treatments, until my head was spinning. I didn't fully understand everything that I read. What I did understand was that it wasn't a psychiatrist or a therapist that was going to help our son. What we needed to know was in his blood.

It was a long holiday weekend as I waited for business hours to open on Tuesday. When I talked with Hans's teacher on Monday, I let her know that I wasn't planning on following through with the recommendation made and that we would update her when we had more information. Tuesday morning, I called and scheduled another appointment with our pediatrician, Dr. Jordana Hawkins, and I cancelled our next appointments with both the psychiatrist and the therapist. I was on the road to getting answers, and I had direction. I was still terrified and unsure, but I was hopeful for the first time!

CHAPTER FOURTEEN

MY ANGELS

"**H**ans! I think I know what's wrong! I think you have something called PANS. It's when your immune system, your army that's supposed to kill the bad germs in your body, gets confused and starts attacking good things in your body. I've scheduled an appointment with Dr. Hawkins again so we can talk with her about it and find out what we can do to get you better."

Our appointment was scheduled two weeks out. Hans went willingly, I think because he saw the hope in us that we might get answers. When Dr. Hawkins came into the room to meet us, she smiled.

"So, have things gotten any better?"

"No, in fact they've gotten worse, but I think I know what Hans has. Have you ever heard of PANS or PANDAS?"

"I've heard of PANDAS, but I'm not familiar with PANS. I've never had a patient with it before."

"It stands for Pediatric Acute-onset Neuropsychiatric Syndrome, and it's a sudden onset of psychiatric symptoms that can't be explained by any other neurological cause. PANDAS is associated with Strep, but it's not always Strep. PANS is what it's being called now because it could be a result of some other infection that has caused the immune system to malfunction. I will send you links so you don't have to research this yourself."

I shared with her the symptoms and recommended diagnostics that I had pulled off of the PANDAS Network website. I told her that he was continuing to have emotional outbursts, sometimes presenting as rages. He was having severe anxiety attacks and couldn't go to school, and he wanted me to be at home. When he would come out of his anxiety attacks, it presented as almost seizure-like, with him staring off before coming to and asking us what just happened.

"We've got a system, so when his anxiety is a 3, Arnold texts me, and I come home. This has been helping."

I shared that he was overly afraid of bugs, especially bees, flies, and spiders. He wasn't eating, probably a quarter of what he used to eat, and ad lost 4 pounds. His pupils were dilated. His joints ached, and he would ask me to rub his arms and legs, but a certain way, and I had to start over if I didn't do it right. He complains that he feels weird in his body and head and begs me to make it stop and that he can't do it any more, that it's too much.

"Arnold and I completed the PANS Symptoms Checklist. We got it off the PANDAS Network website, but it was developed by Dr. Susan Swedo with the National Institute of Mental Health. We filled it out independently to make sure we were both seeing the same thing, and our scores were only 2 points off from each other. I've got copies here, but pre-onset scores were 18 – 20, and post-onset scores were 95 – 97 out of 100."

I handed her the checklists, and she looked at them briefly.

"Can we please just do the diagnostics?"

"Absolutely," she didn't even hesitate.

I was in tears as I thanked her. That began a close relationship with the doctor who first diagnosed my son with PANDAS. What I appreciated most about Dr. Jordana Hawkins was her willingness to explore further without making us feel like we were crazy. I also appreciated her honesty about not knowing what she was doing, but she was willing to give it her best effort. She was my first angel in this hell we had been living.

We scheduled an MRI and decided to do the extensive lab work while he was sedated for that procedure. I emailed Dr. Hawkins the information I had researched and the list of labs to perform that I got off the PANDAS Network website. Essentially, we were ruling out other neurological conditions that could explain his behaviors while also looking to see if there were elevated antibodies to any infections that might indicate an autoimmune reaction. Antibodies, also known as immunoglobulins, are Y-shaped proteins that are produced by the immune system to help stop intruders from harming the body. When an intruder enters the body, the immune system responds. These invaders, which are called antigens, can be viruses, bacteria, or other chemicals. The current hypothesis about autoimmunity is that, in response to an infection, the immune system may be mistaking the body's own healthy cells as invaders and repeatedly attacking them, or it may be attacking a pathogen that is embedded in the cells themselves. Autoimmune diseases can affect almost any part of the body, including the heart, brain, nerves, muscles, skin, eyes, joints, lungs, kidneys, pancreatic beta cells, glands, the digestive tract, and blood vessels. Once you get an autoimmune condition you are more susceptible to developing others.

The classic sign of an autoimmune response is inflammation, which can cause redness, heat, pain, and swelling. How an autoimmune disease affects you depends on what part of the body is targeted. If the disease affects the joints, as in rheumatoid arthritis, you might have joint pain, stiffness, and loss of function. If it affects the thyroid, as in Graves' disease and Hashimoto's Thyroiditis, it might cause tiredness, weight gain, cold hands and feet, and muscle aches. If it attacks the skin, as it does in scleroderma/systemic sclerosis, vitiligo, and systemic lupus erythematosus, it can cause rashes, blisters, and skin discoloration.

In the case of PANDAS, the originating infection is streptococcus, and the current understanding is that antibodies cross the blood-brain barrier attacking the basal ganglia. The result is a sudden onset of obsessive compulsive behaviors. Dr. Susan Swedo, with the National Institute of Mental Health, had been researching this since the early 1990's. In 2012, Susan Swedo, James Leckman at Yale, and Joel Rose at Johns Hopkins proposed PANS, which builds on and subsumes PANDAS.[1] It includes youth who experience acute onset of OCD or anorexia symptoms mixed with a varying profile of other neuropsychiatric symptoms where the cause is unspecified. It also acknowledges that the triggering pathogen may be something other than streptococcus. Today, there are those who recognize that this is autoimmune encephalitis. Encephalitis is inflammation in the brain caused by infection or an allergic reaction. Autoimmune encephalitis refers to a group of conditions that occur when the body's immune system mistakenly attacks healthy brain cells, leading to inflammation of the brain. This is a field within medicine that is expanding rapidly since the first antibody-mediated AE was identified in 2005. [2] As of early 2017, there have been 22 antibodies discovered and, according to one prominent researcher, a new antibody is being discovered roughly every six months.

Our task was to rule out any other causes and check Hans's blood for antibodies. We waited for the scheduled MRI and blood draw. We were hoping we would get answers from both. Rage, confusion, anxiety attacks, and a drastic loss of appetite were the daily norm for Hans. We were homeschooling, if you could call it that, while I was continuing to try to work. Expectations at home were minimal in order to reduce any triggers that might result in the symptoms he was experiencing. Hans's daily goals were to complete 5 math problems on Kahn Academy, read to himself or listen to Arnold or I read to him, and water the plants on the back deck. Watering the plants was simply to get him outside. On some days he would crawl off the couch, across the floor, and onto the deck, then into a chair, and hold the watering can over the pots before crawling back into the house and back onto the couch where he spent his days propped on his pillows with an iPad in his grip. The iPad use was a particularly difficult accommodation for us to make. Previously, the boys had one hour of screen time a week, and they had had to earn that time. Now, Hans was either playing games or watching shows on the iPad close to 10, sometimes 12 hours a day. The tech consumption seemed to soothe him and keep him out of his mind, where he seemed to be so troubled.

He continued to eat only a quarter of what he used to. Quantity and variety were significantly diminished. Things he used to love he would refuse. He began a pattern of only wanting to eat the same thing for days until he was sick of it: English muffin and strawberries, bagel with cream cheese, quesadilla or macaroni and cheese with carrot sticks, chicken and noodles with carrot sticks. He wasn't eating anything green, and his protein and vegetable and fruit intake were significantly limited.

He was also refusing to bathe or cut his nails. Bathing had never been his favorite thing to do, but it got done with hair washed. Now he said that the water was too wet and his fingertips felt funny. Neither of these were things I wanted to battle over, and I began to wash his hands and feet from a large bowl of warm water, ignoring the dirty looking hair and long nails. This was difficult to look past. Andre thought his nails were creepy, Arnold wanted his hair trimmed up and clean, and I was concerned that he might get an infection. Extended family and friends noticed right away, the nails in particular, but everyone was willing to look past that and simply acknowledged Hans and let him be.

We were trying to keep Hans connected in some way to school. His good friend, Connor, came to visit after school with his younger brother. Just prior to their arrival, Hans began to have what I had been calling anxiety attacks. I later came to understand that these were panic attacks. He was sitting in the corner of the couch, rocking back and forth, trying to pull the cushions over him. He began banging his head against the back of the couch and was begging me to make it stop. He was crying and pleading.

"It's too much, it's too much! I can't take it anymore! Please, make it stop! I can't do this anymore, just kill me!"

All I could do during these episodes was sit next to him, making sure he didn't bang his head on anything hard, which sometimes required strategic placement of pillows.

When I heard the knock on the door, I went to greet our friends.

"I'm afraid it's not going to work out today. I'm so sorry, but we can't receive any visitors."

Arnold was outside and called to them to shoot hoops with Andre. I saw Connor look past me at Hans with such compassion and worry. His mom, Jenny, gave me a huge hug, and said they would come again. I choked back the tears and thanked them. Then I returned to sit next to Hans while I watched outside as the kids shot the basketball and Arnold and Jenny talked. After a short period, they piled into their car and drove off.

We tried a visit a couple of other times, none of which worked. After the third attempt, Hans was angry.

"Why can't I see my friend? Why do I always do this? I'm so tired of being like this! Can't you do something?"

"You can have a good visit with Connor. I've been paying attention to these visits and I've noticed something. Every time, right before he gets here, something has happened that upset you and you weren't able to control how you felt and it hasn't worked out. I am going to make sure that the next visit happens when nothing will get you upset ahead of time. Then you will have a good visit. I promise!"

I hoped I was right and that I could make good my promise; I really did feel confident about this observation. And Jenny, my second angel, was willing to do whatever it would take to get Connor and Hans together in a positive way.

CHAPTER FIFTEEN
WILL HE MIND YOU?

That night, Hans was very agitated. He had been continuing to have panic attacks off and on for several hours. His pupils were dilated, his pulse was at 150, and he was breathing rapidly. He was begging me to make it stop. It was the weekend, and I didn't know who to contact. I had the number of the psychiatrist we had fired, and I decided to page him and ask what to do. He told me to take him to the Emergency Room. I went into Hans's room where he was wedged into the corner sitting on his bed holding his head.

"Hans, we are going to the Emergency Room at St. Joe's to see if they can help us make this stop."

He went willingly and seemed to calm down as soon as we got there. It was a quiet night at the ER; very different from the visit we had had three years earlier when Andre had needed stitches. We were taken to a room immediately after checking in. Hans looked around, taking note of the surroundings just as he had at Seattle Children's Hospital. His observations were not so positive, and he was not reassured. He called the place a dump and said he didn't want to stay in this dirty place, but we had checked in, and I felt that we had to go through the process. I talked with the doctor on call and told him my concerns. He ordered a blood draw. Hans looked at me, terrified, and pulled his sweat shirt down over his hands. The nurse tried to cajole him to no avail.

"What do you do when the patient refuses?"

"There are things we can do if we have to."

"Is there something you can give him that might help?"

She ordered Lorazepam, a sedative that is often used to treat anxiety. Hans took it in liquid form. He seemed to settle after that and actually let them draw his blood. When they had finished, we waited. A counselor came in and told me that the doctor had asked her to give me information. She asked questions and then provided me with a list of resources in our community, all of which I had already exhausted. I thanked her and knew that I was way past this list she had given me, but she was just doing her job. We waited even longer. It was now 11:00 pm, and we were both tired and wanted to be home. The doctor returned and told me the lab work was normal and that one of the nurses would bring us the discharge papers so we could go. He also gave me a prescription for Ativan to keep on hand at home if we needed it.

We continued to wait. I watched the nurses sitting just outside our room at their station as they chatted about different things in their lives. I wanted to scream at them. *What are we waiting for while you sit around and chat?* Finally, I went out and told them that we were just waiting for our discharge papers, could they check to see if those were done? They looked up at me and said they would check as soon as they could. One of them then went over to what looked like a fax machine, pulled the papers off, and came into our room to release us. I was so frustrated and tired. I felt like this visit had all been a waste of time. A generic blood draw had been taken, a counselor had given me resources I had already exhausted, I had a prescription for a medication that would *maybe* soothe my son, and I had had to advocate myself to have my son released while hospital staff sat around doing nothing. We went home. Hans climbed into bed and was asleep almost immediately.

He awoke the next day right where he left off, agitated, banging his head, begging for me to make it all stop. By 11:15, Arnold had picked up the Ativan prescription, and I gave him a 0.25 mg pill. At 12:15, I gave him another one as he continued to be agitated. Then I consulted with the on-call doctor, and at 6:00 pm, I gave him four more, totaling 1.0 mg. By 7:45, our new routine of eating dinner while watching a movie was over. With the distraction of the movie over, he continued to be agitated, and then it shifted to anger. Unprovoked, he raged at me, kicking and hitting at me. Soon he was lying on the ground, arching his back and kicking his feet into the air. This was something I had never seen before, and I assumed it was an uncoordinated attempt to kick me. Many months later, I would wonder if this had been a chorea movement. After several minutes of this, he got up and lunged at me. I easily stepped out of the way. As he continued to swing at me, I evaded and moved towards the stairway and led his attack upstairs to his room. Once in his room, his attack stopped, and he climbed into bed complaining that he was hot. I brought up a fan and aimed it at him.

"Get away from me, or I will kill you!"

He closed his eyes and, thankfully, was asleep within five minutes.

This pattern continued for days. One morning, he woke up and told me he hoped he would have a good day like the day before, except the going crazy part in the morning.

"Do you remember the going crazy part?"

"No, I just know that sometimes I feel like I'm going crazy."

Arnold and I were concerned about the upcoming MRI and his current panic and rage attacks. We were wondering how we were going to get him into the MRI machine and to stay still. Again, I consulted with the doctor. We tried a different benzodiazepine, Clonazepam, to calm him. I gave him .25 mg, and that evening he had another meltdown. I was feeling completely lost, and I couldn't even imagine how he was feeling--clearly not well! The next day, the day before the scheduled MRI, we gave him .25 mg Clonazepam in the am and again in the pm, and he seemed to be less agitated, but we had no way of knowing if it was the effect of the medication or if he was just having less of a bad day. We discussed how we were going to keep him from having anything to eat for the required 8 hours before a 3:00 pm procedure. We decided not to mention food.

He awoke the next day, and I didn't offer him any break-fast. Later in the day, I didn't offer lunch. Not once did he ask for food. I realized that all the prodding I had been doing to get him to eat, trying anything that might appeal to him, holding the food up to his mouth, was really the only reason I was getting food into him at all! We gave him .25 mg of Clonazepam and then prepared to leave at 1:30. I had told him about the procedure over the past several days as best I could. I had tried to explain that he would lie on a bed and a donut shaped machine would move around the bed and take a picture of his brain. As I had explained, he had seemed only partially aware of what I was saying.

"It's time to go, Hans."

"Oh, I'm not going!" he said with conviction, and then he climbed behind the couch.

Arnold was pulling the car out into the driveway as I prepared the room in order to secure Hans and carry him out of the house. I moved furniture that would impede our path towards the door, predicting it would be a two-person escort. Arnold had the side door of the minivan open, engine running, and then came in to support me.

"Hans, it's time to go, please come out from behind the couch."

"No! I'm not going, and that's final!"

As I reflect back on this, I can only imagine the terror that he was experiencing. Someone was going to take a picture of his brain. What did that really mean? How would they do that? Would it hurt? Even though I had tried to explain the procedure to him, I knew he wasn't able to think like he used to and that he hadn't really been paying attention to me. What followed was horrific.

I carefully pulled him out from behind the couch and secured his upper body while Arnold secured his lower body. He tried to kick and wiggle free. Arnold and I worked together, carrying our precious son out the door screaming and fighting, as if for his life. We got him into the car, and then I restrained him, no seat belts, as Arnold drove to St. Joseph Hospital to check in. The restraint in the car was very difficult. I was sitting in the back seat with him in front of me between my knees. I had his arms crossed in front, and I secured a grip between his wrists and elbows. He was trying to kick me, and since he couldn't hit me, he began to try to bite me, with success. My first thought was *I can't believe my arm is in my son's mouth. I know better than to let my arm end up in someone's mouth! I'm trained to prevent this.* As I pushed my lower arm into his mouth and rolled out to release the bite, I then thought to myself: *hey, it really works!* I had taught this release many times, but had never needed to use it, myself. It was then that I noticed blood on my white sweater sleeve and was concerned that he had broken my skin. I would later determine that it was from a loose molar in his mouth.

I made the decision to release him to see if he would stop fighting, knowing that this sometimes is the case as the fight is often against the feeling of being trapped. He quickly scrambled to the back of the minivan, sobbing with rage and fear on his face. He found an umbrella stowed under the back seat and was gesturing as if to hit with it, but stayed put. Arnold pulled up to the entrance where we would check in. I told Arnold he would need to go in, explain the situation, and request a room. A few minutes later, a nurse came out to the car. Hans was in the back corner with the umbrella raised and was seething, spittle coming from the side of his mouth.

She looked at him and asked me, "will he mind you?"

I looked back at her with disbelief, "does he look like he'll mind me? A month ago he would, but now he won't. That's why we are here. We are trying to figure out what's wrong."

"Well, maybe we should reschedule."

"That is not an option. We have an MRI scheduled, and we are not leaving until that gets done today."

"Well, I've never done this before," she told me as she pointed to my terrified and seething son.

"We haven't either, but we got him here, and we aren't leaving until we have done an MRI. We just need a room."

She left and immediately returned with two security officers. I did not want to have to use them. Arnold went over to talk with them and assured them that we could get him in, but we wanted a room to take him to; we did not want to sit in the waiting room.

I turned to Hans. "We can either carry you in or you can walk yourself in, but we are going in."

With terror in his eyes, and a tear-streaked face, he said to me between sobs, "Please, just let me get dressed." I gave him sweat pants, and he pulled them on over the pajamas he had been in for weeks. He walked in with us, and we followed the nurse to a room.

Once we were in the room, I gave him his iPad and helped him find a game to play. A different nurse began to take his vitals. We consulted outside the room as Hans was now de-escalated and playing games. I let her know what we had already given him. She got the sedative ready to administer, 3 syringes filled with a liquid Midazolam, a sedative that was supposed to help him go to sleep. I explained this to him and put the first syringe in his mouth, aiming it to the back, just as I had done when putting meds in my mom's mouth when she was unconscious and dying of cancer. The third one made him choke.

"Hans, I'm so sorry! You have been so brave, and I'm so proud of you!"

Thirty minutes later, the anesthesiologist came in. Thom was a personal friend of ours. We had requested him to be our anesthesiologist because he was the best. He looked at Hans.

"He doesn't look sleepy at all. He should be drowsy by now."

"No, he doesn't look tired at all," I agreed and made a mental note that the benzodiazepines didn't seem to affect my son.

Thom called for a different anesthetic, which was brought in liquid form, but this time Hans refused.

"I am not taking any more medicine," and he pinched his lips tight shut.

I pleaded, tried to bribe, but he refused, standing up on the bed and pointing at Thom.

"You're not a real doctor. Get away from me! Let me go!"

Thom looked at me. "There are other ways we can do this; we do it all the time for the developmentally delayed. He probably won't even remember it."

"Yes, let's get this done."

As the nurse prepared the syringe with a needle, Arnold and I moved to either side of Hans. We pulled him down on the bed, rolled him over, and pulled his pants down to expose his bottom. He was screaming.

"No! Stop! I'll drink it, please don't do this!"

And then the shot was administered as I felt my insides wanting to wretch.

Arnold and I released Hans. He sat up and looked at me.

"What's happening? I demand to know what's happening to me?"

Then he fell into my arms. I was overcome and began to cry myself as I laid him down on the bed. The nurse began to prepare the bed for transit and asked if I wanted to ride with him.

"Will he know I'm with him? If so, then yes, but if he doesn't know, then I can walk."

She assured me that he was completely sedated, wouldn't remember a thing, and that they were going to take excellent care of him. Arnold and I followed them down the white, windowless hall, and I leaned on him as I sobbed. I knew Hans was safe and that we were going to get answers, but I was feeling terrified and so broken over the battle it had been to get here. As they wheeled him through the last set of double doors, I called out to the nurse.

"Don't forget to do the blood draw while he's sedated. We need that lab work done as well."

We waited in a small room. For forty-five minutes we waited. Thom came out to let us know that Hans was in the recovery room and that it would be a while before he would wake up as the Ketamine they had administered was fairly strong. He told us that, ideally, he would have been able to get Hans to drink Midazolam and Ketamine together, and for a short procedure would use 50-75 mg of Ketamine, but because this procedure might have taken a while, he had administered 150 mg of Ketamine to ensure he didn't wake up during the MRI. He then told us that we could go in and sit with him.

Our ten-year old boy was so peaceful laying there attached to all the monitors. The nurse who was recording his vitals was reassuring us. "Everything looks good!"

He finally roused a bit, trying to lift his head.

"Mom? You're here!" Then his head flopped back down on his pillow.

The tears spilled from my eyes. I held his hand and waited. Again, he tried to lift his head just as Thom came over to see how he was coming along.

"Do you have a wake up pill?" he asked, then flopped back onto his pillow.

Thom explained to us that it might be a while before he was completely awake. I watched as he struggled to wake up. His spirit was so strong. Even drugged, he was fighting! During one of his "wake ups," the nurse asked him if he wanted a Popsicle.

"Are you kidding? In this state?" he said, and then again, his head fell to his pillow. I appreciated his humor even in this drug induced state of anesthesia.

After thirty minutes of coming in and out of consciousness, he was finally awake enough to sit up. We were taken back to our first room, and the nurse gave him some crackers to eat and some juice to drink. He needed to use the toilet, so I helped him from his bed into the adjoining bathroom. As soon as he stood up from the toilet and began to walk towards the sink, he vomited all over the floor. I helped him rinse his mouth out and got him back into bed. The nurse gave him another cracker. Once he finished it and could stand up on his own, we could go.

She looked over at all the vials of blood that had been drawn.

"What labs are being ordered?" *She didn't have any orders?!*

"I can tell you exactly what we want checked," Arnold pulled up the list from his phone. We had put this list together from the PANDAS Network website and had given it to Dr. Hawkins so we knew exactly what we were wanting drawn.

"That's fine, but I need orders from your doctor."

She called over to Dr. Hawkins' office, but Dr. Hawkins wasn't there. She asked to be given the doctor's home number. She was not going to take no for an answer. She finally got the information she needed; I don't know if it was from Dr. Hawkins or a nurse. She was looking up codes as Arnold and I looked over her shoulder to make sure she got it all. She then explained to us that these labs were going to need to go to the University of Washington for testing so it might take longer than usual. Our doctor would call us with the results. Arnold took a picture of the lab paperwork so we would have it to reference later if we needed to.

It was late when we got home. Nana had picked Andre up from school, and they had already eaten dinner. She had explained to him that we would all be exhausted and to try to understand that we would need to be taking care of Hans when we got home. Hans was tired and just a little hungry. He drank some chicken broth and went to bed, falling asleep easily. We were all ready for a good night's sleep. That night, I lay in bed going over the day in my head. It had been awful, but we were going to find out what was going on in my precious boy's body. I hoped that I was right. I hoped that there was an explanation for what he was experiencing. I hoped that we would be able to get him relief. I hoped, and I fell asleep.

CHAPTER SIXTEEN
STREP!

D r. Hawkins had recommended seeing a neurologist at Seattle Children's who had an expressed 'interest' in PANS. When I called to schedule the appointment, I was told it would be at least 3 months before the first available appointment. I immediately burst into tears on the phone, explaining our situation. The very kind lady asked if I would be willing to go to any of the satellite hospitals if an appointment opened up earlier and if I would be willing to see any doctor with an 'interest' in PANS. I assured her I would, and I felt very fortunate when she called the next day with an opening at the Everett Children's Hospital with a neurologist that Dr. Hawkins had worked with during her internship. She had favorable things to say, so we were eager to meet him.

Two days after the MRI, Arnold picked up the image and report and joined me for another trip with Hans. Again, he was resistant. This time we had tried Risperidon, hoping that a different family of drug would have a sedating effect. Risperidon is an antipsychotic medication mainly used to treat schizophrenia, bipolar disorder, and irritability associated with autism. I couldn't believe that this was what we were giving our child, but we needed to be able to get him calm for travel. It didn't seem to make a difference. I called Everett Children's and told them we were having difficulty leaving and that we might show up with a combative child. They were incredibly understanding and kind, said they saw this every day, and to bring him on in. Hans alternated between crying, begging us not to make him go, and raging. Again, we had to carry Hans out to the car, resisting, but this time I didn't restrain him, and he crawled under the bench seat with his huge stuffed dog and cried. I assured him that there would be no needles and no sleep medicine. He eventually calmed, and when we arrived, Arnold went in to check us in and let them know that Hans did not want to wait in the waiting room. They let us wait in the car and then called me on my phone when they had a room ready for us. I felt understood, and I appreciated that.

Hans was able to walk himself in. We met the neurologist, and he shared with us that the MRI looked normal, other than a notable mild sinus inflammation, which he said we could take with a grain of salt as that is very common in children. I would find out later, from many other moms, that their children also had this. It may have been an indication of infection, possibly strep, potentially triggering an autoimmune response.[3] He examined Hans while he talked with us, finally reporting that everything checked out normal. I explained the sudden onset of his symptoms and shared with him the symptoms checklist that Arnold and I had completed.

"It could be PANS, but we won't know until we get the labs back."

He asked if there was any history of mental illness in the family, and I ran down the list of people in our extended family with anxiety and depression.

He then looked at me and asked, "what about you?"

I sat there with my folder open, daily notes and charts, symptoms checklist, list of questions and looked back at him, shrugging, "luck of the draw?"

He smiled at me and suggested, "no perfectionist tendencies?"

I could read into that question, OCD perhaps? I smiled, "you got me there."

We thanked him for his time and left. I was feeling like we still didn't have any answers, and I was hoping the lab results would give us something. On the way out, Hans wanted to stop in the gift shop to buy a big stuffed dog for Andre so he would have one like his own Baxter. I appreciated his thoughtfulness. I hesitated. Part of me wanted to honor this request because he was showing kindness towards his brother *and* I was afraid he might rage if I said no. On the other hand, we didn't need another stuffed animal at home.

"Let's look for a stuffed dog another time with Andre." I waited for his reply, ready to respond if I needed to.

"Ok." I had an inner sigh of relief, and we walked past the gift shop, out the door, and got back into our minivan to begin the drive home. We were just getting onto the freeway when my phone rang. It was Dr. Hawkins.

"Hi Heather, I wanted to let you know right away that Hans's labs came back and everything looked fine except his ASO titers and DNase B titers were both high!" she told me.

"Okay, so now we know he had strep!" I answered. I looked up to Arnold who was watching me in the rear view mirror and gave him a thumbs up.

"I've never been so glad to get back positive labs before. I've called in a prescription for an antibiotic. I would like you to start him on a 10-day course of Amoxicillin right away."

"Yes, of course. We've just left Everett Children's Hospital, nothing remarkable to report. We'll pick up the prescription on our way home."

I hung up and sat there quietly for a moment. Then I looked at Hans.

"Sweetie, you've got PANDAS and we're going to get you better!"

At that moment, I was filled with so much hope. I didn't yet know what a long journey recovery would be. I had only watched the youTube video of the little boy who had recovered after 8 days of antibiotics, and I was hoping for that same outcome.

The rest of that week felt pleasant just having an answer and some direction. Andre, Arnold, and I were all swabbed for strep, and it turned up that Andre was an asymptomatic carrier of strep. He started a course of Amoxicillin, as well. The last weeks of the school year, Hans worked on his goals of watering the flowers on the back deck and taking a bath at least once a week. He spent most of his time on the couch or in his bed watching cartoons or playing games on his iPad. However, he still became angry when limits were set, sometimes going to his room and kicking his wall and swearing at us. He was easily set off by Andre and would attempt to hit him or push him, and I would have to intervene. His panic attacks were lasting late into the night and wee hours of the morning; I would continue to sit with him until they subsided, and he would eventually fall asleep.

At our request, Dr. Hawkins consulted with Dr. Frankovich with the Stanford PANS Clinic, who suggested a standard antibiotic protocol for kids with PANS. One week into the Amoxicillin, we switched to a different antibiotic, Augmentin, an Amoxicillin/Clavulanate, 875/125 two times a day for three weeks. We also started a probiotic to protect his gut. He took this in the middle of the day between the doses of antibiotics so as to not interfere. We didn't see any improvement. I was recording every day in a log with details about when he awoke and went to sleep, if he slept through the night, what he ate, how he was feeling physically, what he did, and any other factors that I thought might give us information. We were seeing the same saw tooth pattern of easy days where there was no incident followed by days with raging or panic attacks. It had gotten to the point that I was doing whatever I could to prevent both of those, which meant fewer expectations and fewer triggers. Hans was frustrated that he was taking medicine and not getting any better. He was having headaches, nausea, achy joints, and would need me to rub his arms and legs to get the blood back into his fingers and toes.

The end of June he had a sore throat, and I was afraid that he had strep. It didn't look red or inflamed, and I gave him ibuprofen to take away the pain. I began to research causes for aches and pain in the joints and limbs as well as changes in hair texture. I had noticed that he was growing tight cork-screw hairs amidst his fine straight hair. I was worried that he might have a thyroid problem on top of everything else. I asked Dr. Hawkins if we should do another round of labs, and she didn't think so. I couldn't imagine how we would accomplish it even if she thought we should, but I was worried. He wasn't getting better, and it seemed that he was developing additional symptoms.

PART 3

Treatment:
The Long Journey

"Even darkness must pass. A new day will come. And when the sun shines it will shine out the clearer."

J.R.R. Tolkien,
Lord of the Rings: The Two Towers

CHAPTER SEVENTEEN
LOST SUMMER

Summer vacation was beginning, and I didn't know what to expect. Typically, we planned a month of travelling, but this summer we hadn't made any plans as we were completely consumed by this change in Hans and our family. The neighborhood children were out playing, enjoying the freedoms of an open schedule. On our block are six other children all about the same age as Hans and Andre. Over the years, we had enjoyed a sort of open door between homes, with kids running in to use the bathroom or get a drink of water at whichever house they were closest to. When the kids came to ask if Hans and Andre wanted to play, Hans would decline. He couldn't explain to me why, just that he didn't want to leave the house. Soon the neighbor kids only asked for Andre and would peak in, sometimes saying "hi" to Hans if they saw him. Even when they were playing in our yard, Hans would no longer join them.

July was a rough month. Instead of enjoying the revelry of Independence Day with our neighbors and friends as we had so many years in the past, we were stuck in our home. Andre spent the 4th of July swimming in our neighbor's pool. Arnold and I took turns between being home with Hans and joining the party. I couldn't enjoy myself and was constantly on the verge of tears as I saw all the kids swimming, laughing, and enjoying this day while my oldest son was at home tormented. I didn't blame anyone for having fun, but it didn't feel fair, and I couldn't share in the festivities, either. Andre wanted to go down to the harbor to watch the fireworks. Bellingham puts on an amazing fireworks show. It is a beautiful display of pyrotechnic artistry that draws the community to the waterfront, and we had spent many years with the rest of the "hamsters" on our blankets at Zuanich Park gazing in awe at the sky as it exploded in color. Since Hans couldn't go this year, we asked our friends if Andre could join them and their two boys. They agreed.

I had picked up some small fireworks to do at home so Hans could enjoy a little bit of the fun. Late in the afternoon, Andre and his buddy asked if they could head over to our house and set off the fireworks with Hans. I checked in with Hans and he was eager to do that. He got dressed and joined Andre and Trevor on the back deck. I was thrilled that he was going to engage with another kid and get outside. He wanted to light one of his smoke bombs and throw it. Just as he was about to do that, Arnold told him to stop and started to go over the safety rules. His presentation was direct and rough, pointing his finger.

"No one will be setting off any fireworks without following the rules."

Hans took immediate offense, yelling at Arnold, "I hate you, you ruin everything!"

He ran to his room, changed back into his pajamas, kicking his wall, and screaming that everyone needed to leave *now*! Andre and Trevor returned to the party, and later Andre went with them to the harbor to watch the fireworks show.

I was furious with Arnold, feeling that he should have known that Hans would respond in this way and why couldn't he have been gentler in his presentation. It seemed that Arnold and I were fighting more often as I was trying to keep Hans from escalations, and Arnold was trying to keep things the way they had been. The stress between us did not help things around the house as Hans was very sensitive to our interactions. Whenever we would disagree, Hans would say, "stop fighting you two!" It felt like we were all walking on eggshells all of the time.

To make things worse, we weren't seeing any real improvement in Hans. After the three week course of Augmentin, we had switched to 150 mg of Clindamycin, yet another antibiotic, which he took three times a day. We also started him on 5 mg of Celexa, a selective serotonin reuptake inhibitor. With an SSRI, you start with a small dose and slowly increase. I had read that some kids with PANDAS/PANS had good results with a low dose of an SSRI.[4] After a month, we had completed the Clindamycin and started him on prophylactic antibiotics, switching to 500 mg Cephalexin two times a day and increased the Celexa to 10 mg a day. We still weren't seeing the results we were hoping for. He couldn't leave the house, he was easily set off in a rage, he had stopped bathing completely, and he wouldn't eat much. We had a safety plan in place for Andre. If Hans became aggressive, Andre knew to either go outside or to his room and lock the door.

Our neighbors knew what we were dealing with and were very sympathetic, offering to take Andre at a moments' notice. He spent a lot of time in the neighbor's pool with their girls and the other kids from the neighborhood. Extended family also offered to have Andre come and visit for a week or more, but he didn't want to leave home for any long trips. My heart ached for him, wishing I could give him back his brother, his summer, his sense of safety.

Arnold would offer to do things with him, go bike riding or camping, but Andre didn't want to unless I could go also, and I couldn't. I was housebound, caring for Hans, a prisoner in my own home. I was angry at Arnold. If it had been me, I would have planned an awesome trip that Andre couldn't say no to, something that I knew he would love. I wanted Arnold to do that, but he didn't. I had sympathy for Andre and understood that he didn't want to be away from me and the entire family, as dysfunctional as it was. He was just eight years old and didn't fully understand what was going on. None of us did.

It wasn't just that Hans couldn't leave the house. We couldn't have visitors the way we used to either. A friend came up from Seattle for the afternoon, and we had to stay outside, dining on the back deck. That would have been fine, except that it wasn't because it was an especially nice day. It was because, if he came in the house, our son would have a panic attack or rage. There were many times with friends and family when we would cut visits short or ask everyone to stay outside so we could reduce Hans's stress. I knew it sounded crazy that our child would be dictating our social lives. I knew that it would appear we were enabling him. I also knew what could happen, the hours of physical restraint or destruction in his room, and those were not situations I wanted to allow.

I was exhausted from researching. I read everything I could find on PANS and PANDAS. I took notes, wrote questions, and kept Dr. Hawkins apprised of any changes or lack of changes. She was very honest with us, stating that she really didn't know what to do. We were on a waiting list to get in to the Stanford PANS clinic, and it was expected to be four or five months before that would happen. I was impatient and stressed and angry.

And then, to make matters worse, we got fleas. I didn't know how I was going to get rid of them. I was hoping we could all stay overnight in the RV that we hadn't been able to use all summer so I could bomb. I talked with Hans about it. He hated the fleas in the carpet, but he just couldn't leave the house.

"I'm sorry mom, I can't explain it, but I just can't stay in the RV. You have to get rid of the fleas some other way."

I hit the internet again, this time searching for natural ways to rid the house of fleas. Arnold bought a five pound bag of salt, and I sprinkled it on the carpet, swept it in, and then three days later I vacuumed the carpets. I repeated this process six times, going through fifteen pounds of salt. Every night, we would sweep the non-carpeted floors and count the jumping critters in the dirt, so happy when it went down from twenty to twelve, to two or three, until finally there were none. During those weeks, when Hans would be up late having a hard time falling asleep and would need me to be with him, I would place pillows on the floor to lay on and pull my knees up to my chest so I could be on my little island away from any potential fleas.

Outside our home, Arnold sprayed a non-toxic flea repellant on the grass and shrubs along the perimeter of the property and spread cedar bark around the base of the house and by the entrances. We didn't want any more fleas coming in the house! This process took us three weeks, but we were rid of the fleas and had been able to do so without making Hans uncomfortable and without using any toxic chemicals. It felt like a small victory, and I would take any victory I could get! Later, I would understand what a good thing it had been that I couldn't bomb the house. Those toxic chemicals could have wreaked havoc on Hans's already compromised immune system.

I was supposed to co-teach at a week-long conference in Seattle. It was my third and final training in becoming a Senior Trainer for Life Space Crisis Intervention. I loved these conferences! They were emotionally intense as we would support the participants in role playing how to support individuals in crisis and take stressful situations and turn them into powerful teaching opportunities, but they were also incredibly fulfilling as we spent time with like-minded individuals who care deeply about our students, especially those who present with challenging behaviors. I knew I wasn't going to be able to be away for a week, and Hans couldn't leave the house to go to Nana's. In the past, Arnold and the boys had enjoyed the many fun things for families to do in Seattle, but that wasn't going to happen this year. I contacted one of the Master Trainers, a friend of mine, and explained what was going on. I felt so badly; my training had been paid for, and now I wasn't going to be able to complete it. She was incredibly understanding and also intrigued by what we were experiencing. She told me to keep in touch, there would be other opportunities, and then she said, "I foresee a book in your future."

I was reading *My Brain on Fire*[6] and *Saving Sammy*[7] and was blown away by the similar and yet different experiences. Susannah Cahalan does an amazing job in *My Brain on Fire* explaining how she felt and what she thought as her brain inflamed. It was so good for me to read what might be going on in my own son's mind, as outwardly, he was raging or panicking. It definitely gave me a perspective that would help me to be more empathetic and understanding of how he was feeling. And Beth Alison Maloney described the sudden onset of OCD and anxiety in a way that I understood, though her son's presentation was certainly different from what we were experiencing. At one point, as I read about her son's tics, I thought to myself, *I would so rather have those tics than the rages*! But I quickly checked myself. Who was I to judge someone else's experience as less awful than mine? I reminded myself that no one's experience is harder or easier than anyone else's; it's all relative. Crisis is simply not having the resources to manage the situation. I had many skills and resources to help me manage what we were going through. I was not going to feel sorry for myself or compare my situation to someone else's. And, most importantly, I wasn't about to challenge the universe. I didn't need to be shown that there were plenty of things that could be harder or worse than what we were dealing with. I began to shift my thinking, searching for and finding gratitude. My child didn't have a terminal illness. I had the skills to manage his rages and panic attacks. We hadn't had to wait years for a diagnosis as so many had. Others had gone before us and paved the way to make access to diagnosis and treatment more readily available. I had found information when I needed it. Reading both of these books gave me inspiration and hope for healing.

It was this hope that I had experienced that would later nudge me to share our story. I wanted other parents to know that the symptoms could look a little different than typical OCD or tics. The symptoms could easily be misdiagnosed as a behavior disorder, anxiety, depression, anorexia, or autism to name a few. I knew, from our experience, how easy it was to be lead down the path of psychiatry. I knew that parents might be told they were enabling their child's behavior and that they were part of the problem. I knew that they might be given psychotropics to address their child's symptoms and told to get their child into cognitive behavioral therapy[8] or applied behavior analysis[9]. I also knew that when these didn't work, when the parent couldn't even get their child out of the house, they would feel lost and scared, and that it could be years before their child received proper diagnosis and treatment. During this time, children could have such severe symptoms that they might end up in an emergency room and a pediatric psych bed. Again, more psychotropic medicationss or hospitalization in a treatment facility. I knew this because of what we had been told and because I had heard all of these scenarios from parents I connected with during our journey of healing. And worst case scenario, a child might take their own life just to escape the torture they were experiencing. This should never happen, but it does.

I decided I would write. I wanted to give parents permission to challenge their doctors, therapists, or psychiatrists when their intuition told them that something was wrong and that what the "experts" were saying didn't make sense or wasn't enough. I wanted to remind parents that they are the experts of their child and that it is okay and their right to ask their providers to dig a little deeper, to get at the root cause, and not just treat symptoms. It was even okay to fire their providers and find someone who would listen to them. I needed to share that even though cognitive behavioral therapy was listed as a treatment for these symptoms, it wouldn't work when a child was in a flare, when their brain was inflamed. Without proper medical intervention directly addressing the inflammation in the brain and the root causes for this inflammation, these other common psychiatric treatments were a condemnation to a lifetime of mental illness. I knew that some of what I would write might not be popular and might even be criticized, but I had to tell our story.

There was still a window of summer left, and I really wanted Andre to have something that was his and that was fun. I spent an afternoon on the internet looking at different options. He knew that I wouldn't be able to come because I would need to stay home and take care of Hans. I remembered a friend telling me how much her boys had enjoyed a weekend at Great Wolf Lodge, and I pulled up their website. Andre loved being in the water, so I thought maybe that would be a fun option.

"What do you think of this?"

Andre and I snuggled in bed looking at the photos of happy kids frolicking in the pools, climbing on the ropes course, and exploring the hotel. Then we looked at the different room options.

"It looks pretty cool, but it wouldn't be as much fun without you."

"What if your cousins could go? Then you'd have some other kids to play with. Would that make it more fun?"

"Totally!"

He cheered up a bit. We then looked at the rooms again and decided a big suite that everyone could stay in would be the most fun! He seemed excited about this trip, and I was so happy that he would have something joy-filled! My sister and her family and my brother and his kids were all on board to help Andre experience some light-hearted fun! I reserved the suite for two nights and then told Arnold the plans. He was a little taken aback at the cost, but I explained that Andre deserved to have something that was his. Arnold agreed and the plans were set in motion. We asked Hans if he thought he would like to go, though the idea terrified me. He didn't, or couldn't. Hans and I stayed home while Arnold and Andre left for a boisterous and fun-filled excursion with our extended family.

The fact that Hans couldn't leave the house for something fun had me problem solving. My youngest sister, Nicole, was getting married the end of August, and I was the Maid of Honor. She knew what we were going through and was supportive of whatever would need to happen. Arnold and I were trying to figure out how to pull it off. This was a very important event for me, and Hans knew that. With my dad's death the week before Hans was born, my baby sister would be walking down the aisle alone. As the oldest sister, I wanted to be there for her as she took that step into committing her love to Colin, the man who had won her heart. Hans wanted to try.

I thought maybe having something special to look forward to in Seattle would help us get Hans there. I found a Chima Lego set that he had been wanting and had it sent to Nana's house where we were planning to stay for two nights as we had done so many times before when life was normal. I told Hans it would be waiting for him. I talked with him about what would make the drive easier. He wanted his huge stuffed dog, his quilt, his pillow, the iPad, and the fan. We prepared the car, allowing him to lie in the back bench seat without a seatbelt as it was too uncomfortable. The fan was secured and wasn't running, but he would have it at Nana's house. We brought food I knew he would eat.

When we arrived, we got Hans settled in a room upstairs. He was very agitated, crying that he wanted to go home. Nana gave him the Chima Lego set and that distracted him. I came downstairs and fell into her open arms crying with tears of mixed emotions. I was so happy to be there.

"We did it. We got here."

My aunt and her boyfriend were sitting in the room, and as I walked back upstairs, I heard my aunt ask with genuine curiosity, "What's that all about?"

"They've been having a rough time with Hans lately," she told them. I smirked to myself. Rough time didn't seem to do it justice, but how do you explain this to someone who has never lived it, never witnessed it? I was too exhausted to try and explain to anyone that it felt just short of a miracle to even be here. And I felt like I didn't care what others might think, but I did. I just didn't have the emotional capacity to register that feeling.

Arnold and I discussed the rehearsal and the dinner to follow. We decided that I would go to the rehearsal while he stayed home with Hans, and then I would come home and Arnold and Andre would go to the rehearsal dinner while I stayed home with Hans and help him build his Lego set. The rehearsal was emotional for me. My sister, Oriana, shared with me a written letter from our dad that she had found after he had passed just ten years prior. He had left many written scraps of paper around his place, all of them having meaning to one person or another. This one was a letter he had written to Nicole for her wedding day, knowing that he wouldn't be there. He had walked his middle daughter down the aisle, performed the service for his eldest, and this was his way of being with his youngest daughter in spirit if he wasn't able to be there physically. Oriana showed it to me, and I read it. I didn't understand yet that it was actually from him.

"Oh sweetheart, it's beautiful. You've really captured his voice. It sounds just like him."

She looked puzzled, and then realized my mistake.

"That's because it *is* his voice. He wrote this for Nicole. I found it when I was going through more of his papers, and I've kept it all these years waiting for this day. I'm going to read it during the toasts."

My eyes welled up with tears, and I hugged Oriana tight. Somehow, that letter was physical representation of our dad, and I felt his presence, wishing so much that I could lean into him and feel his strength. I tried to tap into that strength so I could be joyful during this celebratory rehearsal, smiling and giving hugs and making light conversation.

When the rehearsal was over, I returned to Nana's. After Arnold and Andre left for the dinner, Hans and I worked together on his Lego set and discussed the next day. I told him that there were pictures before the wedding and that I would like to be with Nicole and Colin for those pictures. He agreed that he would try. He ate some food and continued building.

"I'm not going to bed until this is finished."

I hoped that wouldn't be too late. Arnold and Andre returned from the dinner and were getting ready for bed. Arnold told Hans it was time to stop and go to bed, also. I hadn't had the foresight to let him know that we had already discussed this.

"No! I'm not going to bed until I finish this!"

"It's late," Arnold said, "you can finish it in the morning."

Hans began to scream. I was so afraid he would start to rage, and I didn't want him to break anything in Nana's home.

"Arnold, Hans and I already talked about this, and I agreed to let Hans work on this until he's finished it," I interjected. "Hans, I am going to help you finish this tonight."

He settled down, and I set up the next set of pieces. I had been sorting pieces while he built to move the process along.

"Fine," Arnold replied. "I'm going to bed. It's late, and I'm tired."

I took a break from helping Hans and helped Andre get ready for bed. I tucked him in and lay with him for a few minutes.

"Is Hans going to the wedding tomorrow, mom?"

"I don't think so, sweetheart. If he can make it, we'll take him. We'll see how he's doing tomorrow. Get some rest. You've got a big day ahead of you. You will be up late tomorrow, and I want you to have fun. Your cousins will be there, and you can hang out with them."

"Okay," he said, and I kissed him on his nose.

"I love you," I told him, as I did every night.

"I love you more," he answered, with his standard reply.

"I love you most," and our routine was complete.

Hans built for another hour until he was finished. I helped him into my bed knowing that I would need to be there if he woke up in a panic.

"Mom, I'm scared. This house is so big, and it's scary."

He had never felt this way at Nana's before, and I was saddened that this home away from home felt scary to him now.

"Let's watch a show to get your mind off of it, and then we'll go to sleep."

We watched several episodes of Woody Woodpecker, and I hoped he would fall asleep easily. I just wanted to get through the night. Finally, sleep overtook him. I allowed myself to go over the plans for the next day in my head, and then I also gave in to the gift of sleep.

The next day was cloudy. The wedding was set to be outside at the Seattle Aquarium overlooking Elliot Bay, unless it rained. It wasn't one of those bright sunny days that so many brides hope for. It was, however, that perfect day that photographers love. The clouds made a dramatic backdrop for the scheduled photo shoot along the Seattle waterfront, and the lighting was perfect. No squinting, just happy faces would grace the photos that I was supposed to be in, but would only see later in an album.

Nicole was scheduled for makeup and hair at her hotel room downtown. I was going to meet her there. As I was gathering my things and letting Hans know that I would be gone for a few hours before the wedding, he began to have a panic attack, banging his head against the floor. I was supporting him, trying to coach him to breathe.

As he was lying in my lap, gasping for breath and holding his head, he sobbed, "Why do I ruin everything?"

"Oh honey, you're not ruining anything. This is hard for you. I am here to help you. I don't have to get my hair and makeup done. I can stay here."

He began to calm as I stroked his hair along his forehead. I texted Nicole and let her know I wouldn't make it to the hotel. She assured me that it was okay and let me know when and where pictures would be.

Again, as I got ready to go, he had another panic attack. This time, it took much longer for him to settle. While I was trying to support him, I was texting Nicole to let her know that at this point I didn't think I was going to be able to do anything but be at the ceremony. She was so gracious and understanding. She told me that Oriana had offered to stand in for the pictures and could also stand in for the ceremony if needed. I choked back tears when I read that text. The grace and love of both my sisters overwhelmed me in that moment. I was so grateful for the support of my family, and I was aching that I couldn't be part of this celebratory event.

Arnold and I discussed how we could make it work. We decided that Andre would go with my brother, Eric, and his family. I would leave at the last minute for the ceremony.

Arnold would stay home with Hans and pack up the car. Andre would sit with his uncle and cousins, which he would love. As soon as the ceremony was over, I would let Arnold know, and he would drive down with Hans and text me when they arrived. I would come out and drive Hans home to Bellingham, and Arnold would stay for the reception. We shared this plan with Hans.

"Okay," he said quietly. "I'm so sorry. I know how important this is for you." And then he sobbed in my lap, "I ruin everything. Why can't I stop this?"

I assured him that nothing was ruined and that we had a good plan. He could watch cartoons on his iPad or play with his new Lego set. It would be a short amount of time and then he would be going home. He settled, and I set him up on the sofa in the front living room.

When it was time, I slipped out the front door without saying goodbye and took an Uber to the Aquarium just in time to meet up with the wedding party. As we were waiting in the side room, I read my toast to the bride and groom. I told them Arnold would read for me at the reception. We hugged and cried. I was so proud of these two amazing people, and I was so happy that I could be a part of their special day, though it wasn't as ideal as I would have liked.

The ceremony was perfect. Nicole's elegant and simple lace sheath dress emphasized her tall athletic frame, and she radiated strength and beauty as she walked alone down the aisle to meet her husband. I felt my dad's presence embodied in this woman, as though he was there with her as she stepped into another chapter of her life. As I stood at the end of Pier 59, I was filled with such love and gratitude in my heart for all those gathered that day to bear witness and for those who were missing in body. And I ached. For my son, for my family, and for all who experience hardship that others just can't understand. It was a most bittersweet moment that I will never forget.

After the ceremony, we gathered in the side room again and toasted the bride and groom. I texted Arnold to meet me, then joined the party downstairs. I had time to briefly connect with extended family who were in town. I hugged Andre and told him how proud I was that he was flexible and independent. I told him to have fun with his cousins, and I smiled as he ran off to enjoy his family and the party. When I met Arnold and Hans outside, the car was packed, just the way it had been, to help Hans feel comfortable.

I hugged Arnold, "Thank you for helping to make this work for me. It was a beautiful ceremony. I want it to work out for us. I love you, and I don't want to lose us."

"I love you, too," he held me for a moment. "Have a safe drive home with Hans. We'll see you tomorrow."

I got into the car to make our drive north, reflecting on what an emotional few days this had been.

"Thank you, mom," Hans said to me from the back of the car. "I'm sorry I couldn't go and that you don't get to go to the party."

"Oh sweetheart, I got to do the part that was most important to me. You are one of the most courageous people I know. I know this was hard for you, and I'm so grateful to you for making this work for me." I smiled at him. "Let's get something to eat on our way home. We'll just drive through so it's easy for both of us."

"Okay, mom, I can do that."

It was a quiet ride home as we left the city and made the familiar trip north through the Skagit Valley and into the hills of the Chuckanuts to our place in this world. As the miles flew by, I allowed myself to replay the past few days, and I was open to receiving the triumph of the accomplishment we had achieved. My heart was full.

Many months later, a cognitive behavioral therapist would write in her notes that Hans had attended a wedding. I would hardly consider this attending a wedding, and I learned that some professionals don't really listen to parents. This same therapist would tell us that our son was too far gone, that she couldn't help us, and that we would need to hospitalize him. She was supposed to be the best in our area. It is hard, at times, to forgive the misinterpretation of our reporting or the judgment. It is hard to forgive those who don't believe in this illness. I can overlook ignorance, but for those who have heard of this illness and don't believe it is real...that makes me angry. I am forever grateful that I trusted my intuition and never gave up on my belief that Hans would be healed. I am forever grateful that we fired those who were not meeting our needs and found providers who believed in the diagnosis and would treat the illness, not just the symptoms. I try to allow the gratitude to be greater than the anger, but sometimes anger creeps in, and I have to look at it, then put it away, and choose gratitude.

CHAPTER EIGHTEEN

FMLA

The long days of summer were slowly coming to an end. The transition to autumn in the Pacific Northwest is one of my favorite times of year. The days get shorter and cooler, but there's still that warm sun shining in an eye-blinking blue sky. You start wearing long sleeves, but no jacket, yet. The children begin to anticipate reconnecting with friends they haven't seen over the summer months. There is usually a palpable excitement in the air; but not for me this year. It was evident that Hans would not be able to attend school. We let his teacher of four years know that he would not be returning for the 5th grade. She was understanding and hoped he would be feeling better soon. I contacted several of my colleagues in the school district to find out about different options available. Home Hospital[1] seemed the best choice. He would get four hours of tutoring a week. I just needed to get paperwork signed by his pediatrician. Dr. Hawkins was on maternity leave. She had gone over Hans's case with the doctor covering her patients while she was out. I contacted her replacement for the paperwork. She completed it without hesitation. Then I had to enroll him in his neighborhood school. I completed that the day before school was scheduled to start. But the more I thought about it, four hours didn't seem like much. I talked with another colleague and learned about online learning through Washington Virtual Academy. After looking into that, I felt that it would better meet our needs. I would be his learning coach at home, and we would do all of his academic work online. I would need to un-enroll him and sign up for homeschooling, then enroll him online. More paperwork to fill out, but my contacts in the district office helped me get the right forms to the right people without delay.

At the same time, work was gearing up for me. There were the before school meetings and trainings. I was late to several of them as I had to reassure Hans and go over our plan: if his anxious feelings got to a 3, he was to have Arnold text me, and I would come home. At one of our Leadership Team meetings, I spoke to my supervisors and told them if they felt I wasn't fulfilling my job as needed, to please let me know. I explained that things were still rough at home, that Hans was unable to attend school, and that I may need to go home at any given moment. They expressed their understanding and told me they would support me if I felt that I needed to take time to care for my son, that family comes first.

It was the first day of school, and I was spending the morning at one of the elementary schools in anticipation of a potentially rocky start. I was called into the gym to assist with a boy who was having a hard time. When I arrived, I could see him rolling on the floor in the distance, making moaning sounds. The school counselor, who was new to this building, came up to me and explained that he had been in PE, and on the way out, he fell to the ground and started kicking and wouldn't leave.

"What do we do?" she asked me.

I could see that there were only two exits.

"Are you concerned that he might bolt?"

"Yes. I've been told that he was having problems at the end of last year and that he had run away several times."

"Okay, you stand between him and that exit, and I will see what I can get from him."

I asked the principal, who had requested my assistance, to stand by the other door. I approached the boy.

"Hi, I'm Heather. I'm here to help you feel safe."

I kneeled next to him and just watched him for a minute. He was pulling the hair on his head, rolling on the floor, kicking at the wall, and sort of screaming softly. His eyes were scrunched up tight. This was not a boy who was being naughty. This was a boy who was feeling tortured. I felt in my gut that I knew what was going on.

"I'm wondering if it feels too big in here. I'm wondering if it wouldn't feel better to go somewhere smaller and quieter."

I spoke softly near the boy so he could hear my inner thinking. I then asked the principal if they still had a quiet room in their building, and she said they did. I asked her if she could make sure there was a soft pillow in there and some food.

The boy continued to writhe on the floor for a few more minutes, then he got up and tried to run away, but stumbled, crying out, *leave me alone*! He continued to kick aimlessly, holding his head, and crying.

"I'm only going to help you get somewhere quiet and safe when you are ready."

The PE teacher told me there wasn't another class coming in for an hour. That was good news! We could take our time and wouldn't have to physically escort him out for safety reasons. I continued to talk softly to the school counselor.

"I suspect that a small quiet room would feel much better than this big room. I would like our friend to walk with us to the quiet room where he will have a pillow and some food. When he is ready to walk, he will get up, and we will walk with him." I wanted him to know what the expectations would be and that we were there to support him when he was ready.

As I sat there watching him, I was wondering what I would do if Arnold texted me and needed me to come home because

Hans was having a similar episode. How could I leave this boy? But how could I not go care for my own son? After another twenty minutes of quietly waiting while he rolled around on the floor, kicking at the wall, he stopped. He lay there quietly, breathing hard as if he were exhausted. I knew this as well. He would be able to be responsive now.

"We're going to walk to a quiet room and rest and have something to eat."

He was able to get up. I asked the counselor to lead the way and said I would follow. We walked down the hallway to the quiet room. Once inside, I sat next to him while he ate some food.

"Can you tell me what happened?"

After several more bites, he told me, "a boy tripped me, and then I got mad, and when I got mad I couldn't stop."

"Do you remember what happened after that?"

He shook his head no. I observed that he had small patches of hair missing on his head.

"Do you pull your hair out when you're mad?"

"I don't know, I guess so."

"Do you get mad often?"

"I don't know," he answered, and this I knew, also.

He really didn't know, and pushing it would only make him feel stressed. We made a plan that if he got mad he could come to this quiet room. He didn't even need to tell anyone, he could use a pass, put it on his desk or just hand it to an adult, and he could come to this room. He finished his food and said he was ready to go back to class. I walked with him back to his classroom, and then I met up with the principal and the counselor.

"Is he new to our district? What grade is he in? Why haven't I ever heard of him before? Those were pretty extreme behaviors."

"He's in 5th grade, and he's not new. We've had him since Kindergarten and never had any problems until last spring. He's the kiddo I was telling you about at the very end of last year."

I vaguely remembered her telling me they had a kid with some severe behaviors, but I hadn't been able to get to him as it was the end of the year, and my own world had been falling apart.

"I know what's wrong with him. He has PANS, I know it. I've sat with my own son presenting like that."

"Well, we can't manage that kind of behavior. We've already started a referral for Special Education. We're going to need help to manage him."

"I need to work with your school psychologist on this one. If I'm right, he's going to need a lot more than Special Education. He's going to need a good doctor."

I spent the next hour talking with the school psychologist about what my suspicion was and going over the PANS symptoms checklist found on the PANDAS Network website. I asked her to have the mom fill it out and to help her score it as part of her assessment so the mom could take it to her doctor. Over the next several days, I was in communication with the family's case worker. As it turned out, they were "in system," and assumptions were being made about the boy's problems. I sent information about PANS, including labs to run for diagnostics, and treatment options currently available. I was told that the psychiatrist had reviewed what I sent and said there had to be a history of strep in his medical record and that there wasn't. I told him that wasn't true, the evidence was in his blood right now and all they needed to do was run lab work.

I was pulled off the team because it was looking like the district was pushing for a medical diagnosis. How could I not be pushing for a medical diagnosis when I was suspicious that that was what he had? I was told to trust the professionals, but I couldn't because I had been taken down that road myself, and the professionals clearly didn't even want to investigate. I felt helpless. Then I heard that the boy had been sent to Seattle Children's Hospital and was in a psych bed. I imagined what this might look like if it were my son. The terror, the screaming, the fighting, and then the inevitable sedation. No answers, just a laundry list of psychotropic medications. It horrified me, and I wished I could make a difference. I never heard the outcome. I think about that boy and his family, and that still haunts me today.

I wasn't even a week into the school year, and I was feeling very distressed about my job. How could I support other people's kids when I couldn't even support my own? I met with a friend of mine whom I had worked closely with for many years. Colleen and I went for a walk along the waterfront. It was a sunny morning; the birds were chirping, there was a light breeze, and the San Juan Islands were a soft blue in the distance. We walked and talked about the changes for us this school year. She had taken a new position, and I was trying to figure out how to make my job and caring for my son work.

She asked me, "What are your plans for Hans?"

"We were going to try Home Hospital, but it's only four hours of tutoring a week. I think we're going to do online learning."

"But what about you working? What about when he needs you?"

"I guess I'll just do what I did at the end of last year. That seemed to work okay."

"No it didn't. I'm just going to tell you. It didn't work. We didn't say anything last year because it was all so horrible for you and your family, but I don't see how you can work."

"Wow."

I had to let that sink in. We walked together quietly, while I wrapped my thinking around this revelation.

"Okay… I'm glad you told me. Arnold was just asking me if I was going to take a leave of absence. I guess that's what I need to do. I'm hearing you say that it didn't work. I've just had this horrible experience in the district, and I've got to take care of Hans first."

Looking back on this courageous conversation, that was the best advice a friend could have given me, and I needed to hear it from someone outside of the family. After returning home, Arnold and I talked about what this would mean for us. He would need to re-enter the workplace, which he felt confident in doing. I scheduled a meeting with my supervisors the next day.

When we sat around the table, I burst into tears. I told them that I loved my job. I was passionate about the work I did. I believed in helping teachers better support kids, but I couldn't do my job effectively and care for Hans at the same time. I told them that this experience with this boy had put me in a very difficult position. I couldn't *not* know what I knew, and I couldn't *not* advocate for a child that I believed had PANS. I told them that I didn't trust the professionals in our area because they didn't know. And I told them that I needed to quit my job.

They listened, and they supported me. They thanked me for my work, for my passion, and for my dedication to my family. Then they did everything to make sure I was taken care of by the school district. I went on a Family Medical Leave of Absence. I had enough sick leave and vacation time to pay through January. And then the amazing teachers of the Bellingham School District donated their shared leave to pay for my FMLA through the end of the school year. The generosity of my colleagues, the professionalism of the district, and the care of my supervisors brought me tears of gratitude as they gave our family some breathing room to try and figure out what was happening to our son. I worked through October 1st while we found a replacement. That gave me almost a month to get as much in order as I could before leaving. And then I could focus my time and energy on getting my son better, on getting my son back!

CHAPTER NINETEEN

TRANSITION

September was coming to a close. I had done what I could to hand over my job to a skilled teacher who would replace me. I was getting all the paperwork in place for online learning for Hans and thinking about what our home schedule would be. I got a call from my stepmom with a most generous and thoughtful offer.

"I'd like to rent a house close by to help you with Hans. I could come by every day and spend some time with him so you can get out, run errands, go for a walk. You need a break."

"Oh, I can't tell you how much I would love that, we would all love that so much."

I had been feeling so alone, so isolated, and so exhausted. I don't think I even knew how exhausted I was. But my family knew, and my stepmom was offering to help us get through this. We were very fortunate when a friend offered her parents' home for Nana to rent. It was a short walk from our house on the trail and was just the right size for a six month stay.

Nana was the only person in our family who had witnessed the intensity of the symptoms. She understood, better than anyone, what we were going through. She wanted us to get the help we needed. With her suggestions, I began to seek out other providers that might be able to prescribe treatments. I went back to the PANDAS Network website and looked up the providers in our area. I began to call everyone on the list. I could tell within minutes if they really knew what they were doing or if they were just "open" to the diagnosis and willing to help. I was coming up empty. And then I called Vital Kids Medicine in Seattle. They scheduled me for a 15 minute free consultation with Dr. Gbedawo that week.

I will never forget that call. Dr. Gbedawo immediately began asking me questions about presentation of symptoms, what labs we had drawn, and what treatment protocol we were currently following. Again, my raw emotions came through as I burst into tears.

"You're the first doctor I've talked to who knows more about this than me. I am so happy to have found you!" I sputtered over the phone.

"You parents are the real heroes in my opinion. This is hard. Let's get you scheduled, and we'll figure out how to help."

She connected me with the front desk to schedule an intake. It would be two weeks before we could get in, and it would mean another drive to Seattle, but I was elated to be seeing someone who knew what she was doing! I could focus now on getting school set up for Hans.

Online classes were scheduled to start in mid-October, just a few weeks after my last day at work and just after our appointment with Dr. Gbedawo. My first day on leave, I went to the Bellingham Food Coop to pick up some groceries. I felt so self-conscious that I might see someone who didn't know that I was on leave and that it would look weird for me to be shopping. I had many days feeling this way until it finally settled in that I was home with my child and no longer working. It felt so foreign.

Hans did some pre-assessment work online with the teacher who places new students. He read for one minute and then answered recall questions. He scored 100% and read above grade level. He was placed with a teacher, and I began the process of helping her understand our situation. I provided information on PANDAS/PANS and explained that we were hopeful he would engage in his learning, but that our primary goal was to reduce stress[1] and to have healing. She told me how sorry she was that we were going through this. She had never heard of this illness before, but she wanted to do whatever she could to support Hans's learning. She asked me to keep her posted on progress and needs. There would be scheduled online learning times where students joined the teacher remotely for instruction. The rest of the work would happen at home with me as the learning coach. I felt very supported.

This all looked good, but Hans was continuing to have huge emotional fluctuations. He could turn on anything. After waking up early one morning, he called me in.

"Mom! I'm tired of waking up so early. I'm scared. Please stay with me. You make everything less scary."

We snuggled for a bit in his bed and then got up. He noticed a Lego set on the floor.

"It's broken! Now I have to take it all apart and put it back together, again." There were only a few pieces off of it, and they were nearby.

"Honey, the pieces are right here. We can just put them back on."

"No, it has to come apart! It's ruined! Fix it now, or I'm going to kill you!"

I had become accustomed to these irrational outbursts and threats. I didn't respond to them. I quietly picked up the few pieces, put them back on and then showed him that it was fixed. He quieted in his bed and asked to watch a show on his iPad. When it was over, he came downstairs.

"Boy want mommy hug."

I hugged him tight, wishing I could hug this away. I was keenly aware of his baby talk, and I thought our visit with Dr. Gbedawo couldn't come soon enough.

CHAPTER TWENTY

CALM IN THE MIDDLE
OF THE STORM

It was one of those perfect Pacific Northwest October days. The sun was bright and warm, the sky was clear, and there was a chill in the air. That morning I snuggled with Hans in his room and talked with him about his birthday coming up. I was hopeful that he would want to do something with his friends. We discussed different ideas, then I made him breakfast while he watched *Kickin' It* on his iPad.

We were scheduled to meet Dr. Gbedawo in Seattle that afternoon where we would draw blood for additional labs. Arnold and I had decided not to tell Hans about the draw, knowing he hated needles. Hans was terrified to go. This time I gave him .5 mg Xanax hoping it would calm him enough to make the trip okay. At noon, I let him know it was time to go, and he became combative. Then he switched to begging us not to take him. Arnold and I stayed as calm as we could, reminding him that we needed to see one more doctor who would be able to help us understand how to help him feel better.

"Honey, this doctor is an expert. She has worked with many kids who are having a hard time. She knows what to do, but we have to meet her before she can help us. We are going. It will be a short visit, and it will be much easier for you to just get in the car on your own"

"No, please don't do this to me. I can't do this. You don't understand," he cried before he hit me and fell to the floor sobbing.

"I have an idea. How about we stop on the way and pick up that Playmobil set you were looking at. We'll get it as an early birthday present. You can build that when we get there so you have something fun to look forward to."

I felt like I was bribing him again. I reasoned with myself, just like before, that I was simply reinforcing him for doing what I was asking him to do. And it was a birthday present.

"No, that's not fair. You know I want that, but I can't do this, Mom. It's too hard."

He continued to sob on the floor. Arnold and I prepared the car to make it as comfortable as possible for him. We had his blanket and pillow in the backseat, his big stuffed dog, his water bottle, and his iPad all set up. We decided we would pick up the set on our way so we would have it available.

"It's time to go, sweetheart. Everything you need is in the car. We are going to stop and pick up your early birthday present."

Hans finally walked to the car on his own with a tear-streaked face and still catching his breath. As soon as he got in the car, he climbed under the bench seat with this stuffed dog and cried quietly. He stayed there as I ran in to get the Playmobil set and for the duration of the ninety minute drive to Seattle. He reminded me several times that he did not want to go.

"I hear that you don't want to go, and I am so proud of you for doing this hard work. We will only stay as long as we have to."

As Arnold drove down the highway, I thought about the fact that we were making this epic and difficult trip down the I-5 corridor, and no one else on the road knew what was going on in our car. No one knew we had a crying child huddled under a seat, not buckled up. No one knew that we were bringing our child to a doctor that we hoped would have answers and a plan for healing. No one knew that we were trying to hold it together as we hurdled down the road with our most precious cargo. I promised myself that I would never judge a driver on the road again. How could I know what was going on in their lives, in their car, in that moment? Again, my perceptions shifted, and I grew a little more in compassion and empathy.

We arrived, parked the car, and Hans went in with us on his own. We were greeted warmly at the front desk. I was on high alert, ready to respond to anything. We did not have to wait long in the small waiting room, just long enough for me to notice the brochure on the counter with the words PANDAS and PANS on the front. In that brief observation, I felt relief and confidence. For the first time, I felt that I would be in the same room with someone who truly understood. We were directed into a bright room streaming with afternoon sunlight, a desk and chairs on one side and an open floor on the other. Arnold, Hans, and I took a seat across from Dr. Gbedawo. She greeted us warmly. She had read through our intake papers and began asking questions. I gave my responses, so familiar with our story now that the details rolled off my tongue.

After ten minutes, Hans interjected, "I'm done with this. I'm leaving. You said it wouldn't be a long visit."

"We still have some more talking to do, Hans; we're not ready to go yet."

Hans got up to leave and then turned and hit at me. I evaded the hit, getting up from my seat. He grabbed some papers I had brought and began throwing them, and then he tried to hit Dr. Gbedawo. I moved behind him, secured him and sat on the floor with him in front of me, his arms crossed over the front of him in a seated hold while he kicked at Dr.

Gbedawo's desk. She continued to ask me questions, and I answered as best I could. Then I remembered the Playmobil set.

"Arnold, would you please get Hans's early birthday present from the car and bring it in here so he has something to do? I can see that he is feeling like he doesn't want to be here anymore."

Arnold quickly went out to the car to retrieve the large box. When he brought it in, Hans immediately settled, crying in my arms.

"Wow! That looks amazing!" Dr. Gbedawo exclaimed. "Do you build that before playing with it?" she asked Hans.

"Yes," he replied quietly, and then he went over to Arnold and helped him take everything out of the box and began working on it with him. Hans looked over at me, "OK, this appointment can take as long as it needs."

"Thank you, Arnold," I looked at him with appreciation, and I'm sure worry on my face. I returned to one of the chairs to continue with Dr. Gbedawo.

"I'm sorry. He was never like this."

She smiled at me with deep understanding in her eyes.

"I've seen worse. We're going to get him well."

Tears spilled over my cheeks as I smiled back at the woman who would become one of the dearest people in my life. She felt like the calm in the middle of this storm called PANDAS that we had been living in for ten months. We continued our conversation. I shared my spreadsheet with his symptoms mapped out, a 5-point rubric for each one that was also color coded. She appreciated this information as it helped us identify which antibiotic had been the most helpful, even though there hadn't been much relief. I was interested in trying Azithromycin, but because he was on 20 mg of Celexa, we couldn't switch. She ordered a corticosteroid. We would give him a Prednisone burst with a 5 day taper to help reduce the inflammation and CBD oil, 25 mg to start. We would continue on the Augmentin. Then it was time for the lab draw.

"Okay, we need to do the lab draw in another room. How do you want to handle that?"

"We will need to hold him. Are you prepared to do that?"

"Yes," she replied and called for two nurses to assist us.

Hans and Arnold had completed much of the set. I told them we were done in here and asked them to put the pieces back in the box. Arnold knew what was coming next, but Hans thought we were getting ready to leave. As we left the room, I directed him down the hall and into another room. He walked in and looked around.

"What's going on? What are we doing in here?"

"We need to draw some blood to find out what's in it," I answered, prepared for the worst.

"You didn't tell me that," he screamed and tried to bolt out of the room.

Arnold was blocking the door. The nurses and Dr. Gbedawo were quickly getting everything set up.

"I'm sorry Hans," I lied, "I didn't know we were going to need to draw blood, but it's important to know what's going on in your body, and this is the only way we can find out. We have to find out what's in your blood."

"I hate you! You lied to me!"

I felt horrible, but it had been the only way I could think of to get him to Seattle in the first place. I knew this terrified him, but I also knew it had to happen.

"I can hold him in the chair. Arnold, you will need to secure his feet."

I secured Hans and brought him to the chair, sitting him in front of me. I had one of his arms secured across his front, and the other arm was secured on a pillow by one of the nurses. Hans was crying and begging us not to do this to him. I was determined and so sad all at the same time, wishing I didn't have to do this to my precious son, wishing that we weren't living this nightmare. They drew 13 vials. Dr. Gbedawo was so kind, telling Hans exactly what she was going to do. She let him know it would only hurt for a moment. I could feel his body stop fighting, and I was able to loosen my hold. He was still crying, but he wasn't fighting anymore. As soon as we were done, Arnold went to the front office to check out and get the things we had been prescribed to start right away.

"I'm never going to a doctor again," Hans told me, in between his leftover sobs.

"I know that was hard, Hans."

"You have no idea," he said, looking me in the eyes.

"No, I don't exactly. I do know that you are one of the bravest people I know and that you have been able to get through all this hard stuff, and I am so proud of you. I also want you to know that our follow up visits with Dr. Gbedawo can be through Skype, so you won't have to come to Seattle."

"I told you, I'm never going to another doctor again."

I knew not to argue this point; he was expressing his emotions, his fear, his anger, his distrust. I had learned to just listen, not to try to convince or explain when he was in this emotional place. I knew this from the work I did, and I definitely knew this from the months of living with this.

"I hear you, sweetheart. You don't ever want to see another doctor again. I understand that feeling. Let's get Poppa and go home."

The ride home was uneventful. We stopped at a drive-through to get some food; Hans didn't want to go to a restaurant for lunch. He didn't want to be in the car. He just wanted to go home.

CHAPTER TWENTY ONE

HARDLY HOME SCHOOLING

I attempted to create a schedule at home for Hans. We had given up on the goals I had set for him at the end of the previous school year. He had stopped showering altogether and wouldn't brush his teeth. I could sometimes get him to brush a little if I brought his toothbrush in to him with a cup of water for rinsing and a separate cup for spitting. He would stay in his room for days, leaving only to use the bathroom. He didn't change his clothes, wearing his pajamas and the same underwear for a week, sometimes more. It broke my heart to do laundry and have no clean clothes to put away in his room, and I appreciated the irony of that.

I scheduled the online class times for every other day. On the alternate days, I tried to do school work at the same time as the scheduled classes in order to create some semblance of a routine. During the first online classes, he sat in the office chair in front of the computer and listened to the instruction. He even volunteered an answer once, and I thought maybe this was going to work.

Doing the work between these online sessions was not so successful, however. On the nights when he would have panic attacks, he could be up until 1 or 2 in the morning, scared and cowering in between watching his cartoons. The next morning we would let him sleep as late as he could, so the daily "schedule" wasn't consistently the same time. Some days, he would refuse to do any work, and I would sit next to him, reading the material out loud that we were supposed to cover. I would assume no expectation, just read and think out loud. Often he would reply to my out loud thinking, answering the questions I was trying to get at. I would later call this 'coming at schooling sideways.' At least I knew he could process information, make inferences, and pay attention to detail, even though he would refuse to do it independently.

I put together one of the science experiments he was scheduled to do, and he complied with the direction of layering rocks and sand and pouring in colored water, but he refused to write up the lab report. I knew that a decrease in handwriting could be one of the symptoms, and I wondered if this was the cause for refusing to do the write-up.

"Is it hard to write?"

"I don't know, leave me alone. I'm not doing this, it's stupid," he cried, running to his room and locking his door.

I let the lab write up go, trying to find comfort in the fact that he had set up and done the experiment component. As the days went on, he began to refuse to come to the computer.

"You can use a laptop in bed."

I brought it to his room so he could listen to the class. He was no longer participating, but he was at least "attending" his classes, sort of. I was having a hard time calling this home schooling. I knew that it was expected that he would do work independently, but he wasn't. I knew that it was expected that he participate weekly. The laptop was in his presence, but when he wasn't having a good day, which was often, he wasn't participating, and sometimes he was telling me to leave and take the laptop with me.

I tried explaining to Hans, "you are too smart to not be learning. We have to do school work."

"I can't, you don't understand," he would cry.

"I'm trying to understand. I understand more than most people. But I've got to figure out how to help you learn."

I was feeling frustrated. We would have this conversation over and over again, always a little differently, always the same outcome. I would feel frustrated and incapable; Hans would be angry or crying.

His online teacher was very sympathetic, and I appreciated her understanding and compassion. She never made me feel pressured to be doing more than we were. She was encouraging and sorry that we were going through this. She monitored our progress, and when it came time for her to assess his reading again, we were having a good day. Hans did a one minute timed reading called a DIBELS.[1] It's a marker to look at his fluency and comprehension. Again, he was above grade level. He would need to do these quarterly.

There were days that we would get through vocabulary worksheets, read short stories, and attempt some math. Hans wasn't writing at all, and I knew not to ask him to do so anymore. It always ended with him raging because he couldn't. The math was another area of great frustration. I was his scribe. I would write down his answers, set up his math problems, and continue to prompt him or model my own thinking out loud. As a special educator, it came natural for me to accommodate his needs. As a behavior specialist, I was constantly second-guessing myself. I was concerned that I was reinforcing little to no work output by allowing him to have access to his iPad when he hadn't completed any school work, yet. I also saw how stressful the work could be for him, especially on days when he had had a bad night. I decided that reducing the stress load was more important to his body healing than pushing through any academic expectations. Learning could come later when his brain wasn't inflamed. I knew that others might not agree with me, but I was confident in my observation that Hans would work when he could. When he was experiencing stress, not only could he not work, but it wasn't helping his body heal. This became very evident to me the day he was supposed to do his fourth quarterly DIBELS. I brought him the laptop, just as we had done the previous times with such success.

"Your teacher is ready for you to read for one minute Hans."

"No, I'm not doing it."

His teacher was online and witnessing this. I immediately felt embarrassed as a parent and as an educator.

"Sweetheart, you've done these before. It's just reading for one minute. You're very good at reading."

"I said I'm not doing it."

"It's just one minute, Hans. You'd be done by now if you had started when I first asked you to."

My embarrassment was guiding my response, and I wasn't being my best supportive self.

He began to kick at me, and I quickly moved the laptop, concerned he would knock it to the floor.

"You don't understand! I am not reading that! I can't do this! Leave me alone!"

He screamed and continued to kick at me.

I walked out of the room mortified by this outburst.

"I guess we won't be reading today," I said to his teacher.

I had seen this before, many times, but it hadn't been witnessed by many others. I was frustrated because I knew that Hans was a capable reader. I knew that he could have easily read that one minute passage and been done. I was worried that I wasn't doing what I needed to do to get through these stuck moments. His teacher continued to be understanding. She suggested that she send me the passage, and I could do the timed reading when he was feeling better and send her the results. I appreciated her continued supportive compassion and accommodation.

Later that day, I had a meeting with his middle school team. Our application to the Waldorf school he had attended from Kindergarten through the 4th grade had been denied. Arnold and I were hoping he would attend his neighborhood brick and mortar school for the 6th grade. I shared our story and information about PANDAS/PANS that was relevant to the school setting[2] that I had pulled from the PANDAS Network website. I went over accommodations that I thought he would need and asked for their support. I couldn't say for sure what he would be like in the classroom setting next year. I offered to be a volunteer at the school, readily available to be a support academically or behaviorally for him and any other students who might need help. I asked that he would have a quiet place he could go if he was feeling stressed. I asked that he be allowed to type his answers, use speech to text, or have a scribe because he couldn't write. I asked for no time limits. I asked that he be allowed to wear his baseball cap because he couldn't leave the house without it. I asked that the district provide Home Hospital tutoring if we should need to do IVIG because we would keep him home for several weeks after the treatment to ensure he wasn't exposed to any triggering pathogen.[3] I asked that the school tell us if there was a strep outbreak so we could keep Hans home. I shared that I was worried that he would be exposed to all kinds of germs as 6th grade was the year that most kids got another round of vaccinations and they would be shedding live viruses all around him. I shared all of this between tears as I sat at the table with people I had worked with for years.

The nurse was very open to learning and shared with me her understanding of IVIG and vaccines and was trying to reassure me that I didn't need to be so worried. Intravenous immunoglobulin is a product made up of antibodies that can be given through a vein. It is prepared from the blood donated by thousands of people to make a super-concentrated collection of antibodies against many possible foreign substances the body might encounter. Individuals receiving IVIG to provide extra antibodies, because their body doesn't make enough, have a stronger immune system post-IVIG. I explained that kids with PANS were different; they are receiving IVIG to essentially block their immune system from attacking their own cells, in this case, their brain.[3] In kids with PANS, any infection could trigger an autoimmune response resulting in a flare and essentially nullifying the IVIG treatment. She asked me to send her information so she could learn more. The team was very supportive and willing to make any accommodations needed to help him be at school.

On my way home, emotionally drained, I suddenly realized that Hans's emotional outburst earlier wasn't a "won't" it was a "can't." I realized that I didn't understand the reason for the "can't," but that in that moment when he was asked to read, he really couldn't. Just as he was saying, he really couldn't. When I got home, I went up to his room.

"Hans, I had a good meeting with your teachers for next year. They are very understanding and supportive. As I was talking with them, I suddenly realized that earlier today when I was asking you to read, that you really couldn't. It felt to me like wouldn't and looked like wouldn't, but I understand now that it was couldn't. I'm sorry I didn't get it earlier."

"Finally, mom. It took you all day."

Hans burst into tears. I held him in my arms and my understanding of his behavior continued to shift dramatically.

As I was learning how to support Hans, it was becoming evident to me that, because of the brain inflammation, there were things that I would have thought would be helpful, but really he couldn't access them. I was so aware how confusing this could be to others and how confusing it would have been to me if I hadn't been living it first-hand. There were times when reinforcement worked, and there were times when all the reinforcement, bribes, incentives, whatever you wanted to call them wouldn't make any difference at all. I was beginning to understand that it must be dependent on the level of inflammation. When there was healing, he could access learning and reasoning. When there was inflammation, he could not.

I had read in my research that Cognitive Behavioral Therapy was one of the recommended treatments. I wondered how I could possibly get him into a good therapist when I couldn't get him to leave the house, or sometimes even his room, without a panic attack or rage. I bought a book written by recommended therapists, March & Mulle, with the intent to do some of my own work at home. *OCD in Children and Adolescents: A Cognitive-Behavioral Treatment Manual*[4] was a clinical read. I knew I couldn't implement the recommended approach with fidelity, but I could use parts of it. I could help Hans give his thoughts a name, and I could teach him how to "talk back" to those thoughts.

I began to research therapists in our area. I went back to the International OCD Foundation website and found *one* therapist recommended in Bellingham. I called to schedule an appointment and was put on another long waiting list. Unfortunately, when we would finally get in for a consult, this therapist would be unable to help us, not really listening to what we were sharing as she misrepresented in her report our story about taking Hans to Seattle for my sister's wedding.

CHAPTER TWENTY TWO

911

Christmas is one of our family's favorite holidays. Since having children, Arnold and I had decided that we would always have Christmas morning in our home. After the morning revelries, we pack up our Kris Kringle gifts for extended family and drive the hour and a half to Nana's house to meet with the rest of our siblings and their children for "Second Christmas." This Christmas Eve, as I was putting the boys to bed, Hans shared with me, "Christmas stresses me out, mom. I want it to be perfect, and there's always so much chaos."

"Thank you for letting me know, Hans. We will try to keep it as calm as we can. What would help you the most do you think?"

"If we can just open one present at a time as you always try to do. That would help."

"Okay sweetheart, we'll try to do that. Have a good sleep. We will have a calm and relaxing Christmas."

The next morning, the boys woke up early and ran into our room. Andre wanted to run downstairs to get his stocking, but Hans was adamant.

"No, let's just have a minute with mom and dad."

Andre could barely contain himself; he was so excited to get this day going. I could see the stress in Hans's face.

"Andre, jump into bed real quick, and let's have a Christmas morning snuggle. This is important."

Andre had become accustomed to knowing that when I said something was important it meant we needed to do this to keep Hans from having a big emotional response.

"Alright," he said a little reluctantly, and then he snuggled in as he loved to do. Hans sat on the side of the bed and took some breaths before directing Andre.

"Andre, we're just going to open our stockings first. And don't tear through it." Hans clearly needed this to be a calm morning. Andre bounded from the bed and down the stairs.

"Yay!"

While the boys went through their stockings, Arnold and I made breakfast. We had learned how important it was to get protein into Hans as early as we could. We took our time with presents that morning. My favorite gift, I had made myself. It was a large glass jar with pieces of prettily colored papers inside and the directions to "write down happy memories to be shared next Christmas." This would be a task I would relish all year! Hans was motivated to go to Nana's for "Second Christmas," but he required all the comforts of home. We packed the usual, his pillow, his blanket, his huge stuffed dog, his iPad, and food we knew he would eat. I was thrilled that we were all going since our last trip to Seattle for my sister's wedding had been so difficult.

Second Christmas was a distinct contrast from the calm morning we had just experienced at home. The excitement was palpable, and the presents were being handed out right and left. Nana picked up on Hans's stress immediately.

"Hans, I have a gift for you," she said as she found the package she had placed under the tree.

Hans opened it excitedly and found a Lego lion. He went upstairs away from the din to begin the process of building his new set. As the commotion died down, and the other kids went off to play, I headed upstairs to check on Hans. I knew that building Legos had become difficult for him. Since starting him on an SSRI, we had noticed hand tremors. These were getting in the way of his ability to put small pieces together. In addition to the hand tremors, he couldn't hold still. He would often flap his legs, climb furniture, or need to bounce on the mini trampoline we had bought years ago for the boys when they were toddlers. In addition to these new symptoms, he had been saying that he wanted to kill himself. This felt different than the many times that he had begged us to kill him because he couldn't take it anymore, and after additional research on some of the side effects of SSRIs, I had discussed with his pediatrician about weaning him off. We hadn't seen huge improvements on the medication, and the side effects weren't worth the slight improvements we'd seen. We had recently begun that process, but he still struggled.

"Hey buddy, want some help sorting the pieces?"

I knew he liked to have his pieces all sorted out, and I enjoyed helping him with this. What had been referred to my whole life as my 'OCD' often helped me find peace with order, and I was very good with details. We worked together for quite a while. Family came up to see how his build was going, and he was focused and determined to finish it before the day ended. The dinner preparations were taking place downstairs, and I was back and forth. I suggested he take a break as his hands were getting tired and sore.

"No. I have to finish this," he insisted, and I knew it was futile to expect him to stop.

The Christmas meal was being served when he came down to tell me he had finished. The timing was perfect! He joined the kids, eating the food that I had brought for him, and everyone seemed to be happily enjoying time together. I relished in the moment. That night, we headed home having enjoyed a family gathering together, and I counted this day as a huge blessing.

Two days after Christmas, Arnold's brother, Bruno, and sister-in-law, Domenique, flew up from California for a visit. I had been looking forward to seeing them, but I was nervous about how it would go. It was hard to explain to family what we had been dealing with, and though I had tried, I was afraid of what might happen and what they would think. What if Hans had a bad panic attack or rage? I wanted to have a positive visit, but our new normal was so unpredictable. I knew this could be hard for family and friends to understand. Several times we had said yes to visits, but only if we could stay outside or call it quits at any given moment. We had asked friends, and even family, to go home more than once. At times, we were able to anticipate and guests would leave before things got bad, but there were a few times when guests witnessed the extreme behaviors and commented on how scary it was. Yes, scary was our new normal. We lived with it every day. How could others, who had not witnessed this, understand?

Hans often felt queasy due to the antibiotics he had been on for the past seven months, even though he was also taking probiotics. We were addressing many of the deficiencies that had emerged from the extensive lab work that Dr. Gbedawo had run. He was now taking 44 pills throughout the day to address these, and he was beginning to get "pill fatigue" and refusing to take his supplements or antibiotics or the SSRI. Thankfully, because we had been weaning him off the SSRI, I wasn't as concerned about missing that as I would have been at the higher dose. But we definitely noticed a difference when he didn't take the CBD oil. That had a calming effect on him, and I knew it also helped with inflammation.[1]

Bruno and Domenique had decided to get a hotel room nearby so they could give us space if we needed it. That eased my worries a bit. Their arrival was met with enthusiasm by the boys as they brought a *third* Christmas! Hans and Andre were beyond excited to get two more controllers for the Xbox they had received the previous Christmas from them, and we enjoyed the next several days watching hilarious replays of our family dancing to the guided movements of "Just Dance." The men and Andre enjoyed racing, and Hans was mesmerized by Halo.

The third morning after their arrival, I went in to greet Hans, and he was seething. "What's wrong, Hans?"

"I had a nightmare about psychiatrists and doctors and the security guards were golems. You were there trying to help, but not really helping."

"I'm so sorry you had that dream, Hans. I'm sorry I wasn't able to help you in your dream, but I'm here now. I can help you think of something else."

He was irrational, "you're the reason all of this happened! I hate you! I'm going to kill you!" he yelled at me and began kicking at me and throwing his pillows at me.

"I love you, Hans. I only want to help you feel better. I'm sorry you are feeling stressed right now. I'm going to leave your room and get you some breakfast."

I tried to stay as calm as I could. I had learned not to take these outbursts personally. I had learned not to argue with his irrational perceptions. I left his room and could hear him pounding on his wall. He already had five holes that we had duct taped, and I was pretty sure there would be another one added today. I quickly made him some breakfast and put together his supplements. I brought them in for him, and he glared at me.

"Go away!"

"I'm just bringing you breakfast, sweetheart. I will leave you alone."

He finally ate and took his supplements by noon. He didn't want to go with the family to the bookstore, which was what we had planned on doing. Andre was in his room getting ready to leave when Hans started kicking Andre's door. I ran upstairs and secured Hans, moving him away from Andre's room. He fought hard and kicked at Andre who was trying to get past him and go downstairs. I put Hans in a hold on the floor so Andre could jump over him. Andre joined the rest of the family, and they left. Hans's body calmed, and I released him. He lay there exhausted. I sat near him saying nothing. Time and space and silence are often good de-escalators, and I wanted him to have as much of all three of those as he needed. After nearly five minutes, he got up and went to his room. As he walked past me, he muttered.

"I really hate you."

I reminded myself that this wasn't him, this was his inflamed brain, and I held back the tears that threatened to spill down my face.

Later, he came down to play Halo. When the rest of the family returned from their excursion, Arnold and his brother wanted to race. They asked Hans if they could have a turn. He refused, and Arnold started to tell him that he had had enough play time on the Xbox and it was time to give up the controller. Hans yelled at him to go away and threw his controller. I didn't want Arnold to engage with him, so I picked up the controller, looking at Arnold directly, and firmly suggested that maybe this wasn't the best time to race. Maybe the men could find another time to do that. It was evident in my body posture and tone that I meant for everyone to leave Hans alone. He had been on edge all day, and I didn't want another escalation. Everyone was compliant, and we made it through a stressful evening.

The next few days were uneventful, and we said our good-byes to Bruno and Domenique. We thanked them for their visit and expressed our gratitude for their flexibility. They hugged us tight before heading to the airport. We didn't celebrate New Year's Eve. I didn't want the boys staying up late if it was at all possible that Hans might be asleep at a reasonable time, and I honestly didn't feel very festive. We just didn't bring it up. I was beginning to be accustomed to our new normal. I was always anticipating the worst that could happen, trying to prevent it, and waiting for the other shoe to drop. I wondered if I would *ever* be able to feel festive, again. I really felt like the carefree joy of celebrations, the abandon of footloose festivities, was gone from my life...forever...and I was too tired to care.

On January 1st Hans suggested we all go to Mt. Baker in our RV. We hadn't been able to do that for nearly a year, and I was elated, but nervous. I prepared the RV with all the comforts from home, and we drove the hour East on 542. Mt. Baker has always been one of my favorite places to be. I love how peaceful it is once everyone has left the mountain, and we are often only one of a few rigs who dry camp at Heather Meadows. That night, I held gratitude in my heart for this opportunity to be outside with my family playing glow-in-the-dark bocce ball. It was beautiful; the colored lights rolling through the snow, the stars bright overhead without the dimming effect of the city glare, the warm glow from inside the RV inviting us back in for a hot cocoa once we finished. This contrasted with the angry words that were later exchanged between the boys, but we got through it without any physical aggression, and I celebrated that. Everyone was asleep by 10 that night, cocooned in our mountain oasis.

The next morning, we played in the snowbank as the parking lot began to fill up around us. Arnold and Andre went skiing, and Hans and I walked to the lodge where we purchased an Experts Only mug for Andre and a warm knit hat for Hans. It made me happy to see Hans out of the house, around other people, and smiling! After lunch in the RV, we headed home. On our way down the mountain, Hans told us he wanted to go swimming. Arnold and I were shocked! I checked the schedule for the public pool, and after arriving home, we grabbed our suits and headed to the Arne & Hannah community swimming pool. Then we went out for dinner. That night, I relished in what an amazing two days we had enjoyed. I was beyond giddy, hoping we were turning a corner.

All that joy came to a screeching halt the next day. Many months later, I would hear that a significant number of parents reported flares in their children after experiencing altitude changes or being exposed to chlorine. We had just done both. Hans woke up edgy. He got mad at Andre when he came downstairs to play Xbox and Andre was already on it. He threw his shot glass of supplements at Andre, hitting him in the head.

"That is not okay," I spoke in a stern voice.

This only enraged Hans, and he yelled at me, "I hate you!"

He ran past me, back up to his room, slamming the door shut behind him. Then he shoved a note under the door, and called me up. I read the note, *You will die* scratched out in his nearly illegible handwriting. I knew that I had handled that situation poorly. It was so hard to constantly keep my calm when he was so irrational and easily set off by the slightest things. And I couldn't tolerate the aggression towards Andre who didn't deserve to be treated so poorly. There were times when Andre was annoying to Hans, but not at the level of retaliation. I was trying to find a balance between helping Andre not bug his brother, and allowing him to be who he was.

Hans called me up again, later that day, asking if he could use the laptop. I brought it to him, not realizing that some of my notes were up on the screen. I took daily notes, translating them into the 5-point scale rubric that I had created for every symptom. I then recorded the symptoms in a spreadsheet. This allowed me to track his responses to interventions. I got this idea from a video I had watched on a presentation by Dr. Cooperstock, and it made perfect sense to me. I was used to charting behavior in my work with the district. To me, this was no different. I had been comparing current notes with previous notes from early onset. It was the early onset notes that were up. He read them and then called me in.

"I read your notes," he told me calmly. "I hate everyone, and I want to kill everyone," he said as he looked over at his wooden rubberband gun. "Perfect. When I said I wanted to kill everyone, well, one of those people is you."

He swung his wooden gun at me. I deflected it, and he tried again. I secured his arm and restrained him as he yelled at me.

"I hate you, leave me alone!"

I looked around his room, scanning for anything that he could use to hurt himself. I wanted to release him in his room and hold the door shut so I could disengage, but I was worried about his mental state, and I didn't want anything in the room that he might use to hurt himself. I saw a belt and two lanyards hanging on his hooks, nothing else. As I prepared to release him, I grabbed the belt and lanyards and threw them out the door, and then I closed the door and held it shut. I could hear that he was raging, kicking his wall, and tearing his bed apart. Andre was terrified. He was crying in his room. I called Arnold up.

"Please take Andre to Nana's house. He does not need to witness this."

But Nana was still in Seattle for the Christmas holiday, and Arnold didn't want to leave me home alone dealing with this. He called my sister, Nicole, and her husband in Seattle and asked them to please drive up to Bellingham so Andre could be with them at Nana's rental house. They agreed immediately. It would be another hour and a half before they would arrive. Hans continued to rage in his room while we waited. He was screaming and crying.

"Make this stop! I can't do this anymore! I just want to die. Please kill me, or I'm going to kill everyone!"

He began kicking the hollow core door that had already been damaged from previous rages and duct taped for reinforcement. Arnold was in the hallway with his feet supporting the door so it wouldn't splinter more than it already had, and I was holding the handle.

"Hans, stop kicking the door. It's going to splinter, and you could get hurt."

"I don't care!"

He continued kicking. His foot was breaking through the door with each kick and the wood was splintering into jagged sharp pieces. I was concerned that I could no longer keep him safe.

"Arnold, we need to call 9-1-1. I can't keep him safe anymore." Arnold immediately left and got on the phone.

Hans heard me say that, and began screaming, "you won't do that. You won't call the police!"

"Honey, I have no choice. If you won't stop, we have to call the police. If I can't keep you safe, we have to get someone who can help us keep you safe."

He continued kicking.

"You won't do that, you won't!"

Arnold was on the phone with the dispatcher explaining that our child had PANS and that he was having a flare, and we couldn't keep him safe because he was kicking his door to pieces. Hans could hear this and stopped kicking. He was still crying and screaming.

"I stopped! I stopped! Don't call the police!"

I could hear the terror in his voice, and I shared his fear. I did not want the police involved if I could avoid it. I knew that most people had never heard of this illness and certainly wouldn't have the compassion or care that I had for my own son.

"Arnold, he stopped. We don't need the police as long as he keeps himself safe."

"Ok."

Arnold explained to the dispatcher that our son was safe.

"So you don't want the police?" he asked me one more time before hanging up.

"No, Hans is going to keep himself safe," I replied with assurance, both for me and so Hans would hear what needed to happen.

I could hear that Hans had removed himself from the door, but he was still yelling. Not words, just a guttural yelling as if it was taking everything he had to keep himself from destroying the door. Arnold gathered some things for Andre and had him lie down on the couch downstairs and try to go to sleep while waiting for my sister and her husband to arrive. I was sitting outside Hans's door, just in case he tried to leave. Finally, Nicole and Colin arrived, and I could hear Arnold greet them quietly. I heard him tell them that things were a little better, but that it would be best for Andre to be with them at Nana's tonight as we didn't know what to expect. I ached in my whole body for both my children. One was out of his mind, and the other was witnessing it and terrified. I just wanted it all to be over. I felt crushed and depleted as I sobbed silently in the hallway.

Arnold came up and quietly asked me what he could do. I told him we just needed to wait until Hans was completely de-escalated before going in or it would likely set him off again. He said ok, and then he went into our room to lie down. Another thirty minutes went by before Hans stopped yelling.

I slowly opened the door and saw the mess in his room. His pillows, blankets, and mattress had all been pulled from the bed. There were two more holes in the wall, and he was in the corner holding his knees to his chest.

"You know how you could make all of this end? Buy Hans something, and you can have Hans back," he said to me with his tear-streaked face.

"What do you mean by that?"

"I'm barely in control."

He lay down on the floor and began to sob. I quietly put his mattress back on his bed with his blankets and pillows. I brushed the dry wall behind the bed with the intention to clean it up in the morning.

"This can all be over for tonight. Get into bed and go to sleep, and you will feel better."

He got into bed and let me sit next to him. I stroked his forehead, applied the Low Dose Naltrexone on his back and the essential oils we had just begun using on his feet and spine. I knew that Low Dose Naltrexone operated as an anti-inflammatory agent on the central nervous system via action on microglial cells. I had read research that LDN was shown to have positive effects on autoimmune conditions similar to PANDAS and PANS.[1] I applied Frankincense to the occipital point at the base of his skull and down his spine. Frankincense has also been shown to have anti-inflammatory properties, can cross the blood brain barrier, and I appreciated that it was natural.

The lamp was on in his room. He could no longer go to sleep without it, because his room was too dark and scary at night. I rubbed out his hands and feet the way he liked with Lavender oil, and I massaged Aromatouch oil into his joints. Lavender oil has calming properties, and I had begun using it to help him go to sleep, and Aromatouch is a wonderful blend for any discomfort. He finally fell asleep shortly after 1:15 in the morning. I sat there, and I was furious. I was furious that I couldn't fix this for my son. I was furious that my other son had to witness all of this. I was furious that I had been waiting for more than seven months and I still didn't have an appointment to see a PANS specialist. I got on my computer, and I wrote a lengthy rage email to the Stanford PANS clinic. I told them what we had just gone through and that if I sounded like an irrational mother it was because I was at my breaking point. This was the third time this month that we had had to send Andre to Nana's house because of Hans's raging, and I needed answers and direction. I begged, please, just let us know how long before we can get in. I copied Arnold and Nana on the email, and the response I got from Nana in the morning was, "that's the email I've been waiting to read. You've been so clinical about all of this in your description; it's never really sounded so desperate." I *was* desperate. And then I received a response from Stanford; we had an appointment in March. That was a month away.

I was continuing to research and read everything I could find about the immune system, the brain, the gut, and healing. I wished I was a brain scientist and that I better understood the workings of the body. As I researched, I learned that there was still so much that we didn't know and that some of the smartest scientists, doctors, and researchers were continuing to ask questions about how the immune system works. I stumbled across an online seminar, The Children's and Teen Health Summit, organized by Carla Atherton. I watched many of the presentations put on by health providers who looked at the body with a slightly different lens. I learned about the gut and brain connection. I learned about functional medicine and treating underlying causes, not symptoms and labels. I made a long list of labs I wanted to run. I learned about the impact of gluten and glyphosate on the body and the inflammation they can cause. I learned what healthy food really meant and how important it is to read labels. I learned about toxic overload and all the ways that toxins get into our home. I had always considered us a healthy family, but I was spurred on to go through our home and get rid of anything that had a toxic load and replace it with something that wasn't harmful. I became aware of the idea that an overloaded system that has been exposed to toxins can have a poor response to a triggering pathogen. This all made sense to me as I had continued to ask myself *why*? Why did my child get a strep infection that wreaked havoc on his immune system?

I enrolled in Carla's Lotus Health Program,[2] and I studied more. She was such a kind and gentle guide on my journey of learning. I will be forever indebted to her knowledge and compassion in helping me understand how to peel away the layers and be patient and forgiving. I had wanted a quick fix, and instead I was unraveling a puzzle as I learned ways to help my son's body heal itself and be the miracle that it is designed to be. I was cleaning up our home environment in ways I had never considered before. I got rid of all plastics, aluminum, nonstick coatings. I replaced chemically laden cleaning products with doTERRA cleaning products or products I made myself using essential oils. I made more of my food from scratch and read labels very carefully. And I was learning how to combine medical modalities. I knew I wouldn't stop searching for answers until my son was well.

CHAPTER TWENTY THREE

THE FLOOD

We were doing our best to get through each day, making things as easy as possible to reduce stress. Arnold had a business trip and would be away for ten days. Nana was coming over daily and spending time with Hans. On one of these days, I came home from the grocery store to find Nana cleaning up an accident in the bathroom. Too much toilet paper had clogged the toilet, and the chain in the tank got stuck resulting in the toilet overflowing. It had been going on for several minutes before Nana was called up to help. I jumped into action and collected the towels to put in the washing machine downstairs as Nana started to clean the floor. I was loading the machine when I heard dripping overhead. After some inspection, Nana and I discovered that the water had gone out into the upstairs hallway, into our bedroom, and down the heating vent into the bathroom below. I was trying to find where the dripping was coming from.

"Don't touch anything, call your homeowners insurance. This is a bigger mess than I thought."

I called our homeowners insurance, and they sent out a team to begin the process of cleaning up the mess. This was incredibly stressful for Hans. There were strangers in our home late into the night, lifting up the carpets, placing loud fans, and taping off the bathroom. They determined there was asbestos in the vinyl flooring that was under the wood we had placed down when we moved in. After they left that night, I turned off the fans so Hans could settle enough to get to sleep. The next morning he told me that if anyone else came over he was going to shoot them with his Nerf gun. I could tell this was not going to work for us to be home with all of this going on, and I knew there was going to be a lot of repairs that needed to be made. I told Hans we were going to get a nice hotel to stay in while they worked on our home, and I made a reservation for the corner suite at the Chrysalis. Leaving the house was hard for Hans, and I hoped that by staying somewhere nice it would alleviate the stress. It seemed to be okay. We had a beautiful view of Bellingham Bay, I had the Xbox hooked up, and I had brought all of Hans's comforts from home. Room service was a nice diversion. Andre was enjoying playing at the beach just outside the hotel after school, and we had our standing weekly ice cream homework date at the ice cream shop just down the street. Nana was staying in a room down the hall just in case Andre needed somewhere to go if Hans was having a hard time, and again, I so appreciated her being there for us. Andre had a sleep over at a friend's house scheduled that Friday night; so I decided to take advantage of the novelty of being in the hotel and invited one of Hans's friends from school to spend the night with us at the hotel. It all worked out, and we enjoyed pizza and a movie in. It almost felt normal, even though there was nothing normal about any of it.

The repairs were going to take longer than I had hoped, and we couldn't stay at the hotel past the week because the room was booked. I got onto VRBO and found a house nearby on the lake that would be a wonderful home away from home. By the time Arnold returned from his business trip, we were set to move into our lake home where we would live for the next month. We discussed the irony in all of this. It had been recommended by Dr. Gbedawo that we remove the carpet in our home due to allergens. At the time, I couldn't imagine how we would do this as Hans couldn't leave the house. This was our answer. With so much damage done to the carpet, it had to be removed. We decided to pull all of it out and replace with wood flooring. I felt gratitude for having this opportunity to do something that previously had felt impossible. I was reminded how blessings can come in strange ways, and I wondered what other blessings would come from this whole experience we were having.

Hans liked the lake house, and on our first day there, he went out on the water with Andre in a double canoe. I watched them from the dock, thrilled to see him outside, physically active, and having a good time with his brother. When he came in, he told me it was wet, and he didn't like the feeling. He wasn't interested in going out, again. I didn't mind. I was determined to let the joy of that moment carry me for a while.

Even though Hans liked the house, its big rooms, vaulted ceilings, and sweeping view of the lake, he wanted to be in his own home and in his own bed. He was still easily set off, and there were a number of times when I had to use all my de-escalation strategies to get him calm. I was so worried he was going to damage something in this home as he had done in ours. I had to remind myself, even if that happened, it's all repairable. That helped me feel less stressed, which I knew reduced his stress level during these occurrences. I would assure him that I heard he was upset, and I was going to help him problem solve. Then I would talk through ways he could ask for what he needed.

There were some nights when he said he needed to be on his iPad until late into the evening. Andre had long since given up asking why Hans could stay up on his iPad when he had to go to bed. He understood that there was nothing fair about what we were dealing with. One night in particular,

Hans was refusing to go to bed and was on the Xbox with the volume really loud.

"Hans, turn the volume down, it's too loud, and Andre is trying to go to sleep," Arnold directed.

"No, I'm not going to turn it down. I don't care if Andre can't go to sleep."

"You will turn the volume down."

Arnold proceeded to turn it down himself.

"I hate you," Hans yelled, kicking over the chair and running to pull a speaker off the wall.

I stepped in front of the speaker, deflecting Hans as he began to kick at me.

"Hans, I see that you want the volume up. How about you go back to your game, and I will see if it's really so loud in Andre's room."

Hans stopped and returned to his game. I went into Andre's room and observed that he couldn't hear a thing. Arnold and I discussed this quietly in the other bedroom. Arnold felt that Hans was getting away with whatever he wanted to do and that it wasn't healthy. I agreed, but I wasn't willing to have the escalation that would follow over turning the volume down when it wasn't bothering Andre. Arnold agreed to let it go. Scenarios like this had played out time and time again, and we were concerned about what we were inadvertently teaching Hans. Yet I believed, intuitively, that this was something entirely different. I understood that there was brain inflammation affecting Hans's reasoning and responses. I didn't feel that he had the capacity to learn from putting restrictions in place and reinforcing good decision making. Everything that I would have done to shape his behavior didn't make sense to me in this condition. It all felt so contrary, and I was constantly questioning myself, and yet I believed that when his body healed, we would return to normal responses to requests and boundaries. I hoped I was right.

We were scheduled to go to Stanford for Hans'sevaluation after our first week in the lake house. I explained to the homeowner that we would be gone for two days. Andre was going to stay with Nana in town. This was another one of those things that had felt impossible to me. I had been trying to imagine how we were going to get Hans on a plane. This time, it was my brother who intervened to help us out. He had his private plane pick us up at our small local airport and fly us directly to a small airport near Stanford where we had a rental car waiting for us. Hans did not want to go see another doctor, but the thought of flying in a private plane seemed pretty cool to him. I was so nervous the day we left. I didn't want him to have an episode on the plane. It was an open cockpit, and I was worried about what might happen if he began to rage. I did everything I could to keep Hans occupied and appease him. We downloaded several movies onto his iPad, had snacks and his water bottle, and I kept a vigilant eye on him.

We were mid-flight when Hans began running his fingers up and down the window blinds.

"Stop doing that Hans," Arnold directed.

I was immediately on high alert and looked at Arnold, slightly shaking my head no.

"Why should I?"

"Because you could bend them."

I interjected, "It's fine, they're not getting bent."

I was so afraid that Hans would get mad and escalate. I did not want to have to restrain him on the plane. I could tell that Arnold was not happy with my contradiction, but I felt that I couldn't risk what might happen.

We made it to the airport with no incident, disembarked, and got into the rental car. The palm trees lined the street, and for a moment, I was again taken back to my childhood days visiting my Grandma during the summer breaks. But this visit didn't have that joy-filled feeling. We drove to a hotel nearby where we had reserved a suite with a separate bedroom so Hans could have space. We set up the Xbox and made a trip to Toys R Us to get a promised Lego set that he could build while we were at our appointment. Again, I was hoping to use the incentive to give him something to do while I talked with the doctors.

We ordered in Mexican food from a restaurant listed on the hotel directory. Hans ate a plain beef and bean burrito with avocado. I was exhausted and was hoping for a restful sleep, but Hans had a hard time getting to sleep that night. He stayed up late watching *Chicken Little*. I stayed up with him and was relieved when he finally turned his iPad off and went to sleep. The next morning, Arnold brought some food in from the continental breakfast.

Hans didn't like it and began to yell angrily, "this hotel is awful!"

He kicked over a standing lamp before coming after me. I evaded him and asked Arnold to please go back and get some bacon and fruit. I knew that Hans would eat those two things.

"Hans, Poppa is going to get you some food that you like. You are going to be safe."

"I'm not going to this doctor, I hate doctors!"

I knew that he was stressed.

"I hear you saying you don't like doctors. I am going to keep you safe. We have a fun Lego set to build when we get there. Let's watch a show and eat some food."

Arnold returned with a plate full of bacon and some apple slices and oranges. Hans settled on the sofa, put a show on his iPad, and began to eat some of the food. Arnold and I packed our things into the car and prepared for the long awaited visit.

I was surprised when we pulled up to the clinic. I had expected it to be on the main grounds, but found that it was part of a smaller medical building off campus. It was shared with me that there was controversy around this clinic, just as there was controversy around the diagnosis. As we sat in the waiting room, I looked around at the other parents and their children. I wondered where they were in their healing process. I imagined we all had similar thoughts, *when will this nightmare end? Why my child? How long can we endure this?* Hans wanted to build his Lego set, and I assured him that as soon as we were in with the doctor, he would have time to build his set.

We were called back to a bright and clean examination room. Hans sat on the floor and opened his box and began building. I met Dr. Chang. I was almost star struck. I had read everything I could find that Dr. Chang and Dr. Frankovich had published. I had waited so long for this appointment, and I could hardly believe it was finally happening. Dr. Chang went through the detailed history we had provided as part of the extensive intake paperwork. He watched Hans build and exchanged some small talk with Hans, admiring his creation. Dr. Frankovich joined us. She asked Hans to sit up on the bed, which he did.

"I want you to squeeze my thumbs as hard as you can and hold it."

Hans complied.

"Keep squeezing," she urged. She then asked him to walk up and down the hallway as she watched him walk. I asked her what she was looking for. She explained that many kids with PANS have what they called a "milkmaid" grip and a distinctive gait.[1] She had me hold my thumbs up and she squeezed my thumbs with slight pulsing pressure so I could feel what she was looking for.

"Your son has both of these. I've read your history and looked at your lab work. I am confident in confirming the diagnosis of PANDAS." I understood that Hans met the diagnosis of PANDAS because his lab work indicated that he had had a strep infection. That, paired with his medical history and his current presentation of symptoms, allowed for the clinical diagnosis.

We discussed what we had been doing so far for treatment. He had been on prophylactic antibiotics, trying several different ones over a seven month period with some decrease in symptoms, but not anywhere close to baseline. We had some success with steroid bursts when things were at their worst, getting him out of the extreme rages and panic attacks, but it was temporary. He was on a lot of supplements addressing inflammation. He was taking CBD oil daily, and that helped reduce the anxiety, panic attacks, and rages. I rubbed Low Dose Naltrexone cream on his back every night, I applied essential oils daily to help support his immune function, calm him, and reduce inflammation. We had reduced the toxic load in our home by removing anything that was laden with chemicals. We ran an air purifier in his room, had special covers on his bed, pillow, and blankets, and I dusted weekly to reduce allergens. And we were in the process of getting rid of the carpet. We had cleaned up our diet as best we could, considering he was such a picky eater. We were trying as much as possible to eat mostly a paleo diet. Although we were doing all of these things, he had not returned to baseline, and our data indicated that he was only 50% better.

"Your son is a good candidate for IVIG."

Intravenous immunoglobulin is a transfusion of healthy antibodies. There was evidence that high dose IVIG had positive effects in rebooting the immune system in some kids with PANDAS or PANS. It was typically administered over two days in a hospital setting.

We discussed that we would need to do the IVIG in Washington state and that we couldn't be part of the ongoing research at Stanford as the stress to get here was too high. We shared all our data and agreed to keep them informed of our treatment choices and outcomes. It felt good to get the confirmed diagnosis from the experts and to know what their recommendation was. To be honest, I had hoped they were going to have some new idea that I hadn't yet read about, and they were going to tell us that we would have our son back soon. Instead, they were very straightforward in letting us know that there was currently no way to predict which child would respond favorably to IVIG and for how long. We thanked them for their time, and left to meet the plane to return home.

CHAPTER TWENTY FOUR

INTRAVENOUS
IMMUNOGLOBULIN

We skyped with Dr. Gbedawo the following week and discussed the recommendations of the Stanford PANS Clinic team. She agreed that IVIG should be our next treatment option. I was nervous about this, knowing that we would be injecting the antibodies of thousands of donors and that there was the risk of introducing something else. I remembered reading a piece on the PANDAS Network site written by a parent who shared that the parents of a child with PANDAS or PANS will stop at nothing to help their child heal, that we don't ever try a treatment without knowing the risks, but that the illness is so horrific we will try anything. Arnold and I were definitely at that point. We had tried a lot of treatment options, already, and we were ready for the next step. We had done what we could to eradicate infection and reduce inflammation, and now it was time to reboot the immune system. I asked about the possibility of doing a home infusion, and Dr. Gbedawo explained that, for the first infusion, it would need to be in the hospital in case there was an adverse reaction. We decided to have Dr. Hawkins order the IVIG in Bellingham so we didn't have to add a long drive to an already potentially stressful procedure. I was so grateful that these two doctors were collaborating for our son's care and that they were willing to work together to help us manage this.

Again, I hit the internet, this time to look into ways to reduce the stress of IVIG for Hans. I found a recommendation of getting a practice kit for the child so they can perform IVIG on a stuffed animal. I thought this was a good idea as I really wanted to make sure I did a better job of educating Hans on what to expect, hoping it would make it a smoother experience than the MRI had been. I also read up on IVIG on the PANDAS Physicians Network site, and I reached out to Diana Pohlman with the PANDAS Network to see what tips I might glean to ensure that we did this right. Through my research, and Diana's advice, I learned that I had to make sure that high dose IVIG was ordered and that it followed the recommendation of 2 grams per kilogram of the child's weight administered slowly over two days. I also learned that I would want to keep Hans hydrated to help avoid headaches and that I should administer ibuprofen and Benadryl the day before, the day of, and the day after to help reduce side effects.

Hans's infusion was scheduled in Bellingham at the St. Joe's Infusion Center. I talked with the head nurse, explaining what the symptoms of PANDAS and PANS were and that we didn't know what our arrival would look like, but I wanted her to be prepared for the worst. She told us that she would be assigning a nurse to Hans for both days to be consistent and that the nurse was very good with children and could handle the situation. She also assigned him a private room with a bathroom and promised to try and get a TV so we could bring his Xbox to distract him and fill his time. She agreed to put together a kit and even offered two so that Andre could have his own kit, as well. Her cooperation gave me tremendous comfort.

A week before the appointment, I called to make sure the proper dosage was ordered, and I was told that the pharmacist ordered 1 gram per kilogram because that's the usual dosage.

I explained to the nurse who took my call that it must be 2 grams. She kindly let me know that she would leave a note for the pharmacist, but that she didn't make those decisions.

"If it's not 2 grams per kilogram, we will not come in for the procedure. It has to be 2 grams per kilogram, or he could have a flare."

I knew I sounded like that difficult parent, but that was my job, to be my child's advocate and to make sure he got what he needed. I asked for an email that I could send the recommendations to, and I was told to put it in the patient portal. Next, I contacted Dr. Hawkins' office, and she responded immediately, letting me know that she ordered it according to the PPN recommendations and she would make sure it was the proper dose. I decided at this point that I would also print the dosage and administration recommendations found on the PPN website to have with me when we went in for the procedure. I was not going to let this get screwed up.

The day of the procedure, I prepared myself mentally to assist Hans in any way needed to get him in for this treatment. As I was going over what I might say or need to do, the phone rang.

"Hi, this is the front desk at the infusion center. We just got word that the procedure scheduled for today has been approved, but the medicine was denied. If you come in for the procedure you will have to pay out of pocket for the medicine, and it will cost $17,000."

I was stunned. Who would approve a procedure but not the medicine?

"I don't know what to say," I stammered.

"I just need to know if you will be bringing Hans in or not."

"No, we won't be coming in today," I mumbled, overcome with a range of emotions. I hung up the phone and burst into tears.

"What's going on? What do you mean we won't be coming in today?" Arnold asked me as I turned to him in disbelief.

"Insurance denied payment for the medicine. They approved the procedure, but denied the medicine."

"That's bullshit!"

"It certainly is. I'm going to call right now and figure out what's going on."

I put my emotions in check and called Molina, our state insurance carrier. I was connected with someone who helped me understand why it was denied and the procedure for appealing our case. IVIG had not yet been determined to be a safe treatment for PANDAS or PANS, which were not even coded diagnoses. Our pediatrician could request a peer to peer appeal in which she would explain to the insurance doctor why this procedure was necessary. She could also re-order the treatment, coding it for something that would be approved such as encephalitis, but because it had already been ordered this way, it would mostly likely be denied as well and could get confusing. Additionally, I could email in a request to overturn the decision explaining why this treatment was necessary.

I contacted Dr. Hawkins' office and requested that she do a peer to peer appeal. I was told that a peer to peer appeal was very time consuming. I explained that I appreciated that, but this treatment was necessary for my son's recovery. I asked the receptionist to please ask Dr. Hawkins to appeal on our behalf. Later that day, I got an email from Dr. Hawkins, of course she would appeal on our behalf. We received word within two weeks that the peer to peer appeal had been denied. It was now my turn to attempt to get this decision overturned. I did more research on IVIG. I found all the information I could that supported IVIG as a treatment option for kids with PANS. I put together a concise, but thorough email with bulleted points explaining what my son had already tried, what the outcomes of each treatment were, why he was a good candidate for IVIG, and I cited all my arguments. I sent off my email, and I waited and I hoped.

Several weeks later, my brother contacted us and offered to pay for the IVIG. I was beyond grateful to him, but I was also furious that insurance wasn't covering this! I found myself asking again, *why should we get what we need just because we are connected?* It wasn't right that families should have to fight so hard to get treatment that could heal their children. I was furious, not just for us, but for others, as well. I felt so fortunate to have a family member who could help offset the cost, and I knew that most families don't have that. I told my brother that Arnold and I would consider his generous offer, but that I wasn't done fighting with the insurance company, yet. The next day, I got a call from Nana.

"Your brother doesn't understand why you don't just schedule the IVIG if you think it's going to work, and quite frankly, I don't understand, either."

"I feel that I need to fight this. It's wrong that insurance won't pay for it."

"But Heather, this could take a long time, and Hans needs this treatment. Your brother can pay for it, you should accept his offer."

I sat with this, and I had to agree. I believed that IVIG could save my son. I knew that the appeal process could take a long time. We had to do this. After discussing it with Arnold, I called my brother to make the arrangements and give our deepest thanks.

I called Dr. Hawkins' office to reschedule the IVIG. The nurse explained to me again that we would have to pay the $17,000 for the medicine. I told her that my brother was paying for the medicine, and she scheduled us several weeks out. I hung up the phone and felt tremendous relief. We were going to get IVIG! A few hours later, I got a call from the insurance company.

"Hello, may I speak to Heather? This is Molina," I was prepared to receive the message that our request to overturn the decision had been denied, but I was okay with this as I had already scheduled his IVIG.

"I just wanted to let you know that your appeal to overturn the decision has been approved," the young man on the other end of the line told me. I was speechless. I couldn't believe it. Again, I burst into tears, but this time they were tears of disbelief mixed with triumph!

"You're kidding me," I sputtered, "thank you so much! I can't believe it. Our doctor tried and was denied."

"Well, you must have written a very convincing argument. We hope your son gets better."

I was overwhelmed with emotion. I didn't know why this was so important to me, but I felt vindicated that insurance was covering this. It gave me hope that other kids would get this treatment when they needed it, too. I called my brother and let him know that we wouldn't need his gift, that insurance had overturned the denial, and that we continued to be so grateful to him for offering. All of the preparations I had made would be put into place as we moved forward with this treatment.

The day of the scheduled procedure, Hans was agitated. He did not want to go in and he was ready to fight.

"Hans, this is a non-negotiable," I told him. He had heard me say this before. He knew that I wouldn't force anything that didn't have to happen, but a non-negotiable meant it would happen, easy or hard. He was terrified, and he wrapped his fingers around the slats on the head of his bed. Arnold and I were prepared to carry him out of the house and restrain him in the car if we had to. We were confident that the infusion center was prepared for us to bring our son in one way or another. I remained calm as I peeled his fingers from his bed frame while he cried and screamed.

"Please, no. I can't do this. You don't understand!"

I can only imagine how this must have felt to him. He couldn't think rationally about this, and even though we'd done everything we could to prepare him for what to expect, this was an unknown. What he did know was that someone was going to put a needle in his arm and he would have to sit like that for many hours. And so he fought, as if for his life.

Arnold and I had to work together to pry his fingers from his bed frame, and then we wrestled to carry him like a log between us, as he continued to cry and scream and beg. Finally, he settled, exhausted.

"Ok, just let me get dressed," he sobbed.

We released him and he scrambled back into his room trying to shut the door behind him, but we were right there, and the struggle began, again.

"Hans, I know this is scary."

"You have no idea!" he spat at me.

"Maybe I don't, but I do know that we have to do this. We will be with you the entire time. We have the Xbox, your iPad, and yummy food. Andre is with us to play games with you. We're all here to support you. We can either walk out to the car, or Poppa and I will carry you."

He cried, and we waited. After a few long minutes, he wiped his eyes, got out of bed, and looked at me.

"I really hate you." And then he got dressed and walked out to the car with us.

Upon arriving at the infusion center, we were greeted by a friendly nurse. She would be with us all day, both days. She guided us to our room and started to get Hans set up. As she prepared for the infusion, I gave her the paperwork that I had printed from the PANDAS Physician Network site. I double checked with her that we had a high dose infusion and that we would go slowly. She read over the directions I handed her and confirmed that it matched what she was ordered to deliver. She gave Hans acetaminophen and diphenhydramine. This would help prevent headaches, a common side effect.

I had applied an analgesic cream to the inside of Hans's elbow when we were in the car hoping that it would alleviate the "stick" feeling of the needle insertion. It did not. When she put the needle in his arm, he screamed. As she taped everything down and checked that it was properly placed, he continued to scream. This was distressing to Andre who began to cry. I asked Arnold to take Andre to go get some treats at the café in the lobby. I was second guessing myself, thinking that bringing Andre might have been a bad idea because of the stress on him. I had thought it would be good for him to support his brother and for Hans to have a playmate to help him keep his mind off of the many hours he would need to be in the hospital.

"It hurts," Hans cried to me. He looked at me with terrified eyes. "You said once it was in, it wouldn't hurt anymore. It hurts. You lied to me! Take it out now!"

I felt terrible. I really had believed it wouldn't hurt after insertion. I asked the nurse if there was anything we could do to relieve the discomfort of the needle. She assured us it should stop feeling uncomfortable soon. She began the infusion, and I tried distracting Hans with his iPad. The nurse left to bring a TV in so we could set up the Xbox. Hans continued to cry.

"Hans, you are so brave. I am so proud of you!" I tried to encourage him. The nurse checked his vitals every 15 minutes, following the infusion protocol. Hans continued to be upset saying it hurt.

"I'm going to take this thing out, it hurts!" he threatened.

"Hans, if you take it out, it will hurt even more. The nurse is the only one who can take it out without it hurting, and she isn't going to do that. We've started this, and we must finish it. Let's get your mind off of it by doing something else."

I tried to distract him. He finally settled into compliance. Arnold and Andre returned with muffins, the nurse returned with the TV, and Arnold began to set up the Xbox. Andre asked Hans if he wanted to play Bloons TD5 on their iPads, and Hans did. I took a breath and began to relax. We were doing this! Six hours later, Hans's first infusion was complete.

"Do you want to keep the port in overnight?" the nurse asked Hans.

"No!"

"We'll need a new poke tomorrow."

"I do not want anything in my arm when I leave here. It is too painful."

I asked the nurse if there was anything we could do differently the next day to help it not be so uncomfortable. She suggested I apply more analgesic cream to the inside of his arm earlier on and that I cover it. She would try using a butterfly port instead. It was smaller, but she was pretty confident she would be able to access his vein and it would definitely be more comfortable. Hans was glad to hear this.

The next day was much easier. Hans understood that he had to complete the two days of infusion or things could potentially be much worse. I had read that a partial infusion could actually cause a flare and had told him this. Nobody wanted that. He also knew that the needle was going to be smaller. The second infusion was easy. I was so impressed with everyone's efforts to make this happen. That afternoon, we returned home after another six hours, and I was very hopeful.

CHAPTER TWENTY FIVE

HE'S BACK!

Recovery after IVIG can be overnight, or it can take weeks to see the benefits. It can take three to six months for the healthy antibodies to do their job and then another three to six months for the system to settle. We were prepared to observe Hans's progress over the course of the next year, knowing that at that time we would have all the benefit we were going to get.

Several weeks after IVIG, Hans was sitting at the kitchen table. I brought him some breakfast to eat, delighted that he was eating at the table and not in his bed. He looked up at me.

"Thank you, mom."

"You're welcome, sweetheart. I love you," I kissed him on the head.

"I love you too," he replied and turned to eat his food.

I was overcome. This was the first time I had heard these words come from his mouth in over a year. I stood there and let those words wash over me. I felt the joy of those three simple words envelope me, and I knew we had our son back!

Over the next few months, we observed that he was no longer having the severe panic attacks or rages. We made a trip to Seattle together to visit with family. I was nervous, but everything went well. We planned as if we might spend the night, but Hans preferred to be in his own bed, and we returned home that night. I was elated.

As we watched Hans healing, we saw the changes in subtle ways. One of the first things I noticed was that I had laundry of his to do, and I was so happy! Again, I was struck by the irony of this. I reflected on how there had been a time when doing laundry seemed like a chore, but now I found joy in this task because having laundry to do meant that Hans wasn't stuck in his pajamas and in his bed. I hoped for more of these ironic happenings to unfold. I promised myself never to take these seemingly mundane things for granted, again. I was keenly aware of my own transformation that had taken place as my rigid parenting beliefs had been overturned and replaced with a desire for my children to be happy, to have joy and laughter in my home, and to live every day as if it might be the last. I didn't want to miss any opportunity to experience a blessing.

Now that we were seeing real healing, I was inspired again to get things in place for Hans with schooling and counseling. I was hopeful that he might be able to access Cognitive Behavioral Therapy as he continued to have stress around the concept of school and continued to want things just so, but not to the degree of panic attacks or rages. I reached out to a counselor I had once worked with in the school setting whom I had been very impressed with. He agreed to come to our home and try to meet with Hans. We tried several times, but Hans wouldn't leave his room. I took away his iPad, but he still wouldn't leave his room. He told me that he didn't like counselors and he didn't trust them. This understanding counselor tried reaching out through email, but Hans refused to reply. We decided to postpone any CBT until a later date.

I contacted the school district and applied for Home Hospital services. I worked with their coordinating nurse; filled out the appropriate paperwork, got it signed by Dr. Hawkins, and we were granted 18 weeks of tutoring, 4 hours per week. The first tutor to come to our home was a kind older gentleman. He contacted the 6th grade teachers that Hans had been assigned to in order to request material. He was told by one of the teachers that there was no way of knowing what to give for school work because he'd never met Hans. The tutor and I decided to use the history book as a starting point, choosing the cradle of civilization as our focus. Hans was enjoying Halo and through his gaming had learned about the Spartans, though he didn't know the historical context, yet. I thought that maybe we could spark an interest by making that connection for him.

Hans refused to meet the tutor. After several sessions of the tutor and I discussing how we might engage Hans, the tutor suggested that it wasn't working. I agreed. He suggested that maybe there might be a better fit with someone else. Fate stepped in. Through an accidental run-in with a former colleague, I found out that a dear friend and retired administrator from the school district was tutoring. If anyone was going to reach Hans, it was Gigi. She had over twenty years working at the middle and high school levels, connecting with many of our fringe kids. I reached out to her, and she enthusiastically agreed to give it a try. She did all the right things to engage with him. She brought him a hot cocoa the first day and left it outside his door, letting him know it was there and that she was going to talk with his mom. She brought him a book filled with funny cat poems knowing that he loved his two cats. She sent him emails with interesting YouTube videos about Halo and Legos knowing that he loved both of these. She focused on connecting with him rather than on completing work. She knew that building a relationship was going to be a key component to reducing stress and getting him to do anything. She had done her research on PANDAS, and she knew what we'd been through. She was determined to make it work.

Hans was mildly receptive, at best. He would come out of his room to greet her and he thanked her for the things she brought him. He was polite, but he didn't do anything but the most minimal amount of school work. What he did demonstrate, however, was the ability to synthesize information, make inferences, and problem solve. It was evident that his reading was solidly in place, but he struggled with math, and his writing was still illegible. As the end of the school year neared, Gigi and I put together a plan to help Hans return to school in the fall for his 7th grade year. She helped me identify who his team of teachers would be, reviewed the 504 we had put in place for this year but never used, and identified some steps to try to accomplish. Our goal would be to normalize school as much as possible by driving by the middle school whenever we were out, with the hopes of getting in the building before the first day.

And then Gigi suggested we get a dog. She was the third person to tell us that a dog would be good for Hans, and she thought it would be great "curriculum" as Hans would need to do some research. Arnold and I discussed this reluctantly. Neither of us were "dog people," but we understood that the responsibility would be good for him as well as the connection, since he really had no one that he spent any time with anymore other than his immediate family. When I finally mentioned the idea to Hans, he was elated.

"Mom, I've always wanted a dog, a wolf or a Husky!"

"Really? Why have I never known that?"

"How could you *not* know? Look at my stuffed animals."

I took a moment to examine his observation, and felt foolish that I had never paid attention to the fact that nearly all of his stuffed animals were either huskies or wolves. I felt sheepish.

"You're right Hans, I'm sorry I never noticed that. Let's start doing some research."

Hans and I agreed that we wanted a rescue dog. It turned out that Andre's teacher ran a local dog rescue operation, Happy Tails. I let her know that we were in the market for a rescue dog, that Hans would really like a Husky, and that Arnold and I would really like a dog that would get Hans out into the world. She assured us that she would find the right dog for us. As Hans continued his research, he learned that adult Huskies who have not lived with cats are not good companions for cats because of their predator nature. He learned that Golden Retrievers and Golden Labs are great family dogs. Hans agreed that it would be best to not get a rescue Husky and that he would have to wait until he was older to have a Husky of his own. This compromising was yet another sign of his healing.

We met a couple of available dogs and none of them inspired us. What we did learn through these introductions was that we wanted a medium sized dog that was young enough to still be playful. After meeting one of the rescue dogs who had recently had a litter, Andre asked if we could get a puppy. I adamantly replied, "no." The research that Hans had done had made it very clear to me that having a puppy was like having a baby, and I felt that I already had enough on my plate.

"But they are so cute!" Andre insisted enthusiastically as he bounced around the puppies as if he were one, himself. And they certainly were cute! Hans looked at them from the side, not engaging, but clearly watching. Andre's teacher observed this, and she approached me.

"I think you need a Husky puppy. I can see that your boys would love a puppy, and Hans wants a Husky. If you raised your Husky puppy with your cats, they would be compatible."

I pondered this idea and thought that it wasn't very likely there would be a rescue Husky pup.

"We'll talk about this as a family and get back to you. Thank you for your observations."

On our way home, I shared her thoughts with the boys and Arnold. The boys thought it was a great idea. I offered to take care of the night time potty breaks if the boys promised to walk the dog every day and help with potty-training during the daytime. They enthusiastically agreed.

One week later, I got a call from Andre's teacher. They had just picked up a rescue litter of Husky mix pups. Unbelievable. When I asked her where they were being fostered, she told me the family who was caring for these pups were our neighbors who lived across the street. I felt as though it was meant to be. Later that day, as she was delivering the pups to our neighbor's house, Hans got out of bed, got dressed, and went directly over. He looked over the pups in the pen, and without hesitation, he picked up a puppy.

Hans looked at me smiling, "this is the one, mom. This is the annihilator."

In his arms snuggled the cutest bundle of fluff.

"Can we call her Annie for short?"

"Sure, I was just kidding about the annihilator, but Annie is a good name."

And that was it. Annie, the Annihilator, joined our family. We had a week to prepare for her as she needed to stay with her foster family for temperament assessment. She would prove to be a wonderful layer of healing for Hans and a great addition to our family.

CHAPTER TWENTY SIX

LAYERS OF HEALING

As we moved into the summer months, I was thrilled to see Hans out playing with the neighbor kids on occasion. He didn't always choose to enter into their shenanigans, preferring to play his video games at home, but there wasn't that feeling of being stuck. The previous summer he would tell me, "Mom, don't you think I *want* to go out and play with my friends? I can't. I can't explain it, but I just can't." Now it was a choice, and I was relieved to see the difference. We had gotten our son back to 85 percent of baseline, and we wanted to figure out how to get him to 100 percent.

I reached out to my network of families in our Washington State Facebook parent support group. When I first joined this group, we were 30 members. We were now 60 members and growing weekly. Several parents had found success through genetic testing and addressing variances identified with supplements. We pursued getting Hans's genetic testing done through Courtagen, but we found out that they didn't accept Molina/Medicare, and the cost was thousands of dollars. We were accustomed to having huge out of pocket expenses with the supplements and CBD oil that Hans was taking, but we couldn't afford the testing that Courtagen would provide. The very kind intake nurse suggested I consider the 23andMe test that I could order online for $200.[1] After consulting with Dr. Gbedawo, we decided to order the test. It would take six weeks to get the results back, and then she be would able to interpret the data for us.

Hans had many SNPs in his DNA, which we all have. Single Nucleotide Polymorphisms are variances, or mutations, which can cause problems if they are expressed or not expressed by the environment. Some may impact an individual's response to certain drugs, susceptibility to environmental factors such as toxins, and risk of developing particular diseases. SNPs can also be used to track the inheritance of disease genes within families.[2] Certain SNPs indicate difficulties with methylation, and Hans had many of those. Methylation is a chemical reaction that occurs in every cell and tissue in the body. The methylation process helps the body detoxify, helps the enzymes in the body work efficiently, and is important to overall health. [3] Hans's genetic profile matched much of what we were seeing in his blood workup. He had high homocysteine levels, which are toxic. All of this was a bit over my head, but I trusted Dr. Gbedawo would help us address these issues. My own research helped me to understand that proper methylation could also help with symptoms of depression and anxiety. The body basically takes B vitamins, and through several steps, turns them into balanced neurotransmitters. Balanced neurotransmitters, like serotonin and dopamine, help us feel happy and motivated. We began to add in more supplements, specifically B vitamins, to address Hans's specific variances. We added in one at a time so we could monitor the results. The first supplement we added in was 1 mg of 5-MTHF, and Hans went into a deep depression. He was on it for two weeks and immediately presented depressed, even stating that he felt really down. I stopped the dose after the two week trial, and within a few days, he was back to his "normal." I was confused because I knew he had these variances and that he needed this B vitamin. After conferring with Dr. Gbedawo and also with an applied kinesiologist that I found through my parent support group who muscle tests on dosing, we decided that the dose was too high. This posed a problem for me because the smallest dose I could get was a 1 mg capsule. I started cutting the capsules in half and re-capping them, and we tried again. This time, we saw favorable results. This was the beginning of fine tuning the supplements that Hans's body needed for optimal performance and healing. Each time we added one in, I monitored and adjusted and muscle tested until we got the right dose. I was cutting and encapsulating pills and one of my kitchen cabinets began to look like a pharmacy and supplement shelf, but I was determined to help Hans have maximum healing.

As well as adding in additional supplements, we decided to add in Ketotifen to address his seasonal allergies and to stabilize the mast cells in his body. The mast cells are involved in allergic reactions and initiate inflammation.[4] Hans had always been affected by seasonal allergies and eczema, and we knew that he was dealing with brain inflammation so this seemed a reasonable addition. I saw all of these additions as "keeping the gears oiled" after IVIG. We had done the hard work of rebooting his immune system with IVIG, and now we were addressing the body to maintain optimum health. It was a lot of pills every day for Hans to take, but he did so, and I reminded him that I was also addressing my health with supplements and healthy eating, as well.

I had worked hard to eliminate toxins from our home. I read labels all the time and made healthy food, only bringing home processed foods that were real foods and didn't contain questionable ingredients. I was keenly aware that a stressed immune system couldn't handle toxins, and I was doing everything I could to reduce the toxic load. I was using essential oils to reduce inflammation, fight off any bacteria, viruses, fungi, or microbes, and to create scent memories that assisted with sleeping and calming what I called "big emotions."[5] I used homeopathic treatments to keep Hans's immune system strong and to help anyone else in the family who might come in contact with pathogens outside of our home.[6] Since using these natural remedies, I had been free of any illness, and I had been able to keep Hans from getting sick even when Andre or Arnold came home with a bug, and that was without having to use antibiotics! I was feeling empowered.

People in this community are caring and want to help, but I became disheartened by the "camps" of parents who were dealing with PANDAS/PANS/AE. I had some online parents who told me to *quit doing all of that natural stuff that doesn't work anyway, and just continue with IVIG.* And then I would have the other online parents telling me to *quit using those toxic medicines like steroids and antibiotics that have horrible side effects.* I knew how confusing it was to try and navigate your child's needs when you knew you couldn't trust most providers who would tell you that PANDAS didn't exist, that you were part of the problem, and that your child was mentally ill. So you research, you reach out, you listen to what others are doing, and you do your best to make decisions for your precious child that you are fighting for every day. I wished parents would be gentler with each other, allowing space for dialogue that wasn't judgmental. So many of us had experienced plenty of judgment from professionals, family members, and friends. The road to recovery is not always a straightforward path, and each child is different. For us, antibiotics had not been the answer we had hoped for. They brought the severity of symptoms down from a loud roar to a dull roar. Steroid bursts had helped when symptoms were at their worst, but only temporarily. IVIG definitely had brought our son back from the black hole he had been stuck in. Supplements, CBD oil, Ketotifen, LDN, homeopathy, essential oils, and healthy living kept him from sinking back into that dark place and perhaps helped him heal further, stopped more inflammation from occurring, and addressed root causes.

One night, as Hans was going to bed, he asked me, "Mom, if you could change anything about the human race, what would it be?"

"Oh gosh, Hans, I'd have to think about that one."

"I know what I'd change."

"What's that, honey?"

"I'd make it so the human body couldn't experience illness or disease."

I caught my breath. "Yes, Hans, that would be a great change."

I certainly agreed with this sentiment, and I ached for this boy who had been through so much. I wondered how this experience would affect him. Would this illness form who he would become? Would it direct his life goals? Would it affect how he engaged in the world? Or would it just be a hurdle overcome by the tenacity of a child? My mother's heart wondered, and then my thoughts wandered to how it had changed *my* life.

Anyone who knew me would observe that my parenting had shifted dramatically. I was much less strict than I had been. I frequently asked myself if the limit I was setting was really all that important or was it just something that I thought I should do because others did. My work and my lifestyle had also changed. I was working from home, sharing the power of essential oils and advocating for families who were struggling to get their children's needs met in their schools or who thought their child might have this horrific illness. I continued to teach Right Response classes in the nearby school districts, but I knew I would not go back into the classroom. I would have a better ability to support kids from the outside, and I knew how hard it was to make change from the inside. I observed how every aspect of my life was different. And I was okay with that.

CHAPTER TWENTY SEVEN

ALMOST THERE

The summer was winding down, and we were preparing for the school year. Hans was determined that he was going to attend what we called his brick and mortar middle school. He would be in the seventh grade, and Andre would be starting in the sixth grade. It was an exciting time for us as we went shopping for school clothes and new shoes. Hans hadn't worn much of anything but pajamas, shorts, a few t-shirts, and flip flops for the past two years, so he needed everything. We also got him a backpack and a new lunch bag. Shopping for these things with both of my boys was such a joyful time for me; I could hardly believe that we were doing this.

I contacted the school counselor and requested that Hans be placed with the same team of teachers that a childhood friend of his was with. He didn't know anyone else in his grade at this school, so Arnold and I thought that having that one friend would be helpful. Several weeks before school started, we had their family over for a BBQ. Hans and his buddy played video games and re-connected. I was so grateful to this family for supporting us in this way. As the kids were playing, I talked with these long-time friends of ours about how we might ensure that Hans be able to get past that first day hump. I anticipated that the first day would be the hardest.

We decided that I would drive my boys, and pick up Hans's friend on our way. This would give us a responsibility to get out the door.

I had been in communication with all of Hans's teachers, sending them information about PANDAS/PANS/AE that I had pulled off of the PANDAS Network site. I connected with the counselor to make sure the 504 we had developed the previous year was current and in place. I tried to get a meeting scheduled with Hans's teachers before school started, but I couldn't get in touch with any of the team. I told myself that it was going to be okay. I had high hopes, and I didn't want anything to get in the way of Hans's success.

Hans had been bathing regularly, a huge change after not showering or taking a bath *ever* for the past two years. He asked to have his nails cut, which also hadn't been done for two years. They would get long until they broke, and then they would get long, again. It was the week before school would start, and Hans decided that he wanted a haircut. He hadn't cut his hair in over two years, either, and it was long past his shoulders. I didn't mind his hair being long, but I saw this request as more evidence of his healing. I called the lady who cut my hair, but she was booked. I explained, briefly, what I was trying to accomplish and why. She referred me to a friend, and we were scheduled to get Hans's haircut two days before school would start. Hans told me he hated his hair, and I was surprised. It made the prison of this illness even more clear to me as I imagined hating my hair, but not being able to do anything about it. I was reminded of all the times that Hans had told me, "I can't. I just can't. I can't explain it. If I could I would, but I don't even know why." I had learned to believe him, but somehow this comment about hating his hair really hit that point home for me.

The lady who cut Hans's hair was kind. She didn't know what we'd been through these past two years. She didn't know how incredible it was that Hans was letting her wash his hair.

She didn't know what a feat it was for him to sit in her chair and let her comb out his hair and cut it. She commented on his waxy scalp, telling him he needed to wash his hair more often. I held my breath momentarily, my fear of an episode had become my norm. But there was no response. She cut his locks long so we could donate them if we chose to. When she was done, I looked at this boy that I knew so well, but had lost for the past two years. It took everything in me not to cry and hold him tight. I acted very casual, letting him know it was a good haircut.

I was so excited and so nervous for his first day back. Two of the neighbor boys came by to drop something off.

"Hans is going to school on Monday!" I wanted everyone to know and to be looking out for him.

"That's great!" they replied with sincerity.

It was the night before the first day of school. As I was saying good night to Hans, he confided in me.

"I don't know if I'm excited or nervous about tomorrow."

I thought about this for a moment. "Yes, those two emotions can feel the same way in the body. Let's call it 'excited.' This is a brave step you are taking, and I'm so proud of all the work you've done to heal."

I kissed him good night, and I let myself believe that this nightmare called PANDAS was over.

The next morning we all got up, and I went downstairs to make breakfast and lunches. I went up to Hans's room to check on him, and I found him in front of his closet. He was stuck and crying.

"Mom, I can't do it. I can't get dressed."

"Sure you can, honey. Just put the clothes on that we bought. It's going to be fine."

I tried to hide the panic I was feeling inside.

"I'm making your favorite breakfast. We'll eat and then we'll go out to the car and pick up your friend. He's going to school with you to make sure you know where everything is. And I'll be there to help if you need it, but I won't follow you around. I'm going to give you some space now, and I'll come back and check on you in a few minutes."

My heart was racing and my stomach felt sick. I went downstairs to finish up breakfast. Lunches were packed and in backpacks with water bottles and notebooks. After heading back upstairs, I found Hans in his pajamas and back in his bed. His tear-streaked face looked at me from behind his cover.

"I can't do it, mom. I can't. I just can't do this. It's too hard."

"I understand Hans. It feels hard. The first day can be hard for lots of kids. But I imagine it feels especially hard when you haven't been in school for two years. You've got this. You can do this. I believe in you."

"I can't, mom. I really can't," he was crying.

"We've got to go pick up Freddy. Tell you what, get dressed and go with me to pick him up, and then we'll see how you're doing."

"No. You don't understand! I can't do this! Just leave!"

I stepped out of his room and took a deep breath. I had to go now or Hans's friend and Andre would be late for school.

From the hallway, I called into his room, "Okay Hans, it's okay. I'm going to take Andre and pick up Freddy and take them to school. We'll see how you are doing when I get back."

I was crushed. I got into the car with Andre and drove the five minutes to pick up their friend. I fought hard to hold back the tears. I went into their house and told them that Hans wasn't able to make it out the door and wouldn't be going with us this first day. I drove the boys to school and went in to let attendance know the same thing. I hugged Andre and told him how proud of him I was and that I hoped he had a wonderful first day of middle school.

"Is Hans going to be okay?"

"Yes. He's going to be okay."

"Is he going to go to school?"

"I don't know," I told him honestly. "I hope so, but we will just have to see."

I gave him another hug, and then I left and climbed back into our car. I sat there in the quiet oasis of this space. Other kids were being dropped off by parents around me. My arms encircled the steering wheel, and I sobbed. I had let myself believe that PANDAS was over. I had let myself believe that we were out of the hell. I had let myself believe that Hans was completely healed, that we were through. All of this emotion and disappointment shook through my body. And then I picked my head up, dried off my tears, and I told myself, *I will never make this mistake again.* In that moment, I hardened myself to the reality that this illness was a hard one to get over. I sat there for a few more minutes, and I wondered how many others had gone through this? Why couldn't we be the ones that got better after antibiotics? Why couldn't we be the ones that did IVIG and got up the next day like everything was normal? How many other kids and parents had gone through this roller coaster of not quite healing? What else could we do?

CHAPTER TWENTY EIGHT

TIME IS AN ALLY

Hans and I spent the next several weeks as we had the year before. His first goal was to get dressed as if he were going to school, knowing that he didn't have to. I made him a lunch in his lunch bag, and he would eat it at home as if he were at school. When we'd been doing this for several days, we added in the goal of getting into the car and driving by the school. Next was to drive to the school and park. And then we were going to try and go into the school.

I had been in daily communication with attendance and his teachers. One of his teachers suggested that we come by after school when the kids were gone. He said he would come out to the car and meet Hans. I happily agreed. I didn't tell Hans this until we were halfway there. I was worried he wouldn't get in the car.

"Hans, one of your teachers would like to meet you. You can go into the school and meet him in his classroom or he will come out to the car. Which would you prefer?"

"Neither, but I definitely can't go into the building, so I guess he'll have to come out to the car."

"Okay, we'll do that then."

I parked, and I let him know I was going to go in briefly to let his teacher know that we were here. I found Hans's teacher in his classroom, and he shared with me that his daughter struggled with anxiety and he just wanted his classroom to feel like a safe place for Hans. I appreciated his compassion and empathy. We walked to the car, and I opened the side door so this kind man could say hello.

Hans was polite, but made little eye contact. His teacher told him he hoped he could come to his classroom. He told him about his daughter and that he wanted Hans to feel safe.

"Oh," was all that Hans could reply.

I thanked his teacher and say goodbye, and then closed the side door.

"I'm never doing this again. Take me home."

I said nothing. We drove home silently. The next day, Hans refused to get in the car. This continued for several more days, and now we were at the twenty day mark, and Hans was automatically withdrawn from school. I filled out the homeschool paperwork to keep us out of court. I talked with Hans about our options.

"We can't lose another year of school. We can do online school, you know what that looks like. We can do Kahn Academy, you know what that looks like. Or we can try the homeschool partnership program. You haven't been there yet."

"Mom, if I can go there then I can go to Whatcom Middle School."

"Okay. What about trying one period to start with?"

"It's the same thing. If I can go one period, I can go the whole day. I just can't go right now."

I was feeling at such a loss. I was feeling incapable of providing any kind of proper education. Again, I reached out to my online parent support group. Many of them were in the same situation. We held each other up, focused on our children's healing. We reminded ourselves that time was on our side, that reducing stress was critical to the healing process, and that where we were was okay. I was so grateful for this strong group of women. I told myself, *I will get through this,*

I am strong enough, Hans is strong enough, we are all strong enough. I believed that things happened for a reason and that there was a blessing in this experience. I had become more compassionate, more empathetic than I had been. I wanted to tell all the parents I had ever worked with that I believed they knew their child best. I wanted to tell all the parents that I had ever judged that I was sorry. I was humbled, and I was grateful.

I believed that in this space of gratitude and acceptance, miracles would happen. I received an email from a woman who teaches whole body healing. She had heard about our situation through a friend, and she wanted to help. Dr. Sandy Gluckman offered to provide us counseling. She asked us to check out her website, Parents that Heal,[1] and if it resonated with us, to let her know if we would like to accept her offer. Arnold and I spent some time looking over her philosophy, her background, her materials, and we were impressed. We purchased her book, "Parents, Take CHARGE!"[2], and we scheduled our first session with her and began the process of healing on yet another level. To me, this felt like nothing short of a miracle. An amazing counselor had just brought herself into our lives.

After completing the intake paperwork, we met with her via skype. Sandy told us that she is frank, and that after we had heard what she had to say, we could decide if we wanted to continue to work with her. First, she explained the stress response system. I was familiar with this from the work I did, but this was new information to Arnold. She shared with us that it was evident from our separate intake paperwork that Arnold and I were struggling as a couple. As long as there was discord between Arnold and I, there would be stress on our children, and it would take longer for Hans to heal because his body would continue to have a stress response, which is toxic. We acknowledged that our marriage was in jeopardy and we shared with her that we had begun counseling with a Gottman therapist in town who was well respected.

"That's great! When your relationship heals, real healing can take place for Hans, as well."

I now had an even bigger investment in trying to save our marriage; if not just for us, than for our children. The time we spent in counseling would prove to be the best investment we could have made. We found a renewed connection and commitment and learned how to talk with each other, to listen deeply, to clear our frustrations, to step away when we needed to, and to come back together in a productive way. It was hard work, but it was helping us get through this dark place we had come to, and it was reducing stress for everyone.

With Dr. Gluckman's advice, we agreed to stop using the diagnostic term, PANDAS, in our home. This was hard for me at first. I understood that we didn't want Hans to identify with this label, but I had fought hard for it. It was what had helped me get answers and healing. Dr. Gluckman understood me and helped me move past this clinging. We applied this concept to Andre, as well. Instead of thinking of himself as dyslexic, we identified that he was a 3-dimensional thinker, a problem solver, someone who sees things outside of the box. We began to focus our attention on both of the boys' strengths. We made a photo and word collage for each of them that represented their beautiful traits and strengths so we could all see them every day and acknowledge who they really were. We focused on joy in the moment and things began to feel lighter. I observed more blessings that this journey was bringing to our lives as we had connected with this amazing teacher/counselor.

To address schooling, I set up Home Hospital tutoring for Hans, again. I requested Gigi, the tutor he had had the previous year. Our first meeting with her was over lunch. This could never have happened the previous year. Right away, Gigi noticed a difference. Hans was more engaging and responsive;

yet, still resistant to work that seemed to him to be pointless. She set him up to complete Washington State history online. It is a graduation requirement, and in our school district, kids take this class in the 7th grade. Although he found it to be boring, he understood that it was required, and he was willing to push through the work. This alone felt like a huge breakthrough! She found an online math program, STMath, that taught math concepts visually.[3]

Hans and I tried it out, and even Andre wanted to see how it worked.

"I could learn to hate this, and that's the best it's going to be for math with me," Hans told me. I appreciated his humor and was saddened that he felt this way. Math had been one of his favorite subjects. After completing the diagnostic assessment, he began the lessons. Some of them felt tedious, but once he got into some new learning, he began to appreciate the program.

"This is actually a pretty good program. They do a good job of showing how the math works."

"I am so glad that you are having success with this program! I am also very impressed with the format and will enjoy learning new ways of teaching math concepts with you!".

Gigi continued to put together assignments for Hans, trying to engage him in areas of interest. She was still met with resistance and a constant questioning of why he should do the work. Hans understood that he needed to learn math. Sometimes he would question if he was ever going to use certain concepts, but because it was a prescribed program, he would plow through the lessons in order to get to the next concept. But he didn't see the point in doing the other work that Gigi was giving him. He thought it was a waste of time to compare games or books to movies. He did very little of the work that she spent hours of time putting together for him, and that frustrated me. She continued to meet him where he was at, and I felt so fortunate for her commitment to helping him succeed.

As the year was coming to a close, Gigi and I discussed the coming year. Hans would be in the 8th grade.

"I don't want you to be disappointed next year if Hans doesn't go back to his brick and mortar school. He may not be a traditional education kid."

I laughed, "no kidding. There hasn't been much these past three years that has felt at all traditional."

"I think it would be a good idea to have a backup plan. I just don't want him to feel badly if he doesn't go back to school, and I definitely don't want to see you go through what you did at the beginning of this year."

"No, that won't happen for me. I know that there is nothing textbook about this illness. I will never let myself believe that it's over. It hurt too much when it wasn't. The problem is that we've tried all the options except the Home School Partnership program, and none of them are a perfect fit. You've been the best resource for us, helping us get Washington State History done and finding a math program that engages him. You've seen his ability to read and synthesize information; even though he won't produce the product that demonstrates that, he's able to verbalize it. You've watched him share his learning on complex topics that intrigue him. I know he can learn. I know that being in a school setting feels stressful for him. I'm not sure now what are residual PANS symptoms and what is typical adolescent resistance."

"I have an idea that may be a good fit for him. He can sit for his GED when he's 16. There are several great online GED prep courses. If he can't go back to school in the fall for his 8th grade year, he could do the online prep work, and when he turns 16, he'd be ready to get his GED and be done with school. Then he can focus on what he wants to do next."

I thought about this. It was a decent back-up plan, but I wasn't sure I wanted Hans to expect to do anything but go back to school. Then I thought about reducing stress. I agreed to have a talk with him about it.

After talking with Arnold about this idea first, later that night, I shared our thinking with Hans.

"Poppa and I want to support you in what you feel you can do. We don't want school to be stressful. We have another option that I want to share with you." I explained what Gigi had proposed.

"I want to go back to school, Mom."

"Okay, I hear that, and we will support you one hundred percent in making that happen. We will do whatever we can to help, but we want you to know that there is no pressure to do so. We have a great option if it doesn't work out. We believe in you."

He didn't tell me to leave his room. He just sat with that, and I allowed a little hope to creep in, hope that we were moving into a new place of healing and acceptance.

Several weeks before the school year ended, a parent from one of my online support groups reached out to me. Her son had presented very similarly to Hans with regards to symptoms and was responding to interventions. He also had had chronic sinus problems and both of their MRI's presented with sinusitis or inflammation of the nasal cavity. After three years of treatments that resulted in a state of "chronic static," as she called it, they decided to circle back around to antibiotics, and they were seeing an improvement. She shared this information with me and suggested that we consider trying antibiotics, again. I scheduled an appointment with Dr. Gbedawo. We needed to see her, anyway. It had been nearly a year since our last visit, and we needed refills on the Ketotifen and LDN cream. She would need to see Hans in order to refill those prescriptions.

I told Hans that we needed to see Dr. Gbedawo in person in order to get refills on a few of his prescriptions. I explained what the Ketotifen did for his allergy relief. He hated having itchy eyes and he understood that the Ketotifen helped. I didn't go into the mast cell stabilization that it also provided. I didn't think that would be as important to him as helping with allergies. He thought it was stupid that we had to see Dr. Gbedawo in order to get the prescriptions refilled.

"If we already have plans in Seattle then we can swing by, but I don't want to go to Seattle just for a doctor's appointment."

He had just given me my way to make this appointment easier. I knew seeing doctors was stressful for him. I knew that it brought up the trauma of the many times we had physically forced him to appointments. Countless times he had told me he was never going to another doctor, again. Yet, here he was calmly telling me what would work, and I was very much aware of the difference. This was progress! I scheduled the appointment with Dr. Gbedawo and then made a date with Nana to meet for lunch. We now had plans to go to Seattle and would *swing by* the office afterwards.

It was a beautiful sunny day in Seattle as we walked from Nana's house to one of her favorite local restaurants near Greenlake. We were seated at a table outside under a sun umbrella. We enjoyed a lovely lunch together. Hans ate fish and chips and said it was one of the best he'd had. Walking back to Nana's home, I watched the two of them talking together in the warm afternoon sun. Nana had been there for Hans on such a deep and consistent level. She had been on her own journey of healing the previous year as her body overcame cancer. And yet, she had been a consistent loving presence in his life daily as he had worked on his own healing. I was in awe of their determination to be well. I felt such appreciation for their courage and their unwavering belief in the human body. The human spirit is a beautiful and precious thing, and on that short walk I felt humbled, witnessing these two magnificent beings that I was blessed to have in my life.

Hans and I thanked Nana for meeting us for lunch and said our goodbyes. We drove the 20 minutes to Vital Kids Medicine, and it was a surreal experience for me. The last time we had driven to this office, Hans was fighting for his life as a terrified and combative little boy. Today, he was a typical teenager. His voice was changing, he was developing acne, and he was nearly as tall as me. He'd rather not go see Dr. Gbedawo, but he *chose* to go with me without incident.

We found her office and sat quietly in the waiting room. When Dr. Gbedawo came out to greet us, I hugged her. It's hard to explain the feelings I had developed for this doctor. For me, this was the woman who had saved my son from this horrible illness. She will forever be my champion. She never gave up on us, and I was so happy she got to see the young man Hans was becoming. We sat with her and answered her questions. I updated her on the supplements Hans was taking, the progress that we had seen, and I requested a refill for the Ketotifen and LDN cream as well as a prescription for antibiotics, specifically Augmentin. We had seen the best results with Augmentin when we had tried antibiotics initially. She was hesitant to prescribe the antibiotics without doing a nasal swab. Hans adamantly refused one. I shared the reports I had heard on parent support group calls with doctors at the Stanford PANS clinic and the University of Missouri on the success with antibiotics to address symptoms. I shared the story of the boy similar to Hans who was now doing better with antibiotics. I reminded her of his MRI presentation and the continued difficulty Hans had had with breathing and allergies. I asked her if we could, please, just do a 4 week trial. She finally agreed and asked us to schedule a follow up visit in a month to see how things were progressing. I was hopeful that this would be what got us past this state of "chronic static." I thanked her, then Hans and I left to drive the hour and a half home.

The next day, I picked up the antibiotic and included it with Hans's daily supplements, but he refused to take it.

"It's huge, and I don't really know what it is or what it will do for me," he calmly told me as he took it out of the glass and put it on the table. I explained to him that we were trying it to see if it could help him feel 100% better and that he might be fighting some infection in his nasal passages. For the next several days, I offered it to him, and every time he refused politely. On the third day, Arnold asked me why I didn't just smash it up and put it in a veggie cap since I was already putting the CBD oil in a veggie cap. Brilliant! I mashed it up, and it took three veggie caps to collect all the powder from the pill. Hans took these without even noticing.

Two days later, I was having an essential oil DIY at our home, and Hans came down and hung out for a while, engaging in conversation with one of the neighbor ladies. Arnold and I were both amazed at this. Several days later, when I had another group over, one of the moms brought her twin boys who were Andre's age, and they all played for a while on the Xbox before going to the park to play laser tag. Again, Arnold and I were astounded. I was already so grateful that I could have people in our home as there had previously been the days when we could barely have family in our home. And now, *this*! We were noticing the subtle changes, and we hoped that this time the antibiotic might just be what his body needed to kick him over the edge into full recovery. We'd worked so hard to help his body heal, and if he could continue this healing, than the possibility of returning to school in the fall was real. For now, we would be content to enjoy a summer that felt more normal than we'd had in years.

Grandma drove her trailer up from California to celebrate several graduations and to do some camping with us and extended family. Our first camping stint was just north of us at Birch Bay State Park. We scored a couple of great spots next to each other under the tall pine trees and close to the trail to the beach. As we were setting up camp, Hans and Andre headed to the beach. An hour later, they returned, excited with their discoveries.

"There are literally hundreds, if not thousands, of little crabs along the shore," Hans told us excitedly.

"The tide's way out, Mom, you have to come see it," Andre interjected.

"It sounds awesome! Help Grandma get the rest of the dog fencing up, and then we can all go and bring the dogs." The boys set up the last of the fencing, and I relished in this moment, smiling as we all worked together to set up our spot. We walked to the beach together, and the boys showed us the baby crabs and hermit crabs, turning over rocks and digging in the sand. The dogs splashed in the water and chased each other up and down the beach. After a bit, Grandma and I sat on a large drift log. The sun, in a cloudless blue sky, was warming us as a gentle breeze kept it from being too hot.

"You look like a normal family," Grandma offered with a smile and put her arm around my shoulders.

"Yes, I feel that. It's hard to believe that we're finally at this place. And I have to tell you that I can't completely believe that it's over. It crushed me last year when I believed it was over and it wasn't. I won't let that happen to me, again. I will live these moments deeply with gratitude, but there will always be caution." I watched Hans pick up little crabs, the sand between his toes, and I knew that this was huge. I was also so happy for Andre to be enjoying time with his brother. The smell of the salt air, the warm sun, the beauty of the Pacific Northwest, all of this enveloped me, and I felt so blessed. Time had certainly been an ally. I was filled with hope. I was filled with gratitude. I was filled with determination. I knew how hard and long this journey of healing had been for all of us. We had had to fight for diagnosis, for treatment, for payment, and it had been challenging. But we had persevered, and I was forever changed.

I was now determined to be an advocate for others so they wouldn't have to work so hard to get their children what they needed. I felt a deep obligation to use my training, knowledge, skills, and credentials to help others. I had learned, through my connections with other mothers, that there were politics surrounding this illness. There were doctors with egos who didn't share their research. There was a lack of funding, so sometimes research went unpublished. There were non-believers who thought this illness was purely psychiatric. There were traditional approaches to healing, and there were alternative approaches to healing. There were people with strong opinions and beliefs. It frustrated me that it fell on the parents to figure out what was wrong with their child, to get proper treatment, and to have to pay tens of thousands of dollars for that treatment.

I was so impressed with the parents who had come before me, who had been a voice for change. They had put together wonderful resources to help families navigate the medical and insurance systems. They were getting legislation passed that mandated education and awareness, which required insurance to cover treatment, and was making PANDAS/PANS/AE familiar in some of our states. They had shared their stories, their pictures, their videos, and their courage with others to make a difference. I wanted to be a part of that much-needed change.

Later that night, we were sitting around a roaring campfire waiting for the coals to get just right so we could roast marshmallows. The dogs were worn out, lying on the ground at our feet. Andre was snuggled up on my lap; Hans sitting next to us on the picnic bench. I leaned back and looked up at the night sky. It was late, but the sky still had that dusk light so typical of the Pacific Northwest summer nights. Hans pointed out the first star, and I made a wish. I wished for complete healing, for Hans to go to school in the fall, and for this nightmare to be over. And then I made a promise. I was going to share our story. I was going to write a book. I was going to do my part to make this journey easier for others. I looked at my children, and I felt complete.

PART 4

Resources:
The Road Map

"Sometimes, reaching out and taking someone's hand is the beginning of a journey. At other times, it is allowing another to take yours."

Vera Nazarian,
The Perpetual Calendar of Inspiration

CHAPTER TWENTY NINE

REFLECTIONS

These past four years have been such a roller coaster for our family. The presentation of symptoms that were beyond anything I had ever experienced in my twenty years of working with children with challenging behaviors brought me to my knees in fear, grief, and uncertainty. What we were first told didn't make sense to me as a mother or as a professional. Through research, we found our pathway to understanding, to diagnosis, and to treatment. I know that the decisions we have made along the way won't resonate with some. I know that there are some who still consider this illness to be controversial. I am so grateful to the pioneers who forged a path making it easier for us to even have this conversation. I have deep respect for the scientists, clinical researchers, and providers who are doing everything they can to help our children heal, even in the face of opposition. I am inspired by the parents who raise their voices in advocacy. And I am forever grateful for my family and the friends who stood by our side with understanding, support, guidance, and who witnessed what we were going through with compassion and an offer to assist in any way possible. Not everyone could find their way to do that, and that is understandable. This illness can be isolating, and those who showed up for us helped us get through the nightmare.

I am not a doctor, a medical provider, a researcher, or a psychiatrist. I am a mother. It took courage to advocate for my child, to disagree with the professionals, and to seek out new providers. It took determination at other times to get treatments paid for. It took the love and support of friends and family to get through the crisis. I can't imagine what it would be like to go through this experience without the training, background, experience, support, and love we have had. It is my hope that, by sharing our story, we will help raise awareness so that children don't continue to go misdiagnosed or undiagnosed. It is my vision that our story, coupled with the thousands of other stories that are coming to light, will spur those with the means to finance research so better diagnostics and treatment options become available. It is my belief that traditional medicine, functional medicine, allopathic medicine, homeopathic medicine, and anything else I've missed can truly be complementary, comprehensive, and cooperative so families can find the best path of healing for their children. I am a mother sharing our story. Take from it what resonates with you to aid you on your own journey. Trust your intuition, and never give up on healing. Always believe.

CHAPTER THIRTY
NEW BEGINNINGS

s I finish the writing of this book, I have returned from a wonderful conference on the Common Threads of Post Infectious Autoimmune Diseases of the Brain at Columbia University put on by the PANDAS Network. I have listened to doctors and scientists from around the world share their research and their findings as they continue to work to save children's lives. I have so much hope that real change is coming. I know that money is needed to continue the research, particularly in the face of naysayer doctors who criticize without doing any research of their own, beholden to the big pharmaceutical companies that fund their work. However, there are also doctors who look at the research to date and conclude that PANDAS/PANS/AE is a distinct clinical entity and that it is a useful research field that could open up new insights into the pathogenesis of OCD and other conditions, even in adults. I am aware that legislation is needed to ensure that families get proper diagnosis, effective treatment, and that insurance will cover the costs so that all children can have deep healing. I believe that the regional groups of courageous parents who are fighting for the same thing will come together collectively as one unified voice. I know that all of this can feel overwhelming. But it must be done. It will be done.

Hans did not return to his brick and mortar school for his 8th grade year. After weeks of Exposure Response Therapy, he was able to sit in the car, working on his school assignments, without having a stress response. We discussed what it would take to walk into the building, go into his classroom, sit down, and do the work there. I told him I would push through all of this if it was what he really wanted. He was very clear with me that he wanted nothing to do with traditional schooling. He felt that it was a waste of his time to learn things he had already learned. He wanted to be learning about string theory and why the tides work the way they do. He wanted the freedom to learn what interested him. Arnold and I agreed that he could continue his learning at home for his 8th grade year. We also decided that Hans would attend an accredited online high school as part of his preparation to take the GED test when he turns 16, if that is what he chooses. We decided this was a better plan than just doing a GED prep program, in case he changed his mind. He would be earning credits towards graduation should he decide not to sit for the GED and instead pursue a high school diploma.

I wasn't crushed by these decisions. With the stress of having to "go to school" completely removed, Hans has shown complete healing. We have had regular visits with family in Seattle, spending the night when we decide to. We have traveled in the RV, and we even flew to Mexico for a wonderful family get together over the Thanksgiving holiday. We play games at home and go to movies. We have dinner parties with friends in our home or theirs. We are a functioning family.

I am able to be away from home for extended trips, again. I am getting my life back. I am, however, forever changed. I don't take things for granted. I stop to appreciate the beauty around me. I relish the time we spend together. When I become frustrated, I ask myself, *is this really worth being upset about?* It's usually not, and I try to look for the joy in every moment, instead. I am laughing more often and I love more deeply. I have learned that everything we experience is full of wonder. Even when it feels like a great weight, the experience itself is profound and there is something in it for us. I believe that when we open ourselves to what is possible, incredible things happen. My life path has been altered by an illness that is still being debated. But I have my son back. I have my family back. I have my own life, richer because of all of it. I believe in the power that each of us has to live this life fully and abundantly when we view our experiences with gratitude. That shift changes everything. I am stronger. I am wiser. I am courageous. I am.

CHAPTER THIRTY ONE

THE ROAD MAP

I spent countless hours, as most parents have, combing the internet for any information I could find on this illness. I was acutely aware, during those first few months, that if I was going to get help, I needed to know what to ask for. I searched websites, read research, and watched youTube videos of doctors presenting at conferences or archived on hospital and university sites. Through this search for information, I gathered my diagnostic requests and my questions about treatment options that I would seek as I worked my way to putting together our team of providers.

The outline below is intended to recap the steps we took to get our son properly diagnosed and to list the treatments we chose. It is not intended as a guide to follow, as each child is different. In order to determine what options are best for your child, consult with a professional who is knowledgeable about PANDAS/PANS/AE. If your Primary Care Physician is open to the diagnosis, it is possible to have your PCP run diagnostics and, through consultation with an expert, order treatments for insurance purposes and ease of treatment on the child as we did. You will decide what is best for your child and your family. I share this information to hopefully make your decision process a little easier.

1) Identify symptoms (see Appendix A)

2) Complete symptom scales (see Appendix B)

   Tip: We had two people who knew our child well complete these scales independently of each other to ensure validity; in our case, it was the parents.

3) Get immunological workup done (see Appendix C)

   Tip: We requested this workup be done by our Primary Care Physician.

4) Find an expert (see Appendix D)

   Tip: We sought out a leading physician as well as a local knowledgeable physician. Ultimately, it was our local physician who provided most of our care, collaborating with our PCP to order treatments closer to home.

   Tip: PANDAS Network and PANDAS Physicians Network list leading providers and providers by state. If you are looking for someone in your area, call around and ask questions to determine if they really know what they are doing. They should know more than you do!

5) Implement a treatment plan (see Appendix E)

   We chose a complementary treatment plan that included western medicine, natural remedies, homeopathic remedies, essential oils, and environmental and dietary changes. Seek treatment that fits your beliefs about healing, but don't discount all the options. You may have to try something you wouldn't normally be comfortable utilizing. Ultimately, you want to eradicate infection, reduce inflammation, and reboot the immune system.

"It is good to have an end to journey toward; but it is the journey that matters, in the end."

Ursula K. LeGuin,
The Left Hand of Darkness

APPENDIX A

SYMPTOMS

I first found a list of symptoms on the IOCDF website when I was researching OCD. That list and the diagnostic label led us to the PANDAS Network website. You can read their text in its entirety at those sites, but I've included the current list of symptoms here. "Symptom presentation and severity can vary from child to child. It can also vary in each exacerbation. Not all (symptoms) need to be present. Not all possible symptoms are listed."[1] Symptom presentation depends on which part of the brain is inflamed and to what extent.

OCD (OBSESSIVE/COMPULSIVE DISORDER) - Acute sudden onset of OCD. See the PANDAS Network website to read *OCD in a Young Child* for a description of how OCD might present itself. OCD is not only obsessive hand washing or ordering! (http://www.pandasnetwork.org/your-story/ocd-in-a-young-child/)

RESTRICTIVE EATING - Restrictive eating includes selective eating to full-out food refusal. There can be a variety of reasons why the child experiences this, including contamination fears, sensory sensitivities, trouble swallowing, fear of vomiting or weight gain, and more. If restrictive eating is resulting in severe weight loss, call your provider immediately.

TICS - Tics can be gross motor tics, such as head rolling or chorea movements, or they can be subtler tics such as eye stretching or throat clearing.

ANXIETY - Anxiety may be generalized or separation anxiety.

EMOTIONAL LABILITY - Emotional lability includes not being able to control one's emotional response. It may include uncontrollable crying or laughing. This is a neurological symptom.

DEPRESSION

IRRITABILITY AND AGGRESSION

BEHAVIORAL REGRESSION - Behavioral regression may include baby talk.

DEVELOPMENTAL REGRESSION

DETERIORATION IN SCHOOL PERFORMANCE - This may include deterioration in math skills, inability to concentrate, difficulty retaining information, and school refusal. School performance can also be a result of another contributing symptom, such as OCD or severe separation anxiety.

CHANGES IN HANDWRITING - Changes may include margin drifts and illegibility.

SENSORY SENSITIVITIES - This may include being sensitive to touch, sounds, and noise. Simple touches may feel like they are hurting. One may not be able to stand the way socks feel or the texture or temperature of certain foods. Sensory processing problems can also cause difficulty in finding an item when it is among a vast selection of items. For example, a child may have a hard time finding a shirt in a full dresser or finding words in a word search.

SOMATIC SIGNS - This may include sleeping difficulties, enuresis, frequent urination, and bed wetting.

HYPERACTIVITY

CHOREIFORM MOVEMENTS - See the PANDAS Network website for a video example of Choreiform Movements. (http://www.pandasnetwork.org/understanding-pandaspans/symptoms/)

SEVERE SEPARATION ANXIETY

HALLUCINATIONS - This may include both visual and auditory hallucinations.

FIGHT OR FLIGHT RESPONSE

DILATED PUPILS

URINARY PROBLEMS

http://pandasnetwork.org/

https://kids.iocdf.org/what-is-ocd/pandas/

APPENDIX B

SYMPTOM SCALES

We completed these symptom scales and brought them with us to our appointment with our PCP. Specifically, the PANDAS Symptoms Scale was most beneficial as we filled it out independently of each other and had only a 2 point variance between us and an 85 point difference between pre-onset and post-onset. This information was valid and significant, supporting our request for diagnostics.

In addition to the symptom scales listed here, your PCP may ask you to complete an anxiety symptoms checklist and a depression symptoms checklist as some of the symptoms on both of these may be presenting.

PANDAS/PANS Symptoms Scale

OCD Scale – Children's Yale-Brown Obsessive Compulsive Scale

Tic Scale – Yale Global Tic Severity Scale

http://pandasnetwork.org/

APPENDIX C
IMMUNOLOGICAL WORKUP

I did my research on the immunological workup that would help us understand what was going on in our child's body and brought that information to our PCP, requesting that the lab work and MRI be done. Over time, we did additional lab work to get at underlying issues affecting our child's immune response, including genetic testing. Work with your PCP and PANDAS/PANS/AE provider to get at root causes and triggering pathogens.

Below is a list of the first blood workup we requested. We did not do the Cunningham Panel™ at our initial visit because we didn't know about it. The purpose of the Cunningham Panel™ is to assist physicians in diagnosing infection-induced autoimmune neuropsychiatric disorders. The panel measures the level of circulating antibodies directed against antigens concentrated in the brain, and measures the ability of these, and other autoantibodies, to increase the activity of an enzyme (CaMKII) that upregulates neurotransmitters in the brain. [1] We did run this panel later, after we had been treating for five months with antibiotics. Hans's numbers were elevated, but not crazy high. We didn't have a baseline to compare to. It would have been interesting to have run this lab with our diagnostic blood work and then again after each treatment. We also didn't do an EEG or PET scan. We wouldn't have been able to do the EEG without sedation which defeats the purpose, and we didn't know to ask for a PET Scan at the time. There has been some research indicating that a PET scan could be a good diagnostic tool.[2] It provides information on how the basal ganglia are functioning, not just anatomical information as an MRI does. I am not sure that we would have done the PET scan, however, because of the radioactive liquid injected. I am hopeful that a more sensitive MRI will be coming soon. At the time of the writing of this book, diagnostic guidelines have been published in the Journal of Child and Adolescent Psychopharmacology, February 2015.[3] These may also be useful for you and your provider.

Strep - ASO, Anti-DNase B Titer, Streptozyme

Other Infections - Mycoplasma Pneumonia, Lyme (request the Igenex test), staph, H1N1, Epstein Barr Virus, Herpes Simplex Virus

ANA Test (Antinuclear Antibody Test) - This test measures the presence of autoantibodies

CD4 - This test measures, generally, an over-reactive immune response

IgG - Subclass 1, 2, 3, 4 for total immunoglobulin levels

IgA and IgM

http://pandasnetwork.org/

APPENDIX D

RESOURCES

This is not an exhaustive list. These are the resources that I found to be most helpful in our journey of healing. I do not get any monetary benefit from making these recommendations.

PANDAS/PANS/AE

PANDAS Network – information on diagnosis, treatment, providers, support groups, help with school, and more. http://www.pandasnetwork.org/

PANDAS Physician Network – information for providers and parents on diagnosis and treatment options. https://www.pandasppn.org/

National Institute of Mental Health – history and information on PANDAS and PANS.

https://www.nimh.nih.gov/labs-at-nimh/research-areas/clinics-and-labs/pdnb/web.shtml

Moleculera Labs – information on PANDAS and PANS, informational videos, Cunningham panel for assisting with diagnosis.

http://www.moleculeralabs.com/pans-pandas-diagnosis-treatment/

IOCDF – International OCD Foundation, information on OCD in adults and children, information on PANDAS and PANS, treatment options for OCD, and list of preferred providers. https://kids.iocdf.org/what-is-ocd/pandas/

ACN Latitudes: Association for Comprehensive Neurotherapy – information on a variety of neurological symptoms with diagnostic and treatment discussions, broad forum in each category. https://latitudes.org/category/conditions/pandas-pans/

Advocacy

Beth Maloney – author of *Saving Sammy* and *Childhood Interrupted*, toolkit for diagnosis and treatment guidance, legal advocacy.

http://bethalisonmaloney.com/

CABDA – Children's Autoimmune Brain Disorder Association, supporting families in Texas. https://cabdatexas.org/

MPPPA – Midwest PANDAS/PANS Parent Association, supporting families in the Midwest. http://www.midwestpandas.com/get-help/

NEPPA – New England PANS/PANDAS Association, supporting families in the Northeast. http://www.nepans.org/

PN – PANDAS Network, supporting families worldwide. http://www.pandasnetwork.org/

PAS – PANDAS/PANS Advocacy & Support, supporting families nationwide. http://www.pas.care/

PRAI – Pediatric Research and Advocacy Initiative, supporting families in North Carolina and Virginia. https://praikids.org/

SEPPA – Southeastern PANS/PANDAS Association, supporting families in the Southeast. https://www.sepans.org/

Health Coaching/Counseling/Teaching

Healthy Family Formula – education and support based on functional health and holistic care principles, addresses overall health as well as chronic conditions.

http://healthyfamilyformula.com/

Parenting That Heals – education and support based on neuroscience supporting the powerful healing tool of the parents' relationship with their child.

http://www.drsandygluckman.com/parenting-that-heals.html

Teaching That Heals the Brain – information and tools based on neuroscience for educators at all levels supporting students who are neurotypical, special needs, or gifted.

http://www.teachingthatheals.com/teaching-that-heals-the-brain.html

Ross Greene – education and support with children who present with challenging behaviors. http://drrossgreene.com/

Right Response – education in de-escalation skills. http://rightresponse.org/de-escalation-skills

APPENDIX E

TREATMENT OPTIONS

At the time of the writing of this book, the current understanding is that treatment is three-pronged; eradicate infection, reduce inflammation, and reboot the immune system. I have listed research-based treatment options as well as included the complementary treatment options we chose. This is not intended as a guide. Work with a professional who understands PANDAS/PANS/AE. The PANDAS Network site has guidelines that can assist your decision making, as well, and the PANDAS Physicians Network site is a great resource for your provider. Treatment guidelines have been published in the Journal of Child and Adolescent Psychology, July, 2017. This may be a helpful guide to you and your provider in determining best treatment options to consider.

Eradicate Infection

Antibiotics – Your child may need more than the standard 10-day course. You may also need to use several different antibiotics over a period of time. Many parents choose to use prophylactic antibiotics.

Essential oils – We chose to use essential oils due to their ability to cross the biofilm of the cell wall to get at infection.

[1] Specifically, we used Frankincense, Oregano, Thyme, Melaleuca, OnGuard, and Lemon. Other essential oils to consider are Manuka and Rosemary.

Homeopathy – We chose to use streptococcinum 30C.

Supplements – We chose to use supplements that support the immune system. We worked with our Naturopath to identify deficiencies and addressed those individually. We also worked with an intuitive healer to fine tune dosage and brand of supplements.

Reduce Inflammation

NSAID – We used ibuprofen to address the headaches and the inflammation in the joints.

Steroid burst – We used a 5-day course of prednisone with a taper to address inflammation in the brain.

Essential oils – We chose to use essential oils for long-term treatment of inflammation.[2] Specifically, Frankincense has anti-inflammatory properties and can cross the blood brain barrier.[3]

Homeopathy – We chose to use belladonna for headaches and inflammation.

Supplements – We chose to use turmeric and CBD oil for their anti-inflammatory properties.

Dietary and lifestyle changes – We made a lot of dietary and lifestyle changes, eliminating toxins from our home, eating as much "real" foods as possible, reducing gluten and casein, and eating organic and non-GMO foods. Our family's genetic make-up does not indicate gluten or casein sensitivity, but there's enough evidence to show that high gluten and casein diets are inflammatory.[4] We replaced anything that had any chemicals in it with chemical-free products or made our own using essential oils. I was amazed at how easy that was to do.

Reboot the Immune System

IVIG – Intravenous Immunoglobulin was the clincher for us. We followed the guidelines as they are laid out on the PANDAS Physicians Network site. You may need to have a specialist, such as a neurologist or immunologist, order the IVIG for insurance purposes. You may also ask your provider to consider using the following codes to order the IVIG for insurance purposes: IVIG – 96365 & 96366 Billing and diagnosis ICD 9 code (autoimmune disease 279.49) (obsessive compulsive disorder 300.3) (generalized anxiety disorder 300.2) ICD 10 code M35.9

Essential oils – We chose to use essential oils that have immune boosting properties.[5] Specifically we chose Frankincense, Oregano, Thyme, Melaleuca, Lemon, and On Guard.

Supplements – We chose to support the immune system with supplements tailored to address specific deficiencies. We consider supplements, essential oils, and clean living the "grease on the wheel" once we "got the cog out".

Plasmapheresis – We did not need to use this treatment, but there are cases where this treatment has been shown to be helpful. Essentially, the blood is taken out of the body, washed, and put back in the body, sometimes along with IVIG.

Low Dose Naltrexone – We chose to support the immune system with LDN cream applied nightly and then switched to pills when he was consistently taking them again.

APPENDIX F

OVERTURNING INSURANCE DENIAL

If your insurance denies your medical treatments, don't accept no. You can work with an ombudsman or any other customer support representative with your insurance company. When you find someone who is helpful, get their name and direct contact number so you can stay connected with that person. Your PCP can request a peer-to-peer review. Provide your PCP with information supporting the treatment being ordered, don't expect your PCP to do all the research themselves for the peer-to-peer review. It is a lot of work and they are not as invested as you are in your child. If the peer-to-peer is denied, file your own claim to overturn the denial. Provide relevant treatment that you have already used, with a brief explanation of how it affected or did not affect your child. Provide a brief explanation of why the treatment you are requesting would benefit your child. Cite your reasons. Below is an example of an email I sent when refuting the original denial for IVIG treatment.

To Whom It May Concern (or name of a person is even better):

I am writing on behalf of my son/daughter, (name), who was ordered Intravenous Immunoglobulin by Dr. (name). My child's treatment was recently denied, and I am asking that you overturn this decision.

My child has had the following treatments with some improvement, but he/she has not yet returned to baseline.

Antibiotics – some relief from most severe symptoms

https://www.pandasppn.org/
treatment-of-panspandas-with-antibiotics/

Steroid bursts – immediate relief from most severe symptoms, but not long lasting

https://www.pandasppn.org/ppn-steroid-therapy-use/

In addition to these treatments we have also made many dietary changes and removed toxins that may be a trigger from our home environment.

At this time, it is clear that IVIG is our next course of action, as recommended by all the doctors on our medical team. There is a growing body of research that strongly supports IVIG for children with Autoimmune Encephalitis, particularly when they have been responsive to steroids.

https://www.pandasppn.org/ivig/

https://www.nimh.nih.gov/labs-at-nimh/research-areas/clinics-and-labs/pdnb/web.shtml

http://online.liebertpub.com/doi/pdfplus/10.1089/cap.2014.0067

My son/daughter deserves access to a treatment that could potentially save him/her from being committed to a lifetime of mental illness. Please overturn the denial and allow my child a chance at a healthy life and a return to his/her once normal development.

Sincerely,

Your Name

NOTES

FOREWORD

1. Dileepan, T., et al. (2016). Group A Streptococcus intranasal infection promotes CNS infiltration by streptococcal-specific Th17 cells. *The Journal of Clinical Investigation.* *126*(1), pp. 303-317.

   Weintraub, P. (2017, April). Hidden invaders: Infections can trigger immune attacks on kids' brains, provoking devastating psychiatric disorders. *Discover Magazine,* pp. 50-55.

   Louveau, A., et al. (2015). Structural and functional features of central nervous system lymphatic vessels. *Nature: International Journal of Science. 523,* pp. 337-341.

   Kipnis, J. (2018, August). The Seventh Sense. *Scientific American,* pp. 28-35.

2. Swedo, S.E., et al. (1998). Pediatric autoimmune neuropsychiatric disorders associated with streptococcal infections: Clinical description of the first 50 cases. *The American Journal of Psychiatry. 155*(2), pp. 264-271.

3. Cox, C.J., et al. (2015). Antineuronal antibodies in a heterogeneous group of youth and young adults with tics

and obsessive-compulsive disorder. *Journal of Child and Adolescent Psychopharmacology. 25*(1), pp. 76-85.

Ben-Pazi, H. Stoner, J.A. Cunningham, M.W. et al. (2013, September 20). *Dopamine Receptor Autoantibodies Correlate with Symptoms in Sydenham's Chorea.* Retrieved from https://journals.plos.org/plosone/article?id=10.1371/journal.pone.0073516

4. Chang, K. Koplewicz, H.S. Steingard, R. (2015). Special issue on pediatric acute-onset neuropsychiatric syndrome. *Journal of Child and Adolescent Psychopharmacology. 25*(1), pp. 1-2.

Swedo, S. Frankovich, J. Murphy, T.K. (2017) Overview of treatment of pediatric acute-onset neuropsychiatric syndrome. *Journal of Child and Adolescent Psychopharmacology. 27*(7), pp. 562-565.

5. "In 2010, cases of acute encephalitis in the U.S. (240,000 cases) was reviewed for outcome and etiology. More than 50% of encephalitis cases typically remain without an identified etiology, posing additional challenges in delivering prognosis and treatment." George, B.P. & Schneider, E.B. (2014, September 5). *Encephalitis hospitalization rates and inpatient mortality in the United States.* Retrieved from https://journals.plos.org/plosone/article?id=10.1371/journal.pone.0104169

6. "The cost of hospitalization in the United States in 2010 for encephalitis (2 billion U.S. dollars) illustrates its severe disease burden. Prior epidemiology studies of encephalitis have primarily focused on infectious causes. Autoimmune encephalitis is increasingly recognized as a common treatable cause of encephalitis, yet population-based studies of its incidence and prevalence are lacking...the detection of autoimmune encephalitis is likely to increase over time,

and the prevalence and incidence in our study are likely underestimated. Other contributors to underrepresentation may include the lack of widespread recognition of what we now recognize as classic syndromes (eg, neuropsychiatric, anti-NMDAR) ...and the likelihood of further neural autoantibodies being discovered in the future (is evident)." (emphasis added) Divyanshu, D. et al. (2018, January 2). *Autoimmune encephalitis epidemiology and a comparison to infectious encephalitis.* Retrieved from https://onlinelibrary. wiley.com/doi/abs/10.1002/ana.25131

7. Cullen, A.E. et al. (2018, June 16). *Associations between non-neurological autoimmune disorders and psychosis: A meta-analysis.* Retrieved from https://www.biological-psychiatryjournal.com/article/S0006-3223(18)31630-5/abstract

8. Ponukollu, M. et al. (2015, April 28). *Neuropsychiatric manifestations of Sydenham's chorea: a systematic review.* Retrieved from https://onlinelibrary.wiley.com/doi/abs/10.1111/dmcn.12786

9. Gilbert, D.L et al. (2018). A Pediatric Neurology Perspective on Pediatric Autoimmune Neuropsychiatric Disorder Associated with Streptococcal Infection and Pediatric Acute-Onset Neuropsychiatric Syndrome. *The Journal of Pediatrics, 199,* pp. 243-251.

AUTHOR'S NOTE

1. Gilbert, D.L et al. (2018). A Pediatric Neurology Perspective on Pediatric Autoimmune Neuropsychiatric Disorder Associated with Streptococcal Infection and Pediatric Acute-Onset Neuropsychiatric Syndrome. *The Journal of Pediatrics, 199,* pp. 243-251.

Insel, T. (2013, March 26). *Post by former NIMH director Thomas Insel: From paresis to PANDAS and PANS.* Retrieved from https://www.nimh.nih.gov/about/directors/thomas-insel/blog/2012/from-paresis-to-pandas-and-pans.shtml

2. Lanciego, J.L. et al. (2012, December 12). *Functional neuroanatomy of the basal ganglia.* Retrieved from https://www.ncbi.nlm.nih.gov/pmc/articles/PMC3543080/

3. Naijar,S. et al. (2013, April 1). *Neuroinflammation and psychiatric illness.* Retrieved from https://www.ncbi.nlm.nih.gov/pmc/articles/PMC3626880/

Wallis, J. (2012). Looking Back: This Fascinating and Fatal Disease. *The British Psychological Society, 25,* pp. 790-791.

4. Barney, J. (2016, March 21). *They'll have to rewrite the textbooks.* Retrieved from https://news.virginia.edu/illimitable/discovery/theyll-have-rewrite-textbooks

Collins, F. (2017, October 17). *New imaging approach reveal lymph system in brain.* Retrieved from https://directorsblog.nih.gov/2017/10/17/new-imaging-approach-reveals-lymph-system-in-brain/

CHAPTER THREE – THE FLU

1. Mitchell, D. (nd). *Why do waldorf schools celebrate Michaelmas?* Retrieved from https://www.waldorflibrary.org/images/stories/articles/WJP15_mitchell.pdf

CHAPTER FOUR - DIS-EASE

1. Greene, R. (2014) *The Explosive Child: A New Approach for Understanding and Parenting Easily Frustrated, Chronically Inflexible Children.* New York, NY:Harper Collins.

2. Silver, L (1998) *The Misunderstood Child: Understanding and Coping with Your Child's Learning Disabilities.* New York, NY:Random House Inc.

3. Cain, S. (2013) *Quiet: The Power of Introverts in a World That Can't Stop Talking.* New York, NY:Random House Inc.

4. Tyson, P. (2015, January 1). *Monkey Do, Monkey See.* Retrieved from http://www.pbs.org/wgbh/nova/body/glaser-monkey.html

CHAPTER SIX - IT'S HAPPENING

1. (2018). *Spiritual response therapy: Spiritual restructuring.* Retrieved from https://spiritualresponse.com/srt-class-information/

2. Todeschi, K.J. (n.d.). *Akashic records – the book of life.* Retrieved from https://www.edgarcayce.org/the-readings/akashic-records/

3. (2018, May 8) *What are the differences in evaluations done by school psychologists, clinical psychologists, and neuropsychologists?* Retrieved from http://www.bgcenter.com/bgqa/assessment1.htm

CHAPTER SEVEN - LAS FLORES RANCH

1. Extra Classic: http://extraclassic.blogspot.com/

2. The Donkeys: http://www.donkeysongs.com/

CHAPTER NINE – I WANT RESOURCES

1. Star, K. (2018, July 28). *What you need to know about Celexa for anxiety disorders.* Retrieved fromhttps://www.verywell-mind.com/faqs-about-celexa-for-panic-disorder-2584294

CHAPTER TEN – WHAT'S HAPPENING?

1. The Understood Team. (2017, September 29). *Video: What happens in an occupational therapy evaluation?* Retrieved from https://www.understood.org/en/learn-ing-attention-issues/treatments-approaches/therapies/ot-evaluation

2. Ehmke, R. (n.d.). *What should an evaluation for autism look like?* Retrieved from https://childmind.org/article/what-should-evaluation-autism-look-like/

3. Good Therapy. (2016, May 9) *Family Constellations.* Retrieved from https://www.goodtherapy.org/learn-about-therapy/types/family-constellations

4. NAMI: National Alliance on Mental Illness. Retrieved from https://www.nami.org/

CHAPTER THIRTEEN – COULD THIS BE PANS?

1. Framingham, J. (2016). What is Psychological Assessment?. *Psych Central.* Retrieved from https://psychcentral.com/lib/what-is-psychological-assessment/autoimmunity

2. MedicineNet (2016, May 13). *Medical definition of auto-immunity.* Retrieved from https://www.medicinenet.com/script/main/art.asp?articlekey=18985

CHAPTER FOURTEEN – MY ANGELS

1. Swedo, S. et al. (2012, February 2). *From research sub-group to clinical syndrome: Modifying the PANDAS criteria to describe PANS (Pediatric Acute-onset Neuropsychiatric Syndrome)*. Retrieved from https://www.omicsonline.org/from-research-subgroup-to-clinical-syndrome-modify-ing-the-pandas-criteria-to-describe-pans-pediatric-acute-onset-neuropsychiatric-syndrome-2161-0665.1000113.php?aid=4020

2. (2016). *What is autoimmune encephalitis (AE)?* Retrieved from https://aealliance.org/faq/#what-is-ae

3. Mahony, T. et al. (2017) Improvement of psychiatric symptoms in youth following resolution of sinusitis. *International Journal of Pediatric Otorhinolaryngology, (92)*, pp. 38-44.

4. Murphy, T. et al. (2006). Selective serotonin reuptake inhibitor-induced behavioral activation in the PANDAS subset. *Primary Psychiatry, (13)8*, 87-89.

5. LSCI: Life Space Crisis Intervention. Retrieved from https://www.lsci.org/

6. Cahalan, S. (2013). *Brain on fire: My month of madness.* New York, NY:Simon & Schuster Paperbacks.

7. Maloney, B. (2009). *Saving Sammy: A mother's fight to cure her son's OCD.* New York, NY:Crown Publishers.

8. Martin, B. (2018, April 4). *In-depth: Cognitive behavioral therapy.* Retrieved from https://psychcentral.com/lib/in-depth-cognitive-behavioral-therapy/

9. (2018). *About behavioral analysis.* Retrieved from https://www.bacb.com/about-behavior-analysis/

CHAPTER EIGHTEEN – FMLA

1. *Home/hospital instruction.* Retrieved from http://apps.leg. wa.gov/WAC/default.aspx?cite=392-172A-02100

CHAPTER NINETEEN – TRANSITION

1. Tovian, S. et al. (n. d.). *Stress effects on the body.* Retrieved from http://www.apa.org/helpcenter/stress-body.aspx

2. Legg, TJ. (2017, June 5) *The effects of stress on your body.* Retrieved from https://www.healthline.com/health/stress/ effects-on-body#

CHAPTER TWENTY – CALM IN THE MIDDLE OF THE STORM

1. Shannon, S. & Opila-Lehman, J. (2016). Effectiveness of cannabidiol oil for pediatric anxiety and insomnia as part of posttraumatic stress disorder: A case report. *The Permanent Journal, 20*(4), pp. 108-111.

   Lisbosa, S.F et. al. (2017). The endocannabinoid system and anxiety. *Vitamins and Hormones, 103*, pp. 193-279.

   Prakash, N. et. al. (2009). Cannabinoids as novel anti-inflammatory drugs. *Future Med Chem, 1*(7), pp. 1333-1349.

   Esposito, G. (2011). Cannabidiol reduces Aβ-induced neuroinflammation and promotes hippocampal neurogenesis through PPARγ involvement. *PLoS One, 6*(12).

   Gonzalez-Garcia, C. et. al. (2017). Mechanisms of action of cannabidiol in adoptively transferred experimental autoimmune encephalomyelitis. *Experimental Neurology, 298*(Pt A). pp. 57-67.

CHAPTER TWENTY ONE - HARDLY HOME SCHOOLING

1. Good, R.H. & Kaminski, R. A. (n.d.). *What are dibels?* Retrieved from https://dibels.org/dibels.html

2. (2017) *Resources for school staff.* Retrieved from http://www.pandasnetwork.org/research-resources/school/

3. (2018). *Intravenous Immunoglobulin (IVIG).* Retrieved from https://www.pandasppn.org/ivig/

4. Silvergleid, A.J. (2017, September 21). *Patient education: Intravenous immune globulin (IVIG) (Beyond the basics).* Retrieved from https://www.uptodate.com/contents/intravenous-immune-globulin-ivig-beyond-the-basics

5. March, J.S. & Mulle, K. (1998) *OCD in Children and Adolescents: A Cognitive-Behavioral Treatment Manual.* New York, NY: The Guilford Press.

CHAPTER TWENTY TWO - 911

1. Younger, J., Parkitny, L., & McLain, D. (2014). The use of low-dose naltrexone (LDN) as a novel anti-inflammatory treatment for chronic pain. *Clinical Rheumatology, 33*(4), pp. 451-459.

   Mercola. 2011, September 19. *Low-dose naltrexone (LDN): One of the RARE drugs that actually helps your body to heal itself.* Retrieved from https://articles.mercola.com/sites/articles/archive/2011/09/19/one-of-the-rare-drugs-that-actually-helps-your-body-to-heal-itself.aspx

   2018, June 1. *Low dose naltrexone.* Retrieved from http://www.lowdosenaltrexone.org/

2. (2018). *Healthy Family FormulaI.* Retrieved from https://healthyfamilyformula.com/

CHAPTER TWENTY THREE – THE FLOOD

1. (2017). *Sydenham Chorea.* Retrieved from https://rarediseases.org/rare-diseases/sydenham-chorea/

CHAPTER TWENTY SIX – LAYERS OF HEALING

1. Unknown. (2018). *23 and Me.* Retrieved from https://refer.23andme.com/s/ismck (the author may get a commission).

2. Genetics Home Reference. (2018, October 16). *What are single nucleotide polymorphisms (SNPs)?* Retrieved from https://ghr.nlm.nih.gov/primer/genomicresearch/snp

   Gray, I.C., Campbell, D.A., Spurr, N.K. (2000). Single nucleotide polymorphisms as tools in human genetics. *Human Molecular Genetics 9*(6), pp. 2403-2408.

3. Unknown. (2018). *DNA methylation.* Retrieved from https://www.whatisepigenetics.com/dna-methylation/

   Robertson, S. (2018, August 23). *What is DNA methylation?* Retrieved from http://www.news-medical.net/life-sciences/What-is-DNA-Methylation.aspx

4. Theoharides, T.C. (2012). *Research* Retrieved from http://www.mastcellmaster.com/research.php

   Molderings, G.J. et. al. (2016). Pharmacological treatment options for mast cell activation disease. *Naunyn Schmiedebergs Arch Pharmacology, 389,* pp. 671-694.

Kirshenbaum AS, Goff JP, Semere T, Foster B, Scott LM, Metcalfe DD. (1999). Demonstration that human mast cells arise from a progenitor cell population that is CD34(+), c-kit(+), and expresses aminopeptidase N (CD13). *Blood 94* (7), pp. 2333-2342.

5. Aroma Tools (2018) *Modern Essentials: A Contemporary Guide to the Therapeutic Use of Essential Oils.* Pleasant Grove, UT: Aroma Tools.

   Total Wellness Publishing (2018) *The Essential Life.* Pleasant Grove, UT: Total Wellness Publishing, LLC.

6. Chase, S.M. (2016). *Homeopathy.* Retrieved from https://homeopathyusa.org/homeopathic-medicine.html

CHAPTER TWENTY EIGHT – TIME IS AN ALLY

1. Gluckman, S. (2018). *Parenting that heals.* Retrieved from http://drsandygluckman.com/parenting-that-heals/

2. Gluckman, S. (2013) *Parents Take Charge.* North Charleston, SC: CreateSpace Independent Publishing Platform.

3. MIND Research Institute. (2018) *STMath.* Retrieved from https://www.stmath.com

CHAPTER THIRTY ONE – THE ROAD MAP

1. PANDAS Network. (2018). *Symptoms.* Retrieved from http://www.pandasnetwork.org/understanding-pandaspans/symptoms/

APPENDIX C - IMMUNOLOGICAL WORKUP

1. Moleculera Labs. (2018). *The Cunningham Panel Overview.* Retrieved from https://www.moleculeralabs.com/cunningham-panel-pandas-pans-testing/

2. Kumar, A., et al. (2014). Basal ganglia inflammation in children with neuropsychiatric symptoms. *The Journal of Nuclear Medicine, 55*(306).

3. Koplewicz, H.S. (2015). *Journal of Child and Adolescent Psychopharmacology, 25*(1).

APPENDIX E - TREATMENT OPTIONS

1. Nazzaro, F. et al. (2013). Effect of essential oils on pathogenic bacteria. *Pharmaceuticals, 6*(12). 1451-1474.

   Kavanaugh, N.L. & Ribbeck, K. (2012). Selected antimicrobial essential oils eradicate pseudomonus spp. and staphylococcus aureus biofilms. *Applied and Environmental Microbiology, 78*(11). 4057-4061.

2. Perez, S., et al. (2011). Anti-inflammatory activity of some essential oils. *Journal of Essential Oil Research, 23*(5). 38-44.

3. doTERRA. (2018). *Bioactivity of essential oils.* Retrieved from https://www.doterra.com/US/en/blog/science-safety-physiology-bioactivity-essential-oils

4. Vojdani, A. (2014). A potential link between environmental triggers and autoimmunity. *Autoimmune Diseases 2014.* Pp. 1-18.

5. Goldberg, J.G. (2011, June 9). *More than a scent: Essential oils aid the immune system.* Retrieved from https://www.huffpost.com/entry/essential-oils-health_b_868303

ABOUT THE AUTHOR

Heather Korbmacher's passion is to ensure that children's needs are met. An Author, Educator, Speaker, Coach, and Advocate, she earned a Master's degree in Exceptional Children, is a National Board Certified Teacher, and founder of Courageous Educational Services, LLC. With over 20 years of experience working with children with challenging behaviors, Heather utilizes her practical skills, training, and expertise to help professionals and parents support the children they care for. Heather's advocacy for families living with PANDAS/PANS/AE includes being a member of the PANDAS Network Board of Directors. She lives in Bellingham, Washington, where she resides with her husband and two tenacious children.

BE EMPOWERED

Manage Challenging Behaviors in the Home
and School Settings

AUTHOR, COACH, EDUCATOR, ADVOCATE

Heather knows the importance of managing *our* stress
response so we can better *support* others who are
having a stress response.
Her authentic approach, combined with superb content,
makes her training a must-do for parents, teachers,
and others supporting children whose behaviors
are impeding their success.

CONTACT HEATHER TODAY
CourageousParent.com

FIND THE ANSWERS AND SUPPORT YOU NEED TO RECLAIM YOUR FAMILY'S HEALTH

-Online and in-person weekend workshops and conferences on topics such as Type 1 Diabetes, PANS/PANDAS/AE, mood disorders and mental health, addictions, autism, ADHD, asthma, and other chronic illness

-One-on-one health coaching focused on root cause resolution using the principles of functional medicine, lifestyle interventions, and integrative strategies

-Training for professionals seeking certification in Family Health Coaching

Carla Atherton, MA, FDNP, TNC, is the director of the Healthy Family Formula, an initiative that brings education, resources, and support together to empower families to reverse chronic illness, prevent disease, and basically, live a full-on healthy life. She is also the mother of three children, one of whom has Type 1 Diabetes who has previously experienced the life-altering effects of PANDAS. Almost 7 years after the big D-day, thousands of hours of research, endless study and further education, and becoming a professional in the family health arena, Carla brings all she has learned to other parents who want to lift labels and put into practice the methods and strategies that will help their children to soar.

A Beautiful Testimonial From a Client, Now Trainee:

How I appreciate your thoughtful wisdom and your ability to read between the lines, given a tough scenario. I can't imagine anyone else being as passionate and researched as you when it comes to helping families. You seem to know everything about everything, and if you don't, you have a boatload of resources for assistance. Your drive is contagious! Thank you for educating and feeding us such RICH knowledge, and for equipping us to help others...

EMPOWER YOURSELF. CONTACT CARLA TODAY. SHE IS HERE TO HELP.
healthyfamilyformula.com

Dr. Sandy Gluckman
PARENTING THAT *Heals*

Dr. Gluckman offers a proven and effective medication-free option for healing learning, behavior, and mood problems. She strongly advocates using medication as a last resort for children with these problems. Dr. Sandy believes there is a problem-free child with a healthy spirit, body, and brain, trapped behind the layers of learning, behavior, and mood symptoms. She teaches parents how to free this child by treating underlying causes and using the parent-child connection in a way that changes the brain. Her work is transforming the lives of children, their parents, and their families.

> **Because Parenting That *Heals* is a whole child – whole family healing process, it is a life-saving gift for parent and child alike.**

See Dr. Sandy's Book:
Parents take Charge: Healing Learning and Behavior Challenges
Without Medication
drsandygluckman.com

Ted Putvin, MSS, ATC (Ret.), LMT
360-349-2348
Olympia, WA
www.tedputvin.com

After 20 years of working in the field of Sports Medicine, my oldest daughter was experiencing disabling and painful health issues that no medical provider could explain or alleviate. It took 15 years to finally get to a clinic that could help her heal. During that time, my own skills were called upon, 24/7 sometimes, to help my daughter deal with excruciating pain and debilitating symptoms.

Over that time, I honed my skills in applied kinesiology and energy medicine. These two modalities have been most useful for the most sensitive of clients in navigating their journeys through autoimmune encephalitis, Lyme and other co-infections, cancer, autism, epi-genetic causing conditions, mold and environmental diseases, as well as other conditions.

Sometimes I work directly and solely with a client or the client's caregiver and sometimes I work as part of a team of other medical professionals. Together, we can evaluate and plan a course of action that is unique and specific for the client. For example, many kids with these conditions need mineral and/or vitamin supplementation, but I can help find the right amount and for most of my clients, they NEED a precise brand, due to fillers or other ingredients. What works for one kid in a family, may be toxic or very unhelpful for another kid. My services help decipher this kind of nuance and can make a dramatic difference in their healing.

The other part that is unique in my work, is that I can do "distance" sessions for clients that cannot come to Olympia, WA or are too weak, fragile or sick to come in, and it works very well. I have helped an ER doctor and a family from 3000 miles away figure out what direction to follow, when very vague (to the Western medical world) symptoms of extreme pain of the meninges was occurring and the conventional labs were not showing any helpful reasons. Many providers are grateful to partner as there are MANY rabbits they could chase, and, in the meantime, the patient is getting sicker, in more pain, and missing out on their life.

I have experience in an array of autoimmune conditions, cancer, POTS, PANDAS/PANS, Lyme, injuries that are not healing, chronic fatigue, and autism. Often, clients come see me after years of not finding success. I just happen to offer another way to look at the situation.

Feel free to contact me if you feel drawn. I look forward to seeing how I can support your highest health.

CPSIA information can be obtained
at www.ICGtesting.com
Printed in the USA
FSHW021331120119
54989FS

9 781640 854123